Enclave: Vicksburg & Her Plantations

ENCLAVE
VICKSBURG AND HER PLANTATIONS
1863 – 1870

James T. Currie

University Press of Mississippi : Jackson : 1980

Copyright © 1980 by the University Press of Mississippi
Manufactured in the United States of America
All Rights Reserved
Print-on-Demand Edition

Library of Congress Cataloging in Publication Data

Currie, James T
  Enclave.

  Bibliography: P.
  Includes index.
  1. Vicksburg region, Miss.—History.
2. Plantation life—Mississippi—Vicksburg region.
3. Reconstruction—Mississippi—Vicksburg region.
I. Title.
F349.V6C87   976.2'29   79–9957
ISBN 0–87805–095–7

To my wife and my daughter

Acknowledgments

FIRST OF ALL, I want to express special appreciation to Professor Willie Lee Rose, who as my advisor stayed with me on this and other projects through four years at the University of Virginia and three years in the United States Army.

I would also like to thank Professors Edward Younger and Michael Holt of the University of Virginia for their service as readers of my dissertation on this subject. Special thanks are given to Professor Harry P. Owens of the University of Mississippi, who first stimulated my scholarly interest in the Civil War and Reconstruction during my undergraduate years.

I incurred many debts among those who helped me gather materials for this study. Specific recognition is tendered the superbly professional staff at the National Archives, particularly Mr. Jack Best and Mrs. E. Holkamper. For their help in searching out and supplying manuscript materials I am grateful to the library staffs at the Wisconsin State Historical Society; the Friends Historical Collection at Swarthmore College; Southern Illinois University; Louisiana State University; the Southern Historical Collection at the University of North Carolina, Chapel Hill; and Alderman Library, University of Virginia.

The staff of the Mississippi Department of Archives and History searched their holdings for every possible source of information and then microfilmed it at bargain rates. Going far beyond what any researcher had a right to expect of them, they exemplified Southern hospitality at its best.

Special appreciation is extended to the citizens of Vicksburg who helped me, and especially to Gordon Cotton and his staff at the Old Court House Museum and to the Hon. Mark Chaney, Chancery Clerk of Warren County, and his deputies. I also want to thank my typist, Mrs. Sandra Inman of Clinton, Mississippi. She was fast, efficient, and always ready to meet deadlines.

Finally, I owe special thanks to my wife, Dr. Patricia Sumners, who was there to encourage — even to badger — me whenever I slowed my work or became discouraged. She lived with this study for seven years, and without her forbearance it would never have been completed.

Preface

AN ENCLAVE is a piece of territory that is surrounded by a larger and culturally or politically different one. Such was the Vicksburg and Warren County area from mid-1863, when the city fell to the Union, through the days of Congressional Reconstruction in Mississippi. It was different from the rest of the state and deserving of the title enclave because the continuous concentration of U.S. presence in the area during these seven years gave the native white population less freedom to contest Reconstruction than they enjoyed elsewhere and provided the ex-slave greater protection of his new status.

The siege and capture of Vicksburg were vital to ultimate Union victory in the Civil War, but the period of occupation following the city's capitulation was just as important in the social realm as its conquest had been in the military. Two military results of the successful siege were the removal of Vicksburg as a barrier to navigation of the Mississippi and the separation of the trans-Mississippi Confederate states from those east of the river. The major social impact of the campaign — one which had an immeasurably disquieting effect on Southern-held areas about it — was the creation of an enclave of Union territory in the heart of the Confederacy. This small area, consisting largely of Warren County and the lands immediately north and south of it along the river, continued its status as an enclave even after the War ended in 1865. This occurred because Vicksburg was headquarters for both the Freedmen's Bureau and the Fourth Military District, and the Reconstruction process could therefore be watched and carried out more thoroughly than in any other part of the state.

Vicksburg's story during this time is that of refugee blacks in their initial contact with freedom and of the new lives they began in and around the city. It is the story of agriculture in a non-slave environment; and it is the story of Davis Bend, where largely unnoticed by the rest of the world a group of ex-slaves managed their own plantations. This is also a story of the center of the enclave — Vicksburg itself — and how this city fared under Union occupation and control.

There are numerous questions one might raise about the Vicksburg area during this seven year period. What effect, for example, did Union occupation have on the city? How did the ex-slaves adapt to freedom? Did the continued presence of Union troops in Vicksburg encourage the development of attitudes of black-white toleration/cooperation which lasted past Reconstruction? By what means was an agricultural system reestablished without slavery? What did the crop lien system mean to the individual farmer? What were some of the potential solutions to the problem of the landless freedman? These and other questions implied by them form the basis of this study, though this book does not pretend to offer definitive answers to all of them. It does aim, though, to offer some suggestions as to their solutions, which can then be extrapolated and applied in a larger context.

Table of Contents

Acknowledgments vii
Preface ix
Introduction xiii
1 Occupied City 3
2 The Freedmen of Vicksburg 33
3 Plantations without Slaves 55
4 Davis Bend 83
5 Post-War Agriculture 145
6 Politics in Black and White 178
7 City of Promise 205
Epilogue and Conclusion 225
Selected Bibliography 231
Index 247

List of Maps

Map 1 Vicksburg and the Lower Mississippi Valley *(Front Endsheet)*
Map 2 Vicksburg and the surrounding area vi
Map 3 Davis Bend 1864 84
Map 4 Vicksburg, 1870 *(Back Endsheet)*

Textual Note

Abbreviations used in footnotes:

AL	Abraham Lincoln Papers, microfilm edition.
AMA	American Missionary Association Papers, Mississippi; Amistad Research Center, Dillard University, New Orleans, Louisiana. Microfilm is available.
BRFAL	Bureau of Refugees, Freedmen, and Abandoned Lands, Mississippi; Record Group 105, National Archives, Washington, D.C.
MDAH	Mississippi Department of Archives and History, Jackson, Mississippi.
NA	National Archives, Washington, D.C.
OCHM	Old Court House Museum, Vicksburg, Mississippi.
OR	*War of the Rebellion: A Compilation of the Official Records.*
RG	Record Group within the National Archives or the Mississippi Department of Archives and History.
SHC	Southern Historical Collection, Chapel Hill, North Carolina.
SIU	Southern Illinois University, Carbondale, Illinois.
WSHS	Wisconsin State Historical Society, Madison, Wisconsin.
2nd SA	Second Special Agency, U. S. Treasury Department; Record Group 366, National Archives, Washington, D. C.

Many of the people whose letters are quoted in this study were not well educated, and errors of spelling and grammar are common. Since the errors in most quotations are both numerous and obvious, a distracting *sic* is rarely inserted.

Introduction

HALFWAY BETWEEN Memphis and New Orleans the Yazoo River, having drained one-fourth of Mississippi, empties into the Mississippi River from the east. North of the mouth of the Yazoo and west of the Mississippi the land stretches flatly away for miles. Where these two rivers converge, though, a line of bluffs — composed of an almost impossibly fine, closely packed, wind-blown dust called loess — rises a nearly vertical 250 feet. It is here, where the bluffs meet the Mississippi and Yazoo rivers, that Vicksburg is located.

French missionaries were perhaps the first persons to grasp the strategic significance of the site, erecting a stockade near there in 1719 and calling it Fort St. Pierre. A hundred years later a Methodist parson and would-be planter named Newitt Vick saw promise in the location and acquired land for a city, which was named after him when it was incorporated in 1825. Its potential as a port for shipping cotton was such that within ten years it boasted a population of 2,500 and had begun to take on a somewhat unsavory reputation as a wide-open river town.[1] Vicksburg

---

1. Robert J. Bailey and Priscilla M. Lowrey, eds., *Historic Preservation in Mississippi* (Jackson: Mississippi Department of Archives and History, 1975), 84; Peter F. Walker, *Vicksburg: A People at War, 1860–1865* (Chapel Hill: Univ. of North Carolina Press, 1960), 5–7.

was thirty-five years old by the time of the Civil War, and it possessed, according to the 1860 Census, some 4,591 inhabitants, including 3,158 whites, 31 free blacks, and 1,402 slaves. Approximately one-third of the free inhabitants were foreign born, with Ireland and the German states their most common nativity.[2]

Loess soil has the property of maintaining nearly vertical sides when it is cut, erosion forces not affecting it as readily as they do ordinary topsoil. As a result, the city of Vicksburg was traversed by an intricate network of ravines and ridges, a topography which only enhanced the city's strategic significance. Constructing a city on these hills was not easy, but by 1860 Vicksburg exhibited a well-defined checkerboard street pattern.

For half a mile along the river ran Levee Street, with Mulberry, Washington, Walnut, Monroe, Cherry, Adams, Locust, and others marching parallel to it at one-block intervals up and down the hills. From the north limits of the city other streets lay perpendicular to the river, their steepest parts paved with widely-spaced cobblestones to aid draft animals in keeping their footing. Jackson Street, which became the Jackson-Vicksburg Road after it left the city, was Vicksburg's main east-west thoroughfare, its chief rivals to that distinction being First East, Main, Grove, China, Clay, Crawford, and South streets. The corner of Washington and Jackson was the busiest commercial intersection in town, while politics centered about the new courthouse, three blocks up the hill.[3]

There were a number of impressive public buildings and private residences in Vicksburg, the previously mentioned courthouse, finished in 1858, being the most notable of the first category. Private wealth was apparent in Duff Green's three-story mansion

2. United States Department of the Interior, Bureau of the Census, *Population of the United States in 1860: Compiled from the Original Returns of the Eighth Census, Under the Direction of the Secretary of the Interior* (Washington: Government Printing Office, 1864), I, 271.

3. Walker, *Vicksburg*, 13; Works Progress Administration, *Mississippi: A Guide to the Magnolia State* (New York: Viking Press, 1938), 268.

Antebellum Vicksburg — The city that was soon to become a major battleground was strategically situated atop a high bluff. Courtesy: Mississippi Department of Archives and History

on the corner of Locust and First streets; in the impressive home built by Alexander McNutt, Mississippi's governor from 1838 to 1842; in "Plain Gables," constructed in Greek Revival style about 1835; in "Cedar Grove," whose front lawn reached to the river; and in numerous other residences. The wealth of Vicksburg was scattered over the city, with an opulent dwelling likely to turn up most anywhere. The plain people of the town, in their smaller, less imposing homes, could also be found in any section; and the slave population, too, according to the tax rolls, was widely and evenly dispersed, perhaps because Mississippi law required that slaves live on the property of the owner. Apparently neither economic nor racial exclusivity existed in the residential patterns of antebellum Vicksburg. In addition, judging by the amount of real

xvi *Introduction*

and personal property indicated in the Census, foreign birth was no bar to success in Vicksburg's business world.[4] Commercial success apparently also brought with it social acceptability, for one student found that "the manner in which the immigrants cut across the Vicksburg social strata indicated that the town put as much value on ability and acquisitiveness as it did on the chance of birth."[5]

Ever-growing chances for commercial success in Vicksburg in the years immediately preceding the Civil War made the city one where the wealthiest citizens were not planters but men who owned the great retail businesses, the warehouses for cotton storage, and the manufacturing establishments. Vicksburg had a pre-War economy more diversified than that of any other city in the state. Unlike Natchez, which depended primarily on agriculture, or Holly Springs, whose livelihood was much more tied to manufacturing, Vicksburg's economic success was based on a combination of these enterprises.

In addition to more than 100 mercantile houses which contributed to the city's thriving and heterogeneous economy, Vicksburg supported 24 industries and was the second leading manufacturing center in the state.[6] These industries employed a total of 437 white workers — 436 men and 1 woman — and had

---

4. Works Progress Administration, *Mississippi*, 277–82; "Eighth Census of the United States (1860)," manuscript, original in NA; Jonathan Beasley, "Blacks — Slave and Free — Vicksburg, 1850–1860," *Journal of Mississippi History*, 38 (February 1976), 29–30.

5. Walker, *Vicksburg*, 15.

6. Statistics on manufacturing are listed by county in the *Eighth Census of the United States, 1860, Vol. III, Manufactures*, but any manufacturing in Warren County outside Vicksburg and in Marshall County outside Holly Springs was negligible. Vicksburg's manufacturers were as follows: Agricultural implements (1); Bookbinding (1); Boots and shoes (4); Carriages (1); Clothing (1); Fire-arms (1); Gas (1); Jewelry &c (2); Leather (1); Lumber, sawed (2); Machinery, steam engines &c (3); Millinery (1); Shingles (1); Tin, copper, and sheet-iron (1).

in 1860 a total payroll of $207,540 per year.[7] By 1860 almost 14% of the city's total free population worked in these industrial enterprises, in which wages ranged from a low of $160 per year for shingle makers to $720 for gunsmiths. The median wage was $475 per year, a sum well above the $339 state average.[8]

The extent to which Vicksburg's slaves were used as industrial workers is hard to determine. Almost 200 slaves were owned by corporate interests in the city, including 40 by the foundry and machine shop operation of Reading and Brothers and 46 more by A.M. Paxton, who also owned a machine works.[9] It is also possible that other slaves were hired to work in manufacturing, though no indications are found. None of Vicksburg's 31 free blacks was employed in factories.

Important as commerce and manufacturing were for the city, however, Vicksburg existed how and where it did because of agriculture; and agriculture in antebellum Mississippi meant cotton produced by black slaves. Vicksburg in reality depended for economic growth on her status as a cotton port, but at least in 1860 the majority of her citizens did not see her prosperity as totally bound to slavery, a fact which helps explain the moderate stance of many of her citizens in that presidential election year.

In the 1860 election Vicksburg voted for the antisecessionist presidential candidates by a large majority, giving 816 votes to John Bell and 85 to Stephen Douglas, while casting only 580 for John C. Breckinridge. A month later, even after the election of Abraham Lincoln had become certain, Vicksburg and Warren County together voted by an 805–248 margin to send "cooperationists," rather than secessionists, to the state's secession convention. Only when secession became an accomplished fact did a majority of the city's population accede to it.[10]

7. *Ibid.*
8. *Ibid.*
9. Beasley, "Blacks," 10–11.
10. Walker, *Vicksburg*, 23–34.

General U. S. Grant—He made his reputation in the West and transformed Vicksburg into a Union enclave. Courtesy: National Archives

None of this moderation mattered once the War began; the citizens of Vicksburg might as well have been as ardently secessionist as the most hot-blooded Charlestonian. What mattered were those vine-tangled loess hills which presented at Vicksburg the single most formidable obstacle to Union control of the Mississippi River. The capture of this strategic location became an object of the highest priority for the Union, for as long as Vicksburg held firm the Confederacy could not be severed. The capture of Vicksburg is not itself the subject of this work, but the campaign which ultimately effected this end had its beginnings in the last days of 1862, when U.S. Grant first began his inexorable movement toward the city.

The first months of the campaign were frustrating ones for the Union general, for his initial feint at the city ended in failure at Chickasaw Bayou. He withdrew his forces and pondered new strategy, which after some months was ultimately successful. This intervening period of time, however disconcerting it was to Grant and his staff, was terribly important for the slaves and slaveowners who lived in this part of the Mississippi Valley, as it was for them the first demonstration of what the War would ultimately mean.

Initiating action was not often the prerogative of a mid-nineteenth century black person in the South, but many of the first steps toward freedom in the Vicksburg area were taken by slaves who quite silently, either alone or in small groups, slipped out at night and fled their plantation prison to meet approaching Union forces. Older women and grey-haired men "toting plunder" on their backs came; younger women — mothers — carried babies slung to one side, an older child trailing behind. Leaving the plantations, they picked their way among the cypress trees, carefully avoiding the holes where bull alligators lay mimicking the cottonwood logs which long ago had toppled into the murky waters.[11]

11. Mary A. Livermore, *My Story of the War: A Woman's Narrative of Four Years Personal Experience* . . . (Hartford: A.D. Worthington and Co., 1889), 342–43; Seth J. Wells, *The Siege of Vicksburg from the Diary of Seth*

Escape for the slave family was sometimes more difficult because the younger men, the most able-bodied field hands, were not always part of the fugitive group. Slaveowners near the river had thrown an obstacle into the path of successful escape by removing to more protected areas the most valuable — and most apt to flee — of their human property. As early as the summer of 1862, when U.S. Adm. David G. Farragut first ventured up-river, many hands were transported to Texas or Alabama or even to Georgia. But others remained where they were, sometimes acting "impudent" or "insubordinate" toward their masters as spring became early summer in 1863, then often running away.[12]

Some fugitives were recaptured by their owners, and for these the penalty was sometimes severe; but others succeeded in escaping and made their way to the river, where they hid in the willows and watched and prayed for one of "Massa Linkum's" boats to come, so they might signal it to stop. "Catching up blazing firebrands," reported a passenger on the *Maria Denning*, "they ran up the shore with them, waved them, threw them in the air, and with the most frantic pantomime sought to convey to us a sense of their eagerness to be taken aboard. It seemed pitiful not to stop." Yet the boat, perhaps fearing that the display was a trick designed to lure it close enough to the bank to allow its capture, kept to the channel and steamed past the little group whose feeble torches alone marked their position in the darkness.[13]

J. Wells, including *Weeks of Preparation and of Occupation after the Surrender* (Detroit: Wm. H. Rowe, Publisher, 1915), 60. Wells recorded in his diary that "Alligators, turtles, and snakes abound. The boys have shot a number of alligators."

12. John Q. Anderson, ed., *Brokenburn: The Journal of Kate Stone, 1861–1868* (Baton Rouge: LSU Press, 1955), entry for June 30, 1862, 127; March 5, 1863, 175; Maj. Charles C. Crowe, C.S.A. to Maj. Gen. C.C. Stevenson, C.S.A., March 31, 1863, *OR*, Ser. I, Vol. XXIV, serial 38, 701.

13. A.K. Farrar, the provost marshal at Natchez, informed Mississippi Gov. John Pettus that in the last year "we have had to hang some forty slaves for plotting an insurrection, and there has been about that number put in irons." Farrar to Pettus, July 17, 1862, Governor's Correspondence, RG 27, MDAH; Livermore, *My Story of the War*, 354.

On other occasions the *Maria Denning* did take on a cargo of refugees, filling its middle compartment with a large number of men, women, and children of all ages. "When they were awake," recalled Mary Livermore, a nurse with the Union Army, "they were either cooking, or eating, or holding 'praise meetings.' It would be difficult to say which they most enjoyed." They were occasionally "subdued, impassive, solemn," reported Mrs. Livermore, but their feelings of relief and joy at being rescued could probably have found expression in the words sung by a group of "young darkies" on another boat going upstream at about the same time:

> Oh, praise an' tanks! De Lord he come
>   To set de people free;
> An' Massa tink it day ob doom,
>   An' we ob jubilee.
> De Lord dat heap de Red Sea waves,
>   He jes' as strong as den;
> He say de word - we las' night slaves,
>   To-day de Lord's free men.
>
> CHORUS — De yam will grow, de cotton blow,
>   We'll hab de rice an' corn,
> O nebber you fear if nebber you hear
>   De driber blow his horn.[14]

The coming of freedom was never so swift, however, as when it was brought directly to the plantations by Mr. Lincoln's Army. The ten counties and Louisiana parishes within a hundred miles of Vicksburg produced over one-seventh of the South's cotton crop during the 1860–61 season, and it took a vast agricultural labor force to cultivate and harvest such a crop. Union patrols and foraging details were constantly moving through much of this

---

14. Livermore, *My Story of the War*, pp. 342–43; S. Emma Edmonds, *The Female Spy of the Union Army* (Boston: De Wolfe, Fiske, & Co., Publishers, 1864), 340.

region from late April to early July of 1863, disrupting plantation routine and bringing anxiously awaited freedom to the slaves living there.[15] The diary of Alfred Quine, an overseer who worked for the noted planter Benjamin L.C. Wailes, illustrates the way in which freedom came in late May to one plantation, the 1,200-acre Fonsylvania place, south of Vicksburg: "Clear and warm all hands Plowing and hoeing corn in big manner," began Quine's entry in his diary for May 23, 1863. Because it was Saturday, there was the usual half-day off for the slaves, beginning at noon. Vicksburg was in its fifth day of seige, but the overseer only dittoed his marginal comment from April 3, "Fighting at Vicksburg." There was no entry for Sunday, but the next day Quine sent his hands to the field. There they remained until midday, at which time, he wrote resignedly, "the yankees came and set the Negros All Free and the Work All Stoped." Tuesday he commented on the warm weather and confirmed that "Negros All Free no work dun."[16]

Wednesday brought Union troops back to Fonsylvania, and when they left, "2 waggon loads of corn" went with them, as did "Saulsbery Daniel Little John and Henry with waggon and oxen," the first mention of slaves leaving the plantation. Quine was sorry to see George, Richard, and Jo leave on Friday, but he was delighted when Henry returned "with oxen and waggon." In the next few days other hands left the plantation, and still more livestock was carried off by roving bands of soldiers.[17]

Quine seemed to accept with great equanimity the abolition of slavery at Fonsylvania, as he recorded in his dairy no attempts to prevent the free movement of his former charges. Neither did he attempt to force them to the fields, for he made a notation of "Negroes doing nothing" each day until June 10, when he recorded

15. J.S. McNeily, "War and Reconstruction in Mississippi, 1863–1890," *Publications of the Mississippi Historical Society, Centenary Series*, II (Jackson 1918), 177.

16. Fonsylvania Plantation Diary of Alfred Quine, Overseer, MDAH; Charles S. Sydnor, *A Gentleman of the Old Natchez Region: Benjamin L. C. Wailes* (Durham: Duke Univ. Press, 1938), 92.

17. Fonsylvania Plantation Diary, May 27–31, 1863.

that "The Negros Planted Some Potatoes." Nineteen days after the first soldiers had come to Fonsylvania, Quine made his last entry in the diary. It was a succinct, one-line comment, but it told all that he thought necessary. "Clear and hot," he wrote, "Ritt grinding all the rest doing nothing."[18] Vicksburg was in its twenty-seventh day of seige, and the number of slaves freed by the blueclad troops continued to increase.

The treatment accorded fugitives who went off with U.S. soldiers or trailed into the Army camps, however, did not always coincide with freedom as the slaves had envisioned it; for often as not the Northern soldier was as bitterly anti-Negro as was the "Western Yankee" in Grant's army whose opinion, as reported by a Confederate sympathizer, was that "before I came down here I heard so much talk of the poor slave and the way the poor slave was treated, but since I have been here I have never seen one that I thought was treated bad enough."[19] Reports, indeed, were reaching Washington that some of the officers under Grants's command were so mistreating the refugees that a few were actually returning to their masters.[20] A staunch Southerner keenly noted their condition and even sympathized with slaves who escaped to the Union lines: "Of all the people suffering now, I pity the Negros [sic]. They flocked in to the Yankees, expecting to experience the blessings of freedom. Well, the women were put to washing for the hospital. They washed from daylight to dark on the filthiest of clothes and bandages and were never paid a cent, not even given a place to sleep, only their food. The Yankees engaged some of them to make shirts but never thought of paying for them."[21]

18. *Ibid.*, May 26–June 13, 1863.
19. Anne Shannon to Emmie Crutcher, June 21, 1863, Crutcher-Shannon Papers, MDAH.
20. Gen. H.W. Halleck to Gen. U.S. Grant, March 31, 1863, *OR*, Ser. I, Vol. XXIV, pt. 3, 156–57. Halleck's "Unofficial letter" asked Grant to use his "official and personal influence to remove prejudices on this subject."
21. Anne Shannon to Emmie Crutcher, June 21, 1863, Crutcher-Shannon Papers, MDAH.

Refugees in the area were a problem for Grant's army, but they were a difficulty with which the general had become acquainted even before the commencement of the Vicksburg campaign. In November of 1862, while in southern Tennessee, Grant had been surrounded by thousands of penniless, ill-clad, unhoused fugitives. At that time he appointed John Eaton, a chaplain in the Twenty-seventh Ohio Infantry, as "General Superintendent of Contrabands for the Department," with a primary duty of advising Grant on refugee matters and supervising the blacks as they labored for the Union by picking cotton, cutting wood, and building railroads.[22]

Though a modern historian has described the thirty-three-year-old chaplain as "a Messianic soldier who was long on fanciful dreams . . . and short on a sense of reality," Eaton's contemporaries held a more favorable opinion of him. Assessing his appointee after a year, Grant described him as "practical in his ideas" and "perfectly sincere in his labors." Samuel R. Shipley, President of the Executive Board of the Friends' Freedmens Associations, spoke of Eaton's "great executive ability, combined with a gentle and sympathizing heart," qualities which Shipley felt "eminently fit him for dealing with the interests of this downtrodden race."[23]

The months preceding July 1863 were busy ones for Eaton and his staff, as he had been ordered to "systematize all Government efforts in behalf of refugees. Islands and other points of security on the river will be occupied . . . for the benefit of white and colored refugees." Eaton was further told to "organize

22. John Eaton, *Grant, Lincoln, and the Freedmen* (New York: Longman's Green, and Co., 1907), 26–27.
23. Walker, *Vicksburg*, p. 212; Eaton, *Grant, Lincoln, and the Freedmen*, 114–15; Samuel R. Shipley, quoted in Youra Thelma Qualls, "Friend and Freedman: The Work of the Association of Friends of Philadelphia and Its Vicinity for the Relief and Education of Freedmen during the Civil War and Reconstruction, 1862–1872" (Unpublished Ph.D. Diss. Harvard Univ., 1955).

Colonel John Eaton — First Director of the Freedmen's Department in the Mississippi Valley. Photo taken about 1870. Courtesy: Library of Congress

labor at wood cutting and cultivating the soil, for their [the refugees] own comfort and support and the benefit of the army, navy, and commerce."[24]

Eaton and his Freedmen's Department officials began at once to carry out this directive, and despite the difficulties involved they soon established woodyards at Young's Point, Paw Paw Island, Omega Island, and Island 102, all of which were near Vicksburg. The operation was such a success, reported Col. Samuel Thomas of the Vicksburg District, that by September 1864 "there had been cut in this district and delivered to steamboats, over 60,000 cords of wood, bringing to the freedmen over $125,000, and saving to the Government an expense of about $90,000 more by selling at $1.50 per cord less than the Government could have got the wood from private parties." The men who cut the wood were paid for their work, with the balance of the profits going into a "Freedman Fund," to be used to buy clothing and other articles which the Government did not supply. "Rations were issued to all alike," reported Thomas, "and there was no attempt made to force the chopper to pay for what he received, as he was helping to support and care for the dependent portion of the camp."[25]

The capture of Vicksburg had been almost eight months in the making, the object of a campaign which moved over four states and directly touched the lives of two hundred thousand people. Slaves and slaveowners had been the first to feel its effects, the former to rejoice in newly found freedom, the latter to curse bitterly or silently to accept the destruction of their wealth. Soldiers had of course been a part of it all along. Many in blue would remain as garrison; others on both sides would never leave, for it had been hard fought. The population of the city itself, through forty-seven days of seige, had become active participants in the great event.

---

24. General Orders No. 27, February 25, 1863, *OR*, Ser. I, Vol. XLVIII, serial 101, 978.

25. Eaton, *Grant, Lincoln, and the Freedmen*, 138–40.

Introduction xxvii

July 4, 1863 — Victorious troops of U. S. Grant parade past the bulletmarked Court House at Vicksburg as they enter the city. Courtesy: Mississippi Department of Archives and History

Port Hudson surrendered when its defenders heard the news about Vicksburg, and the Mississippi was opened. Vicksburg was still a powerful fortress, but now the U.S. Flag waved from the cupola of the slave-built courthouse. The "Gibraltar of the Confederacy" was an occupied city.

Enclave: Vicksburg & Her Plantations

Occupied City

WITH THE SIEGE OVER, residents of the Vicksburg area were faced with the prospect of either living out the War in a Union enclave or slipping through the lines into the Confederacy. Most of the city's population chose the first option and remained where they were, there to experience the changes which confronted the city during the last two years of the Civil War. These citizens were soon joined by thousands of others who were drawn to Vicksburg as if it had magnetic attraction.

Because of the siege, residents of Vicksburg had experienced the War more than had most civilians, and the reestablishment of a feeling of loyalty to the Union was a most difficult task for the U.S. commander. This was ironical, for, as previously mentioned, Vicksburg in 1860 and 1861 had been the leader of resistance to the call for secession.[1] Once the War began, however, most who had opposed secession either joined their opponents or maintained a discreet silence, while a minority simply left the state.[2] Duff Green was one who took the oath of allegiance as soon as possible; then he departed for New Orleans. William Lum, another well-known citizen, also subscribed to the oath and even gave his residence to be used as Army headquarters.[3]

1. Walker, *Vicksburg*, 25–34.
2. *Ibid.*, 31–34.
3. Anne Shannon to Emma Crutcher, November 8, 1863, Crutcher-Shannon Papers, MDAH.

4   *Enclave: Vicksburg & Her Plantations*

Some of the yet ardent Confederates among the population were, however, incensed by any compromise with the Yankee invaders and often raged at their neighbors' actions. Alexander Abrams, a newspaperman who had been in the city during the siege, was disgusted by persons who took the oath,⁴ but his feelings were mild compared with the thoughts expressed by Alice Shannon, the impetuous young daughter of Marmaduke Shannon, former editor of the *Vicksburg Whig*. "You remember how Miss Lucy Beaulings wore the secession cockade now she tells the yankees that she always was for the union. . . . Miss Lucy was . . . shot in the ankle by a . . . ball. I wish it had shot her foot off." A Mrs. West also earned Alice's disapproval by giving "several large dancing parties in her house and she invited all the young ladies and yankee officers in town. Lizzie West goes to all the parties given by the yankee women I can't call them ladies."⁵

Other Unionists in town, people whose feelings may have been more genuine than were those of the West family, still kept silent, as Armistead Burwell tried to explain in a letter to President Lincoln:

It is a great error into which ignorant . . . and prejudiced men are liable to fall that those who do not come out boldly for the Union, are its enemies, or in the modern phrase, *disloyal*. There are thousands in Miss. who desire most ardently the restoration of the United States Government, who yet see no way, in which their sentiments can be safely or beneficially expressed. If you wish to hear Jeff: Davis, Wigfall, Toombs, Floyd, etc. etc., cursed from the bottom of the heart and with the whole soul, go disguised to Vicksburg, and converse with the men of Mississippi.⁶

---

4. Alexander Abrams, *A Full and Detailed History of the Siege of Vicksburg* (Atlanta: Intelligencer Steam Power Presses, 1863), 64.

5. Alice Shannon to Emma Crutcher, November 19, 1863, Crutcher-Shannon Papers, MDAH.

6. Armistead Burwell to Abraham Lincoln, August 28, 1863, AL Papers (microfilm), reel 58, #25884.

Some of those who had been the most vigorous opponents of secession, though, had been transformed by the War into men of the most violently anti-Union feeling. Marmaduke Shannon was one of these, and even five months after the capture of the city he refused accommodation with the United States. His daughter Anne quoted her father's sentiments in a letter to her sister. "I shall not go before them unless they send for me," he had sworn, "and if they require me to take the oath, I shall leave."[7]

The young Shannon ladies continued to fulminate about such abominations as the "air of desolation the yankees can give a place," but their comments were largely restricted to letters to their sister Emmie, who with her husband was waiting out the War in Texas.[8] Other women, however, were not so cautious in expressing their opinions of the occupation, a situation which General Grant had expected. In February 1863, for example, he had written to Gen. Stephen A. Hurlbut, operating in the Memphis region, that he would sustain him in "forcing outside of our lines every disloyal person of whatever age or sex."[9] It nevertheless came as some surprise in Vicksburg when in December 1863 Gen. Edward McPherson ordered the banishment of five women for "having acted disrespectfully toward the President and the Government of the United States . . . by abruptly leaving said [Episcopal] Church at that point in the services where the officiating minister prays for the welfare of the President of the United States and all others in authority." The offenders were given forty-eight hours in which to leave the Federal lines, and a warning was issued to

---

7. Anne Shannon to Emma Crutcher, November 8, 1863, Crutcher-Shannon Papers, MDAH. Shannon finally took the oath of allegiance on June 26, 1865.
8. Alice Shannon to Emma Crutcher, November 19, 1863, Crutcher-Shannon Papers, MDAH.
9. Grant to Hurlbut, February 24, 1863, *OR*, Ser. I, Vol. XXIV, 63–66.

all other persons that any behavior disrespectful of "President, Government, or flag of the United States or to any officer or soldier of the United States" while in the performance of his duty, would be punished by fine, banishment, or imprisonment, "according to the grossness of the offense."[10]

McPherson's order was apparently enforced to the hilt by the provost marshal, for several individuals were imprisoned for their public utterances. E. A. Hoenish, for example, was incarcerated for "Disrepectful language to Gov. of U.S. saying 'he wished to God Forest [sic] would come and kill every Yank in Vick.'" C. H. Riley, his tongue loosened by alcohol, found himself in the city guardhouse for suggesting that the officer of the day "Kiss his Mule"; and William Anderson, on July 5, 1865, was arrested for "expressing treasonable sentiments."[11]

Gen. N. J. T. Dana also took swift action against those whose support for the Confederacy consisted of more than mere verbalizations. Two women and three men were arrested in early May 1864 for smuggling mail and other articles through the lines, while four more women were arrested on similar charges in August.[12] General Dana also banished several persons during his tenure, the first such occasion occurring in August 1864 when the wife and family of a Confederate officer were ordered out of the city in retaliation for the way Southern authorities had treated Willie Salmon, Rose Salmon, and Ellen McQuirk.[13] Less than a month

10. Circular, General McPherson, December 27, 1863, *OR*, Ser. II, Vol. VI, 776.
11. Provost Marshal Records, May 7 and 11, 1864, and July 5, 1865, OCHM.
12. Those charged were A. Wenstin, Mrs. G. Claiter ("CSA Cit."), Miss Kline, M. T. Brown, P. T. Yadkins, Mrs. Shuler, Maggie Oliver, Mrs. W. F. Reynolds, and Mrs. M. A. Russell. Provost Marshal Records, May 5, August 18, and August 20, 1864, OCHM.
13. *Vicksburg Daily Herald*, August 30, 1864, 2. There is no record of what the Southern authorities had done.

later the general evicted the H.L. Bond family in "retaliation for the banishment of Mrs. C.R. Bonnie of Yazoo City, Miss., by the Confederate authorities." The Bonds were given five days in which to leave, and $250 was collected from other "disloyal citizens" and given to Mrs. Bonnie, "to reimburse her in part for her losses."[14]

Only a week later General Dana made another attempt to coerce the Confederate government by arresting twenty-two prominent citizens of Vicksburg, "To be held as hostages for the liberation of Certain Union Citizens."[15] Dana did not let up on his campaign against Confederate sympathizers, either; for two months to the day after the Bonds were told to leave, he struck hard at some others among the old families of the city by ordering another five women removed to "beyond the Big Black River."

The charges against each person were stated in the printed order, with "rebel sympathizer" and "rebel mail carrier" the most common offenses listed. Ada DeMoss was also suspected of being a spy, while Mrs. Shuler, for whom this was a second offense, was a "smuggler by association and practice." The most detailed indictment was that against Elizabeth Eggleston, who was, stated General Dana, a "general busybody with rebel interests, rebel philanthropist, mail receiver, carrier of smuggled funds to prisoners in jail &c., &c."[16]

Mrs. Eggleston attempted to gain revocation of the order by appealing through the general's wife and son. George Dana promised to speak with his father, but he held out little hope for success, saying "I know he has decided upon this sad step only because dictated by sense of duty, and not from any *personal* feelings in

---

14. Special Orders #131, Gen. N.J.T. Dana, September 22, 1864, in *Vicksburg Daily Herald*, October 15, 1864.

15. Included in this group was M. Emanuel, later President of the Southern Railroad. Provost Marshal Records, October 2, 1864, OCHM.

16. Gen. Orders #82, November 22, 1864, Gen. N.J.T. Dana, in Roach-Eggleston Papers, SHC, Univ. of North Carolina.

the matter." Mrs. Dana offered sympathy but reported that her husband felt duty bound to act as he had.[17] Elizabeth Eggleston left Vicksburg as required, but she remained away only two months, after which General Dana relented and allowed her, upon taking the oath of allegiance, to return to the city.[18]

In addition to banishing or otherwise punishing individuals for their actions, the military sometimes "encouraged" loyalty among the citizens with what were sometimes less than subtle tactics. When a group from the Oakridge and Milldale precincts outside of Vicksburg protested to General Sherman about the destruction of their property by soldiers and roving bands of freedmen, he replied: "You must first make a government before you can have property. There is no such thing as property without government. Of course we think that our Government (which is still yours) is the best and easiest put in full operation here. . . . Study your real duties . . . and if you remain inert, or passively friendly to the power that threatens our national existence, you must reap the full consequences, but if, like true men, you come out boldly, and plainly assert that the Government of the United States is the only power on earth which can insure . . . protection to life, property, and fame . . . , you will have some reason to ask of us protection and assistance, otherwise not."[19]

U.S. authorities in Vicksburg were faced, however, with more immediate problems than that of squeezing expressions of loyalty

17. George H. Dana to Elizabeth Eggleston, November 22, 1864, and Mrs. N.J.T. Dana to Mrs. M.P.H. Roach, November 22, 1864, both in Roach-Eggleston Papers, SHC.

18. Maj. W.H. Morgan to Mrs. M.P.H. Roach, January 22, 1865, Roach-Eggleston Papers, SHC.

19. Sherman to H.W. Hill, Esq., September 7, 1863, *OR*, Ser. I, Vol. XXX, pt. 3, 401–404; Anne Shannon told her sister Emmie of a Mrs. Messenger who was arrested and held in jail for several weeks. While she was incarcerated, her house was emptied of its furniture — fifty wagon loads. She went to Sherman in protest, but he allegedly turned her back with "A woman who has fifty wagon loads of fine furniture deserves to lose it." Anne Shannon to Emma Crutcher, September 16, 1863, Crutcher-Shannon Papers, MDAH.

from a reluctant population, for the city and its people were in great physical need as a result of the siege. Even Union soldiers who had been part of its destruction were amazed when they saw the results of their handiwork. "The mortars have nearly destroyed the town," wrote Pvt. Seth J. Wells in his diary, while Joseph Skipworth reported, with poorer spelling but more detail, "Thare is a cannon boll through evry house in town and the ground all tore up."[20] The whole city was littered with heaps of rubble, and there were "great holes as big as cellars where the shells had fallen into the ground."[21] There was need for a massive cleanup and rebuilding of the city, but the first priority for Grant and his commanders was that of caring for the 30,000 Confederate soldiers whom they had just taken prisoner. The formal conditions of parole and release were worked out between Grant and Confederate Gen. John C. Pemberton, while among the private soldiers a mutual respect as worthy adversaries quickly became open camaraderie, even to the joining of forces for a bit of petty thievery. "Some of the boys," wrote Seth Wells, "together with several Confeds, broke into a store and stole a large quantity of tobacco and some other things before the guard came around."[22]

Vicksburg's defenders had been on short rations for several weeks, and for many of the Confederate troops such items as coffee had become undreamed-of luxuries. "You better beleve they went into uncle Sams provision as though they was fight for him," recorded Joseph Skipworth. Now, he hoped, "wee will have a good time for a while."[23] The civilian population, too, was largely

20. Wells, *The Siege of Vicksburg*, 89; Joseph Skipworth to wife, July 12, 1863, Skipworth (Joseph) Papers, SIU.
21. Oscar Osborn Winther (Ed.) *With Sherman to the Sea: The Civil War Letters, Diaries, and Reminiscences of Theodore F. Upson* (Bloomington: Indiana Univ. Press, 1958), 61.
22. John C. Pemberton, *Pemberton: Defender of Vicksburg* (Chapel Hill: Univ. of North Carolina Press, 1942), 241–42; Wells, *The Siege of Vicksburg*, 89.
23. Joseph Skipworth to wife, July 12, 1863, Skipworth Papers, SIU.

undernourished, and General McPherson, one of Grant's corps commanders, directed Maj. Gen. John A. Logan to select a U.S. officer, a chaplain, and a citizen of Vicksburg to seek out the "most needy and destitute and issue them provisions."[24] The Western Sanitary Commission sent "anti-scorbutic articles of diet," and the Northwestern Freedmen's Aid Society provided some potatoes and onions. As late as the middle of August, however, Joseph Skipworth observed that "there is a heepe of Sickness going on hear," part of which was undoubtedly caused by the widespread dietary deficiencies. "The cuntry," he noted, "is cleared of every chicken."[25]

The physical destruction caused by the siege had several effects on the city, all of them unfavorable. Vicksburg's economy, for example, had been strangled during the forty-seven days of siege, while many of the city's businesses had been destroyed or severely damaged by the incessant shelling.

Employees in the city's factories, together with those who worked in many of the shops and stores, were thrown out of work as well as out of their homes by the destruction wrought by the siege. Their troubles, moreover, were compounded by the fact that Vicksburg during the last two years of the War was the center of an area where a combination of trade restrictions and rapidly expanding population brought rampant inflation and heartless profiteering. The *Vicksburg Daily Herald*, for example, complained that "the merchants and dealers took advantage of the buyer and have put up many articles necessary for domestic uses at very exorbitant prices — even beyond the reach of persons in good financial circumstances. How the less fortunate will or can live at such prices for the necessaries of life, will become a serious question — so much so that it may require the official action of

24. Special Orders #135, July 11, 1863, General McPherson, *OR*, Ser. I, Vol. XXIV, Pt. 3, 500–501.
25. Eaton, *Grant, Lincoln, and the Freedmen*, 130; Joseph Skipworth to wife, August 17, 1863, Skipworth Papers, SIU.

the military."[26] The situation continued to worsen during the next few weeks, until the commanding general was forced to act.

Echoing the *Daily Herald*, General Dana stated that "Speculators in staple articles of food have monopolized the supply and are grinding the faces of the poor." He thereupon set maximum prices of flour at $16 per barrel, pork at 32¢ per pound, bacon at 33¢ per pound, ham at 43¢ per pound, soap at 15¢ per pound, and salt at 4¢ per pound. He futhermore charged the provost marshal to "encourage complaints" about violations of his order, with penalties ranging from $100 fine for the first offense to "confiscation of stock and imprisonment at discretion" on the third conviction.[27] The prices fixed by Dana were approximately twice those of Cincinnati and St. Louis, but some proprietors of retail food stores who did not feel these amounts were high enough determined to circumvent the order by eliminating from their stock all of the controlled items.[28]

The Treasury Department took note of those merchants who stopped bringing in flour and other staples and warned that such men "must not be surprised if it should be determined to revoke their authorities and issue new ones to more intelligent and patriotic business men."[29] The combination of threat and regulation seemed to take the cutting edge off rising food prices, for there were no more complaints in the newspaper. Profits, however, continued at a high level throughout the next months, one contemporary estimate placing the net rate of return on investment at nearly 30% per year.[30]

26. *Vicksburg Daily Herald*, July 30, 1864.
27. General Orders #23, August 19, 1864, General Dana, in *Vicksburg Daily Herald*, August 20, 1864.
28. *Vicksburg Daily Herald*, October 14, 1864.
29. Letter from T.C. Callicott, Asst. Spec. Agt., Treasury Dept., printed in *Vicksburg Daily Herald*, October 14, 1864.
30. Endorsement, Lt. Stuart Eldridge, May 15, 1865, *Endorsements, Provost Marshal, Vicksburg, Mississippi (1865)*, RG 105 (Miss.), Vol. 73, NA.

12 Enclave: Vicksburg & Her Plantations

Rental fees on real property, too, had a natural tendency to increase as occupation forces moved into the city, and for the use of undamaged or repaired buildings, owners demanded near-usurious rent.[31] Everyone except the property owners suffered as a result of the elevated charges, but few were hurt more than were the black refugees in Vicksburg. "They are greatly oppressed at present," reported the superintendent of freedmen, "by the exorbitant rents they are compelled to pay. Twenty dollars a month being often paid for one small miserable room."[32]

The price of housing continued to rise, so that by mid-September 1864, a month after he had fixed food prices, General Dana found it necessary to act in the matter of rentals, also: "Since the capture of this place by the Federal Authorities, owners of real estate have steadily advanced the rates of rent until they have become extortionate and intolerable. In order to protect loyal men, and the poor, I am directed by the Major General commanding this District to notify all parties concerned that in NO CASE will the lessee of any tenement pay or the landlord receive a sum exceeding twenty-five percent above the rate paid previous to the commencement of the present rebellion."[33] The order remained in effect for five months, with General Dana finally rescinding it on February 20, 1865, by which time the housing situation had become less acute.[34] Helping ease the shortage were the abandoned and confiscated properties held by the Treasury Department, the rents on which were never as high as on privately owned buildings.[35]

31. Walker, *Vicksburg*, 203.
32. Lt. A.M. Brobst to John Eaton, July 16, 1864, Box 35, RG 105 (Miss.), NA.
33. Order from the Office of the Provost Marshal, September 24, 1864, in *Vicksburg Daily Herald*, October 15, 1864.
34. Order from Maj. Gen. N.J.T. Dana, February 20, 1865, in *Vicksburg Daily Herald*, February 21, 1865.
35. List of Abandoned and Confiscated Property, Vicksburg, Mississippi, Box 222A, RG 366, 2nd SA, NA.

In addition to destroying buildings in Vicksburg, the long days and nights of shelling had wrecked the streets of the city and created piles of rubble and craters which fairly blocked many of the thoroughfares. At least as early as July 1864 city authorities began using prisoners from the local jail to repair the streets, working them under guards armed with fixed bayonets.[36] The streets remained, however, in wretched condition, with the *Daily Herald* complaining on numerous occasions of such obstacles as "a hole which is formidable to mules and men" or a pond which had "so encroached upon the narrow strip of road passing by it, as to make baptism a certainty for those who travel that way."[37] The streetlights were also destroyed during the siege, and in June 1864 the military authorities levied a tax of 20¢ per lineal foot per month on business establishments, 10¢ per foot on second floor establishments, and 5¢ per foot on all other buildings in town to pay for the installation and operation of gas street lamps.[38]

Notwithstanding the *Herald*'s description of Vicksburg as "one of the healthiest cities in the United States,"[39] the immense piles of debris and the dank caves left over from the siege created fertile breeding grounds for disease. Measles struck the city hard in June 1864 and caused many deaths, especially among the older people;[40] then only a month later there was an outbreak of yellow fever, and the health authorities closed the public cisterns.[41] Another bout with contagion was fought in the spring of 1865, when a minor smallpox epidemic struck the area, doing most of its damage in sections inhabited by freedmen.[42]

36. *Vicksburg Daily Herald*, July 29, 1864.
37. *Ibid.*, February 26, 1865; March 3, 1865; March 9, 1865.
38. General Orders #1, June 20, 1864, in *Vicksburg Daily Herald*, July 15, 1864.
39. *Vicksburg Daily Herald*, August 4, 1864.
40. *Ibid.*, June 14, 1864.
41. Special Orders #63, July 15, 1864, in *Vicksburg Daily Herald*, August 10, 1864.
42. *Vicksburg Daily Herald*, March 9, 1865.

14   *Enclave: Vicksburg & Her Plantations*

Sanitation was a continuing problem in Vicksburg, and the columns of the *Daily Herald* contained frequent and sometimes humorous appeals for relief. "The pile of thanksgiving from some one's stable which lies just under our window," declared editor James Swords, "is exhaling an aroma not quite equal to Phalon's 'Night Blooming Ceres,' but rich enough to merit the attention of those whose duty it is to cart off the mortified remains of animals and vegetables."[43] Although heavy summer rains helped keep the quantity of filth in the streets from becoming unbearable, report of a haunted house brought the editorial comment that "we can see no reason why . . . any of these departed ones should seek to locate themselves in this region above the ground, especially with the present condition of what should be the city sewage."[44] Health officials attempted to prevent decaying animal matter from becoming a hazard by requiring its removal "immediately after . . . decease," with a fine of $20 for violation of the order. By the end of 1864, however, this regulation was deemed inadequate, and three hours was set as the maximum time allowed for disposal of all carcasses. In addition, a reward of $10 was offered to anyone who informed on an offender.[45] The cemetery was also controlled by U.S. officials, and no burials could take place there without permission from the post surgeon.[46]

As the final sanitation measure the health office ordered in May 1865 the filling in of caves which had been constructed by residents as protection during the siege. Property owners were responsible for the caves on their own land, while the street commissioners would take care of those on public property. These

43. *Ibid.*, June 10, 1864.
44. *Ibid.*, July 22, 1864.
45. Regulations, Office of the Street Commissioner, September 3, 1864, in *Vicksburg Daily Herald*, September 13, 1864; Amendment to City Regulations, issued by Lt. Col. Henry R. Brinkerhoff, December 8, 1864, in *Vicksburg Daily Herald*, December 20, 1864.
46. General Orders #5, December 21, 1864, Brig. Gen. Morgan L. Smith, in *Vicksburg Daily Herald*, December 24, 1864.

burrows, however, which had become in the words of Health Officer Col. Van E. Young "depositories of filth of all kinds to the detriment of the health of all citizens," were still marring the Vicksburg landscape in March of 1866 when journalist John Dennett saw them on his trip through the South.[47]

In addition to the economic and physical disruption caused by their exploding shells, Union forces brought with them to Vicksburg the U.S. Treasury Department's system of trade permits, which was itself a hindrance to full economic recovery and only served to encourage fraud and deception. Within the city of Vicksburg the Treasury Department regulations meant in theory that no one could operate a wholesale or retail establishment or engage in any form of trade without a permit, the number of permits being quite limited. Theoretically, permits were given only to loyal citizens, and especially to "officers and soldiers who have been honorably discharged from the service and are disabled by wounds, loss of health, or limbs."[48] These regulations had been the subject of much discussion between Grant, who wanted no trade at all with areas conquered in the South, and Treasury Secretary Salmon P. Chase, who favored a controlled system of commercial intercourse. Chase's view prevailed, but in practice the system of trade and retailing permits never operated with much efficaciousness.

General Grant in an order of August 1, 1863, had called upon all citizens within the conquered portions of Mississippi to return and "pursue their peaceful avocations, in obedience to the laws of the United States."[49] Four months later, however, after Grant had

47. Order from Col. Van E. Young, May 13, 1865, in *Vicksburg Daily Herald*, May 16, 1865; John R. Dennett, *The South as It Is: 1865–1866*, ed. Henry M. Christman (New York: Viking Press, 1965), 349.
48. T.C. Callicott to William P. Mellen, September 29, 1864, Book 123, RG 366, 2nd SA, NA.
49. General Orders #50, August 1, 1863, *OR*, Ser. I, Vol. XXIV, Pt. 3, 570.

given over to the Treasury Department responsibility for commerce regulation, a perplexed Treasury Department special agent wrote to his superior in Cincinnati, "I find trade has been conducted here . . . with a great deal of looseness and furthermore that citizens are doing business under Gen'l Grant's proclamation."[50] The situation remained in a confused and uncertain status throughout the next year, and Thomas C. Callicott in Vicksburg protested to William Orme, the Treasury Department's supervisory special agent, the order preventing persons without supply store authorizations from selling goods in the district. "If strictly construed and strictly enforced," he suggested, "this rule will cause a great deal of distress among a number of poor people here." Callicott explained that he, as Treasury agent in Vicksburg, had allowed certain persons, "mostly widows having families to support, and sickly or disabled colored people to sell fresh vegetables and fruits, candies, pies, cakes, hot coffee, cigars, etc." He had in addition, he stated, taken certain other liberties with the regulations, for as "disabled soldiers cannot be expected to become milliners and dressmakers," he had granted "authorities to women having proper testimonials of good character and loyalty . . . to operate such establishments."[51]

Although there are in evidence many examples of soldiers who took advantage of the Treasury regulations,[52] questions arose at times as to the means by which certain persons had secured their authorizations. Callicott, who always attempted to stay on top of the situation, wrote William Mellen, one of his superiors, about such an instance. Callicott assured Mellen that he had followed

50. John A. McDowell to William P. Mellen, December 17, 1863, Book 123, RG 366, 2nd SA, NA.
51. T.C. Callicott to William Orme, November 18, 1864, Book 124, RG 366, 2nd SA, NA.
52. See for instance the application of Gardner Allison, a disabled soldier, for a permit to allow him to establish a "restaurant for the sale of wines and cigars and meals." Application dated December 11, 1864, Box 22A, RG 366, 2nd SA, NA.

as carefully as possible the rules about issuing permits to soldiers, but, he stated indignantly on September 29, 1864, "Today I was surprised by the visit of a German Jew who has not been in the United States four years, is not naturalized, and has never served in the United States Army, named Blumensteil, who exhibited to me an authority for a supply store of $1000. per month at Vicksburg granted by our department on Sept. 14th I think to one Henry Hove, a disabled soldier. He also exhibited to me an *irrevocable* power of attorney executed . . . by this Hove virtually transferring his authority to Blumensteil. . . . I look upon the transaction as a fraud."[53]

Callicott investigated further and discovered that the practice of selling official authorizations was not at all uncommon. The result of his discovery was that the Treasury Department issued orders making it mandatory for parties doing business on a disabled soldier's permit to enter into an agreement with the permit-holder and to file a copy of the agreement with the Treasury agent.[54] The result of this order was a rash of partnerships with provisions similar to those in an agreement entered into by John W. Williams, "late a soldier in the Army of the United States," and Moses Cohen on April 7, 1865:

> Whereas the said Williams has obtained a supply store permit . . . , and
> Whereas said Williams has not sufficient capital of his own for said purposes . . . ,
> [It is agreed] that said Cohen is to furnish all of the Capital needed in the business. . . .

The agreement was to run for one year, after which the partnership was to be dissolved and Cohen's investment returned to him. The

---

53. T.C. Callicott to William Mellen, September 29, 1864, Book 123, RG 366, 2nd SA, NA.
54. Notice published by C.A. Montross, Treasury Agent, March 20, 1865, in *Vicksburg Daily Herald*, March 25, 1865.

profits would then be split in a 3:1 ratio, Cohen getting the larger share.[55] This arrangement was within the limits imposed by the regulations, but Callicott preferred that soldiers alone run the supply stores.

In addition to limiting the number of persons authorized to engage in business within the city, restrictions on sales of medicines, drugs, and other valuable commodities were designed to prevent the Confederacy from benefiting from their nearness.[56] The regulations, however, were largely a failure, and the *Vicksburg Daily Herald* commented in July 1864 that "It is a well known fact, that trade from this city has been extensively carried on with the surrounding country, and even beyond our lines in territory not under our control."[57] Trade, indeed, had gotten out of hand, with the small settlement on Milliken's Bend doing over $1,000 daily business, much of it illegal.[58] Finally, in September 1864 General Dana ordered the closing of all supply stores at both Goodrich's Landing and Milliken's Bend, north of the city. In addition, Dana required that no person could work in a store unless he had taken the oath of allegiance to the United States.[59] By the first of November, Skipwith's Landing was also closed to traders, and a blockade of Federal gunboats was established there. This place, stated Callicott, was "one of the ports designated by

---

55. Letter of partnership between John W. Williams and Moses Cohen, April 7, 1865, Box 157, RG 366, 2nd SA, NA; Cohen remained in Vicksburg after the War, and he subsequently got into trouble with the civil authorities there. In December 1867 he was convicted of larceny and sentenced to the state penitentiary. Criminal Court Docket, Vicksburg and Warren County, December 1865–December 1869, OCHM.

56. J. Adam McDowell to General McPherson, March 17, 1864, Book 123, RG 366, 2nd SA, NA.

57. *Vicksburg Daily Herald*, July 30, 1864.

58. E. Merton Coulter, "Commercial Intercourse with the Confederacy in the Mississippi Valley, 1861–1865," *Mississippi Valley Historical Review*, 5 (1919), 386.

59. General Orders #36, September 2, 1864, General Dana, in AL Papers (microfilm), reel 80, #35847.

Vicksburg Wharf, 1864 — The captured city became a major trade center despite Grant's protestations that this hurt the Union war effort. Courtesy: Library of Congress

the Rebel authorities for the exportation of government cotton and the importation of supplies to the Rebel army."[60]

All attempts at stopping illegal trade, however, ultimately failed, with Northern greed and Southern desperation combining to thwart even the most thoroughly laid plans for its control. The benefits derived by the Confederacy from illicit exchange could never be measured accurately, but one historian has estimated that trade in cotton alone prolonged the War by a full year, for

60. T.C. Callicott to J.R. Richardson, November 5, 1864, Box 222A, RG 366, 2nd SA, NA; Callicott to Maj. Gen. E.R.S. Canby, November 26, 1864, Book 124, RG 366, 2nd SA, NA.

through it the South was supplied with much-needed materials from the outside.[61] The incredible irony is that U.S. Army officers were often at the core of the illegal trade in cotton, for they could pass through the lines and explore the country about with a great deal more impunity than could civilians. Pvt. Samuel Glyde Swain was indignant — and perhaps the slightest bit envious — at the workings of the speculators and traders in the armed forces. "Cotton," he explained to his brother George, "can be bought out twenty-five miles in the Confederacy for ten cents a pound in green backs and one dollar in Confed scrip. The rebel soldiers do not hinder its being brought to market as formerly. They are too anxious to see supplies brought out."[62]

General Grant seems to have been proven correct in his assumptions about the harmful effects of trade with conquered areas, though a total ban or prohibition would have been completely unworkable. As long as profits could be made on one side and a dire need existed on the other, some people would sell and others smuggle goods through the lines.

Even before the Civil War Vicksburg had not been a sleepy little river town, but had combined the characteristics of a community on the edge of the frontier: growing, amoral, and unbridled. It now added roles as refugee haven, military enclave, and jumping-off point for adventurers who sought fortune in the aftermath of war. For those persons who had an adequate income and were not lacking life's necessities, occupied Vicksburg was not an altogether unpleasant place in which to pass a year or two as an Army officer or would-be businessman or financier.

The native population of the city apparently accepted quite readily the increasingly frenetic pace of life in Vicksburg, but some of the visitors were not favorably impressed with what they

---

61. A. Sellew Roberts, "The Federal Government and Confederate Cotton," *American Historical Review*, 32 (January 1927), 275.

62. Samuel Glyde Swain to George Swain, February 11, 1865, Swain Papers, WSHS.

found there. For example, Henry Rountree, a Quaker missionary, portrayed the city as one "where sin and wickedness abound with scarcely a solitary redeeming feature, destitute of nearly all the comforts and enjoyments of life."[63] Rountree may have discovered "sin and wickedness" at Belle Forrest's bordello; or perhaps it was in the miscegenation at the Army camps; or perhaps he was incensed by the illegal trade and smuggling which were such an integral part of business in the city.[64] The missionary was certainly correct in some of his observations, for sin and wickedness were as abundant in Vicksburg in 1864 as they had been ten years earlier. Union occupation had not created the conditions, but it provided a fertile ground and stimulus for their growth. The city, however, was not as barren of creature comforts as Rountree's description suggests, and one reason was the influx of Union forces and all that came with them.

The Vicksburg Theater, for example, opened its season on June 14, 1864, with Mary Shaw playing the lead in *Pocahontas*, following which was the suggestively-titled *Child of the Regiment*. The cost of tickets was moderate, with orchestra and white gallery seats going for 50¢ and $1, respectively; a private box for six persons available for $10; and black theatergoers paying 50¢ for the privilege of sitting in a "colored gallery." New plays were presented at regular intervals, and by November the *Daily Herald* felt obliged to comment that "the scattering of green leaves from Lincoln's Treasury tree amongst the soldiers is telling on the receipts at this establishment. The boys in blue now form a respectable proportion of the audiences who nightly assemble there,

63. Henry Rountree to Cincinnati Contraband Relief Commission, March 20, 1864, *Henry Rowntree Letter Book and Record of Capt. Norton's business, Davis Bend, Miss*. RG 105 (Miss.), NA. The name was Rountree, but the bound volume in the National Archives has it spelled Rowntree on the cover.

64. *Criminal Docket, Maj. T.S. Free, A.J.G., Vicksburg, Miss., 1865*, Vol. 279, RG 105 (Miss.), NA; Charles P. Roland, *Louisiana Sugar Plantations during the American Civil War* (Leiden, Netherlands: E.J. Brill, 1957), 99.

and add to the music of the entertainment their enthusiastic applause." Theater managers Holland and Sharpe were good businessmen in addition to being successful thespians, and they garnered much public support by offering benefit performances, such as one for the wife of a Union officer taken prisoner at Franklin, Tennessee. "We are proud of our theater," announced the *Herald* editor, "and do not think a better can be found in this portion of Uncle Sam's domain."[65]

The theater was certainly one of the most popular diversions in the city, but it was by no means the only one. Athletic enthusiasts, for example, could find recreation with the Base Ball Club, which played every Saturday afternoon at three o'clock on the open ground below the arsenal. The Evergreen Race Course, located slightly south of Vicksburg, was also a great attraction, offering such weekly contests as "Gun Boat" vs. "Vicksburg Belle," run for a purse of $400.[66] Probably the greatest spectacle, though, was "S.B. Howe's Great European Circus," which thrilled the population early in 1865 with trained elephants, a kangaroo, and "six enormous lions, fresh from the forest untamed and unsubdued" save by the "magnipotent beast conqueror Crockett." The show played to packed houses, many persons undoubtedly drawn to see the deadly beasts that once had "escaped from their cages and devoured a poor fellow who fell in their way."[67]

Of a more intellectual bent were those who frequented the Union Literary Association, which began in the fall of 1863 and met in the basement of the Presbyterian church. The organization possessed a library of over 2,000 volumes within a year after its founding, and members, who were for the most part Union soldiers, participated in "declamations, discussions, and criticisms, interspersed with songs and music." Debate in the society was usually

---

65. *Vicksburg Daily Herald*, June 14, 1864; October 15, 1864; November 16, 1864; December 20, 1864; December 24, 1864.
66. *Ibid.*, October 15, 1864; August 16, 1864.
67. *Ibid.*, February 26, 1865.

quite vigorous, an example of the sort of topics entertained being "That it is policy for the government of the United States hereafter to keep a standing army of 100,000 men rather than to depend upon volunteers for national defense."[68]

The multitude of schools in Vicksburg provided educational opportunities for those who desired them. Black children and adults went exclusively to schools established and taught by Northern missionaries, as did a minority of the white population. Most white parents in Vicksburg, as in other occupied cities, however, preferred to send their children to private schools, if they could afford them, for reasons partially expressed by a citizen from Natchez: "Billy began school yesterday at the Marshall school. He will probably learn to hold his tongue, for not a word is allowed reflecting on the most beneficent Federal government, and the boys are compelled to join in all the Union songs. If they make the Confederates a nation of liars the sin is at their door, not ours."[69] The other, and most obvious, reason for not attending the missionary schools was of course that the classes were racially mixed.

Marmaduke Shannon sent his daughters Lavinia and Alice to Mr. and Mrs. J.T. Read's school for a few months during the winter and spring of 1863–1864, but at the cost of $6 per month, Lavinia decided it was not worth the money and quit going.[70] At least two other private schools were founded in Vicksburg in 1864 in addition to the refugee schools. The new educational establishments offered work in various subjects, including Latin, Greek, and French. One of the pedagogues was an M.P. Sullivan, "late Professor of Philosophy, Chemistry, and Astronomy, in Loyola

68. *Ibid.*, November 30, 1864; October 29, 1864.
69. Amelia Mandeville to Rebecca Mandeville, January 4, 1864, Mandeville Papers, Louisiana St. Univ. Lib.
70. Lavinia Shannon to Emma Crutcher, July 1, 1864; receipt for tuition payment, signed "J.T. Read," dated March 1864; Lavinia Shannon to Emma Crutcher, April 7, 1864, all in Crutcher-Shannon Papers, MDAH.

College, Baltimore (Md.)," while the other was William B. Anderson, whose "Select school" opened in September of the year. Charges for tuition ranged from $4 to $8 per month, "invariably in advance," as Sullivan phrased it.[71] Some citizens, as might be expected, were satisfied with none of the educational possibilities in Vicksburg, though only a small number went as far as did Eliza Lanier, who sent her daughter "back to Clinton. We got permission from the Federal Headquarters," she stated, "to let them through the lines."[72]

The Masonic Lodge played an important part in the social life of Vicksburg, though two of the Shannon sisters refused to cooperate when "two officers came . . . to invite Babe and I to a ball." The young men offered to send a carriage on the appointed night, but Mrs. Shannon "went into the parlor she told them that we never went in to society they told her that we might' as well commense now." Alice was infuriated at the idea that she and her sister would condescend to go with men in blue, and her comment on the event was a forlorn "I wish I was in Dixie."[73]

Vicksburg was not the desert that Henry Rountree portrayed, but neither was it New York or Boston or New Orleans. It was a city of contrasts, though the siege had leveled, literally, some of the differences. Less genteel than the Union Literary Society or the Masonic Ball, but undoubtedly of interest to more people, was the multitude of grogshops, saloons, and restaurants in the city, which offered everything from a very fine meal to the most terrible whiskey imaginable.[74]

Indeed, drinking seems to have been a favorite pastime in Vicksburg, and hundreds of men and women were arrested for

71. *Vicksburg Daily Herald*, June 8, 1864; June 9, 1864; August 13, December 24, 1864.
72. Manuscript copy of Eliza Ann Lanier's recollections of conditions in Warren County during the Civil War, in Timberlake Papers, MDAH.
73. Alice Shannon to Emma Crutcher, November 19, 1864, Crutcher-Shannon Papers, MDAH.
74. *Vicksburg Daily Herald*, October 14, 1864.

Occupied City 25

public drunkenness. The provost marshal's record book is replete with accounts of individuals who surfeited themselves with alcohol, and terms used to describe their condition — in no particular hierarchy of intoxication — include "drunk," "drunk but lively," "dead drunk," and "too drunk to give his name."[75]

The military commanders for the Vicksburg area were successively Grant, Sherman, McPherson, Henry Slocum, and N.J.T. Dana, and these men had no interest in strangling the city or increasing its growth or cleaning it up or ridding it of the sin and corruption which had always been there; but they had conquered the area and were now responsible for its government, a monumental task for which few Army officers were trained. The mayor and councilmen who served before Union occupation simply faded away, and it was almost exactly two years before Vicksburg experienced civilian rule again. General Dana, the primary administrator in Vicksburg for most of the occupation period, did use some civilians in positions of responsibility, but he customarily relied upon Army officers for most of his personnel needs. Both the city health officer and the street commissioner, for example, were members of the military, and most of the law enforcement duties were performed by details from the local command.[76]

The other instruments of law — primarily courts and judges — could hardly have been left as they were under the Confederate authorities. In both Vicksburg and Natchez local criminal courts were abolished by the military commander, and provost marshal courts were used to try civilian crimes, a system which ended in May 1865 when the U.S. judge advocate general decided that such practice was illegal.[77] The provost marshal at Vicksburg continued, however, to arrest and jail both civilians and soldiers even

75. Provost Marshal Records, OCHM.
76. *Vicksburg Daily Herald*, August 13, 1864; December 20, 1864; May 16, 1865.
77. James E. Sefton, *The United States Army and Reconstruction, 1865–1877* (Baton Rouge: Louisiana St. Univ. Press, 1967), 31–32.

after the War had ended. Extant records cover the period from April 1864 to August 1865, and, excluding arrests for drunkenness, over 500 persons were incarcerated on charges ranging from homicide to stealing pears. The most common crime was larceny (301 arrests), conviction of which usually resulted in a jail term of 10 to 30 days. There were also 22 persons charged with murder, 28 with assault and battery, 5 with rape or attempted rape, and 10 with arson. Other crimes included false pretenses, horse theft, robbery, burglary, breaking and entering, aiding an escape, possession of stolen property, passing counterfeit money, prostitution, wife beating, and cruelty to animals.[78]

Although a modern authority maintains that "the occupation army was fairly free of physical crimes against the civilians,"[79] troop discipline sometimes broke down, and the civilian population — both black and white — suffered as a result. The first major transgression charged against the occupying force occurred when a group of black soldiers was caught in the garden of a white civilian, John H. Bobb. Bobb drove the men from his property, even hitting one of them with a brick, "for his impudence," as Marmaduke Shannon related the story. An unidentified number of the troopers returned later with their guns and killed Bobb, allegedly by bayoneting him.[80] This incident provoked an immediate response from Gen. Henry Slocum, who addressed himself more to the white officers of the regiments than to the men involved. If the experiment of arming and making soldiers of ex-slaves were successful, Slocum asserted, "if these troops prove powerful and efficient in forcing obedience to law, all good officers connected with the organization will receive the credit which will be due them as pioneers in this great work. But if in teaching the colored

---

78. Provost Marshal Records, OCHM; *Criminal Docket, Major T.S. Free*, Vol. 279, RG 105 (Miss.), NA.
79. Walker, *Vicksburg*, 222.
80. Marmaduke Shannon to Emma Crutcher, May 18, 1864, Crutcher-Shannon Papers, MDAH.

man that he is free, and that in becoming a soldier he has become the equal of his former master, we forget to teach him the first duty of a soldier, that of obedience to the law . . . , nothing but disgrace and dishonor can befall all connected with the organization."[81] There is no indication that the parties responsible for the Bobb murder were ever apprehended or punished, but other malefactors were not so fortunate.

Pvt. Cornelius Thompson, Co. A, 48th Regiment, U.S. Colored Infantry, was executed by firing squad after conviction for the murder of an unidentified black civilian more than a month after Bobb's death;[82] and a friend of Samuel G. Swain, writing to him from Vicksburg, related that another member of Thompson's company had recently been hanged, also for committing murder.[83] For the next seven months there were no reports of civilians being killed by military personnel, but enough larcenies and petty thefts were laid at the Army's doorstep to keep the columns of the *Daily Herald* in a continual state of agitation. Soldiers in general — and black soldiers in particular — received much of the blame from local citizens for the "villainy loose in this city." A letter to the editor lamented that it was "sad to see how they are losing their reputation by marauding around and plundering."[84]

Soldiers were themselves sometimes the object of violence in the city, and in November 1864 one of the garrisoning force was found dead in the street, a bullet in his body. The discharge of firearms was so common, reported the *Herald*, that although neighbors had heard the shot about 2:00 A.M., no one had investigated until the next morning.[85] The most notorious crime,

---

81. General Orders #7, May 18, 1864, General Slocum, in *Vicksburg Daily Herald*, June 7, 1864.
82. *Vicksburg Daily Herald*, June 25, 1864.
83. Selden H. Clark to Samuel Glyde Swain, August 31, 1864, Swain Papers, WSHS.
84. *Vicksburg Daily Herald*, June 24, 1864; July 27, 1864.
85. *Ibid.*, November 10, 1864.

however, occurred in the last week of the War, when Mrs. T.K. Cook and her husband were fired on by a group of soldiers, for no reported reason. Mrs. Cook died of her wounds, and General Dana offered a $500 reward for the killers. Three days later the *Herald* announced the arrest of sixteen men and stated that a special commission would be appointed to investigate the case.[86] The commission finished its work by early the next month, and on May 11, 1865, the newspaper reported that twelve soldiers had been found guilty of murder and would hang for the crime.[87]

Soldiers did commit many crimes, but the civilian population of Vicksburg was charged with its fair share also. Indeed, civilians committed more larcenies (187 of 301) and assaults (17 of 28), swindled more people, stole more livestock, picked more pockets, aided more escapes, and broke and entered more frequently than did the soldiers.[88] Soldiers and civilians, too, often cooperated in the commission of crimes. William Smith of Co. H of the 5th Illinois Cavalry and G.W. Gregory and Thomas Burns, civilians, were all arrested on April 16, 1864, and charged with "Rioting firing Pistol in Negroes house to scare of Part of the Wimen and Rafishe the others." Rachel Richards, Jenny Coleman, and Minnie Hamilton were charged with "Keeping Boady [bawdy] House," while Jacob Johnson and other soldiers were arrested when they were "Found in House of Ill fame."[89]

Charges against those put into the city guardhouse were usually couched in language that implied the certain guilt of the arrested party, with very few persons being incarcerated for "allegedly" committing a crime. Thus Thomas Brown and John McGowan were arrested for "Striking and beating a negro," and C.C.

---

86. Marmaduke Shannon to Emma Crutcher, April 9, 1865, Crutcher-Shannon Papers, MDAH: Special Orders #123, April 5, 1865, General Dana, in *Vicksburg Daily Herald*, April 6, 1865.
87. *Vicksburg Daily Herald*, May 11, 1865.
88. Provost Marshal Records, OCHM.
89. *Ibid.*

McDaniel and H.J. Balkston, it was said, "slipped up behind" Joseph H. Boyle, the provost marshal's clerk, and "shot him in the back." The arrest of Barney Sheehan, civilian, was an exception, however. Sheehan, recorded the clerk, was "suspected of having the intention of stealing from William Kelly by putting his hand in the said William Kelly's pocket."[90]

The exact authority for many of the criminal charges — other than the wishes of the commander — is uncertain. There is no Federal common law as such, and many of the offenses charged would normally be statutory ones. Prostitution, for example, was only an ecclesiastical offense at common law, though the keeping of a brothel was a common law nuisance. Nor was Mississippi law apparently the source of authority. Eight men, for example, were arrested for wife beating, an offense on which the common law was not completely clear. Mississippi, however, had recognized as early as 1824 that a husband had authority, "with proper limitations and restrictions," to "use a whip or rattan no bigger than . . . [his] thumb, in order to enforce the salutary restraints of domestic discipline."[91] This Mississippi precedent was not binding on the U.S. authorities at Vicksburg, but it certainly does raise questions about historian James W. Garner's statement that the private law "was not disturbed" in areas under military control.[92] None of this, of course, explains the source of laws that were

90. *Ibid.*; *Criminal Court Docket, Major T.S. Free*, Vol. 279, RG 105 (Miss.), NA.

91. Provost Marshal Records, OCHM; Bradley v. State, 1 Miss. (Walker) 156, 157 (1824). Extreme chastisement could, however, be a battery. The reasoning of the court, as expressed by Justice Powhattan Ellis, was that "it was thought reasonable, to intrust him, with a power, necessary to restrain the indiscretions of one, for whose conduct he was to be made responsible." After the restoration of the civilian court system there are no records of men being arrested for wife beating. Mule beating, however, was still regularly punished. See Criminal Court Docket, December 1865–December 1869, OCHM.

92. James W. Garner, *Reconstruction in Mississippi* (New York: Macmillan, 1901), 29.

enforced in and around Vicksburg, and the lack of such a source must have created much uncertainty among those members of the civilian population who were concerned about such things.

No one in Vicksburg seems to have protested General Dana's criminal court system, though many citizens did sign a petition calling for the establishment of a U.S. district court in the city "of a civil character independent of, yet not in conflict with the military authority."[93] How this seemingly impossible military-judicial relationship was to exist, the petitioners did not indicate, and their request for the court apparently came to nought. Both legal and political matters agitated many of Vicksburg's citizens for the last two years of the War, and those questions which pertained to local law and government were much more satisfactorily answered by General Dana than were ones such as whether Vicksburg and her population could or should serve as the nucleus about which a pro-Union government in Mississippi could be organized.

Maj. Gen. Henry W. Halleck wrote to Grant shortly after the fall of Vicksburg and asked his opinion "in regard to the policy of attempting to organize a civil government in Mississippi."[94] Grant responded to Halleck by averring that "This state and Louisiana would be more easily governed now than Kentucky or Missouri if armed rebels from other states could be kept out." Furthermore, stated Grant, "I am informed that movements are being made through many parts of Mississippi to unite the people in an effort to bring the state into the Union. I receive letters and delegations on the subject myself, and believe the people are sincere."[95] Gen. Stephen A. Hurlbut, headquartered in Memphis, agreed with Grant's estimation, opining that "Mississippi is thoroughly broken-

93. *Vicksburg Daily Herald*, June 11, 1864.
94. Henry W. Halleck to Grant, July 30, 1863, *OR*, Ser. I, Vol. XXIV, Pt. 3, 562.
95. Grant to Halleck, August 11, 1863, *OR*, Ser. I, Vol. XXIV, Pt. 3, 587.

spirited." A group of some fifty "men of mark and position" from the state, Hurlbut informed President Lincoln, had recently sought permission to hold a meeting on the subject of governmental reorganization under the United States.[96] Hurlbut, however, did not allow the gathering, and it appears that both Grant and Halleck let the matter drop.

The citizens of Vicksburg seem not to have been overwhelmingly interested in seeing their state part of the Union again. It is not surprising that someone with the attitude of Marmaduke Shannon would make no mention of the subject; but even J.M. Swords, whose newspaper described itself as the "Largest and best paper published in Vicksburg, official journal of the city, is for the Union unconditionally, just the paper for loyal men," never broached the subject in his columns.[97] Local politicians, however, could hardly allow two years to pass without some sort of activity, and many of them found their outlet in the Vicksburg Union League, which in its periodic meetings affirmed support of President Lincoln and unconditional surrender for the Confederacy and condemned the National Democratic Convention.[98]

The months of military occupation passed slowly for those whose hearts still lay with the Confederacy. The first anniversary of Vicksburg's surrender, and coincidentally the birthdate of the United States, went by without the celebrations which had been so much a part of the pre-War period. There was a certain "sameness" to life, wrote Lavinia Shannon at that time, but she was led to "infinitely prefer it to the changes we have had in the last year or two."[99]

96. Hurlbut to Lincoln, August 11, 1863, *OR*, Ser. I, Vol. XXIV, Pt. 3, 588–89.
97. *Vicksburg Daily Herald*, February 26, 1865. Two years earlier, Swords had been just as rabidly pro-Confederate.
98. Vicksburg Union League to Lincoln, February 15, 1864, AL Papers (microfilm), reel 68, #30556; *Vicksburg Daily Herald*, September 16, 1864.
99. *Vicksburg Daily Herald*, June 29, 1864; Lavinia Shannon to Emma Crutcher, July 5, 1864, Crutcher-Shannon Papers, MDAH.

32   *Enclave: Vicksburg & Her Plantations*

The Shannons undoubtedly felt that the Union occupation was oppressive indeed. There were restrictions on personal liberty, freedom of speech, and commercial transactions. Union authorities were not tolerant of those who sought to aid the Confederacy by smuggling mail, or percussion caps, or medicines through the lines. Even the most ardent Confederate sympathizers must have realized, though, that they were on the losing side of the battle and their conquerors on the other, and that the yoke of occupation rested much lighter than it might have. Vicksburg was a difficult city to control and administer, and the evidence suggests that the U.S. commanders there did a creditable job. They attempted to suppress pro-Rebel expressions of support, but they also tried to control crime in the city. Gen. Benjamin Butler and his occupation of New Orleans must have been the standard against which Southerners could measure the relative harshness of occupation, and against this scale the occupation of Vicksburg was relatively mild.[100]

There were, nevertheless, many people who agreed with Mrs. Shannon, for the War had caused a tremendous upheaval in all that existed within the city. Slaves were free. Civil government was out; military commanders were in. Homes and businesses were destroyed; refugee shacks were erected. And all the old relationships between black and white were no longer accepted out of habit or custom. Many of the older white residents may have yearned for former times, but for black men, women, and children in the area, the commonly and joyfully expressed sentiment was that "de long-looked-fer done came at lass."[101]

100. Provost Marshal Records, July 22 and 23, August 9, September 27, October 18, 1864, and January 9, 1865.
101. Walker, *Vicksburg*, 210.

The Freedmen of Vicksburg

THE ENTIRE POPULATION OF VICKSBURG, plus all the surrounding plantation area, was forced to adjust to changes brought by the Union Army, but no group had their lives more affected by the War than did those who had been slaves when it began. The first rush of freedom was incomparable, and black men who only a few hours earlier had been someone's property lined the streets of Vicksburg on July 4, 1863, and shouted joyfully at the U.S. soldiers who paraded into the conquered city.[1] After the euphoria wore off, however, the freedmen realized that each person, black as well as white, was responsible for his own life. The sheer quantity of refugees who flocked into Vicksburg, however, was enough to overwhelm, in the beginning at least, almost any individual's effort. Even John Eaton, for whom the suffering of ex-slaves had become common, was shaken by the vision before him: "The scenes were appalling; the refugees were crowded together, sickly, disheartened, dying on the streets, not a family of them all either well-sheltered, clad, or fed; no physicians, no medicines, no hospitals; many of the persons who had been charged with feeding them either sick or dead."[2]

---

1. Abrams, *A Full and Detailed History*, 64–65.
2. John Eaton to Levi Coffin, July 5, 1864, printed in Eaton, *Grant, Lincoln, and the Freedmen*, 105.

Eaton and his Freedmen's Department made every attempt to care for the teeming multitudes who had been thrust upon them by the War, but soon over 30,000 persons were clamoring for attention and desperately needing help.[3] Two months after Eaton had begun his work, William Elder, Catholic Bishop of Natchez, visited the city whose inhabitants had suffered so much. "The negroes are dying in the streets of Vicksburg," he recorded in his diary. "The Federal Army expresses a willingness to feed all of them — but there is such a multiplicity of offices in the town that some of the negroes can hardly find out who to apply to. But those who have plenty are exposed to sickness from change of place and diet and water and from want of someone to look after them."[4] White refugees, too, were often in as desperate need as were the freedmen around them, but their condition was frequently overlooked by both military and civilian observers. One man who did not fail to record his impressions of the displaced whites, however, was the Rev. J. P. Bardwell, who described them as "in deplorable condition, sick, suffering, and dying in hovels, sheds, barns, tents on the levee and along the river banks. Helpless and almost hopeless, just as ignorant, poor, and degraded, as the slave, and usually twice as mean, despised by all classes, black, white, bond, and free."[5]

The editor of the *Daily Herald*, too, was touched by a particularly pathetic scene which he witnessed in June of 1864. On the gallery of a house, he reported, "lay a woman and two little children, all soundly sleeping upon the bare floor, without other covering than the garments they had on." These individuals were

   3. John Eaton to Abraham Lincoln, July 18, 1863, AL Papers (microfilm), reel 55, #24978.
   4. Bishop William Henry Elder, *Civil War Diary (1862–1865) of Bishop William Henry Elder Bishop of Natchez* (N.p.: Most Reverend R. O. Gerow, n.d.), 56.
   5. Rev. J. P. Bardwell to Rev. M. E. Strieby, December 24, 1864, American Missionary Association Papers (Miss.), Amistad Research Center, Dillard Univ., New Orleans, Louisiana.

Caucasian, and Swords was dismayed by what he saw. Although he had "read of scenes like this in the over-gorged cities where want and sorrow stalk at noonday, he . . . never expected to witness so sad a sight in Vicksburg."[6] The Unionist editor may have been shocked by such a scene simply because he was viewing three downtrodden members of his own race, but it is doubtful whether many black refugees saw anything particularly noteworthy in the situation, commonplace as it was within their part of Vicksburg's population.

The Treasury Department made an effort to provide for freedmen to the south of Vicksburg by establishing a "Home Farm" near Natchez. This operation, however, was so poorly managed that its sanitary facilities were condemned by the medical director of freedmen, and the majority of governmentally sponsored relief efforts continued under Eaton.[7] Fortunately for the refugees, and of immeasurable help to the government, aid soon began coming from a number of missionary and philanthropic organizations in the Northern states, in the form of both workers and materiel. Though the number of missionaries and teachers in the Vicksburg area could not have exceeded a hundred, their educational and relief work gave them an importance far greater than the size of their group would suggest.

These Northern emissaries were supported by several dozen organizations, from the prestigious American Missionary Association with headquarters in New York, to the "52d U.S. Col'd Inf.," stationed in Vicksburg itself. Most teachers were white, female, and single; though blacks, men, and married persons, usually couples, were also present. The most dedicated among them were like the Misses Beckwith and Whiting of the AMA, who left the relative security and comfort of the city and went out to the plantations to live and work;[8] or they were like Mary O.

6. *Vicksburg Daily Herald*, June 15, 1864.
7. Eaton, *Grant, Lincoln, and the Freedmen*, 162.
8. Thomas Smith to S. G. Wright, May 6, 1864, AMA Papers (Miss.).

Baker who established a school alone on an island in the river and there distributed food and clothing and taught such subjects as spelling, reading, mental arithmetic, singing, and needlework.[9] Despite lofty ideals and qualifications, however, and in spite of the hardships and dangers of the wartime mission field, there were in the group of workers in the Vicksburg area some whose personal qualities were soon called into question.

"Have people no conscience," demanded Samuel Wright of the AMA delegation, "about whom they recommend and send to this work?" Writing angrily to the home office of his organization, Wright explained that he had recently been forced to send back to St. Louis a woman of "loose character" who had been teaching at Vicksburg; and he had just discovered that the sickness of an unmarried teacher at Natchez had been caused by her pregnancy.[10] Henry Rountree of the Cincinnati Contraband Relief Commission felt that the best way to prevent difficulties was to eliminate unmarried women from the area, "seeing that many now here are greatly exposed to influences not at all calculated to adorn the great doctrine of God Our Saviour in all things."[11] Though no group seemed to be free of personal rivalries, accusations, antagonisms, or what John Eaton called "forms of self-seeking strangely at variance with the heroic self-sacrifices" which all were compelled to make, the amount of suffering alleviated by the relief organizations was immeasurable.

Materiel contributions to the work of "contraband relief" began flowing into the Mississippi Valley even before Vicksburg had fallen, and by one estimate over $268,000 in supplies had been

---

9. "Report of Mary O. Baker of School on Island #63, Miss. R. est'd. May 1, 1864," AMA Papers (Miss.).
10. Samuel G. Wright to Geo. Whipple, April 7, 1864, AMA Papers (Miss.).
11. Henry Rountree to Cincinnati Contraband Relief Commission, March 1, 1864, *Henry Rowntree Letter Book*, RG 105 (Miss.), NA.

delivered to the area by July of 1864.[12] The Shaker congregation at South Union, Kentucky, sent boxes of clothing,[13] and other organizations did likewise, so that by the beginning of February 1864 the relief effort had progressed to the point where an AMA worker could report that, "We have succeeded in getting clothing . . . to cover their nakedness and bedding to keep them about half comfortable."[14] Despite the cold winter, when temperatures dropped to an unheard-of eight degrees below zero in Vicksburg,[15] conditions among the freedmen and other refugees continued so much to improve during February that Henry Rountree suggested to his superiors that he might even return to Island No. 10 "there to resume my missionary labours for the next few months."[16]

By the first of March 1864, however, Rountree informed the Commission that, "the Army that lately left this place under Major General Sherman is now returning and have with them no less than eight thousand coloured people just released from slavery."[17] Thus continued the endless stream of helpless and destitute persons, mostly ex-slaves, who flowed into Vicksburg lacking practically every necessity of life. That these refugees appreciated the help given them has not been doubted, but few of their expressions of thanks were recorded as was that of an old woman who, with tears in her eyes, responded to a gift with "God bless you misses. God bless you. I knows de Lord sent you here 'cos I's

---

12. Martha M. Bigelow, "Vicksburg: Experiment in Freedom," *Journal of Mississippi History*, 26 (1964), 33.
13. Henry Rountree to Cincinnati Contraband Relief Commission, March 16, 1864, *Henry Rowntree Letter Book*, RG 105 (Miss.), NA.
14. A. Eberhard to Rev. C. W. Fowler, February 1, 1864, AMA Papers (Miss.).
15. Rev. S. W. Magill to "Brethren," January 8, 1864, AMA Papers (Miss.).
16. Henry Rountree to Cincinnati Contraband Relief Commission, February 22, 1864, *Henry Rowntree Letter Book*, RG 105 (Miss.), NA.
17. *Ibid.*, March 1, 1864.

prayed 'dese many days for Him to send me a friend and prayed all de' night wid de Lord to send me help and now its come. O bless de Lord and you too misses."[18]

Many of the refugees were sick as well as ill-clad and hungry, so one of the priorities had been to establish health-care facilities in Vicksburg. The United Presbyterian Church was first at the task, sending some twenty workers to the city and quickly setting up a "contraband hospital" there.[19] This operation was soon taken over by the Freedmen's Department and was improved to the extent that by July 1865, Dr. D. O. McCord, Medical Director of Freedmen for the Department of Mississippi, felt confident to claim "the finest freedmen's hospital in the United States" and encouraged "a comparison with any Army hospital." Freedmen admitted to the facility from November 15, 1863, to April 5, 1864, experienced a death rate of 164/1,000, with fatalities caused by conditions ranging from "dog bite" to "varicose veins." The number of freedmen dying in the hospital decreased as spring and summer replaced the first hard winter of 1863, but serious maladies continued to afflict a large proportion of the black refugee population.[20]

Relieving the bodily suffering of those with whom they came into contact, however, was only the secondary purpose of many organizations, especially those which were religiously affiliated. The Congregationalist-dominated AMA, for example, according to a student of the society, sought teachers who were "fired with

18. L. A. Eberhart to Rev. C. W. Fowler, February 1, 1864, AMA Papers (Miss.).
19. Rev. S. G. Wright to Bro. Cowles, November 16, 1863, AMA Papers (Miss.).
20. "Annual Report of D. O. McCord, Med. Dir. & Insp. of Freedmen, Dept. of Miss.," Box 36, RG 105 (Miss.), NA; Samuel F. Porter to Geo. Whipple, April 5, 1864, AMA Papers (Miss.); *Morning Report, Freedmen's Hospital, Vicksburg, Miss.*, RG 105 (Miss.), NA; *Register, Freedmen's Hospital, Vicksburg, Miss., 1863*, RG 105 (Miss.), NA.

Primary School for Freedmen — Dedicated teachers like Mrs. Green brought literacy to thousands of ex-slaves. Courtesy: Library of Congress

missionary zeal" and "religious to the point of fanaticism."[21] And the spirit which drove their missionary workers was perhaps best expressed by a supervisor in Vicksburg who maintained unequivocally that, "where the planter can go, the missionary must go — with the school and the gospel."[22]

The American Missionary Association was not, however, the

---

21. Henry Lee Swint, *The Northern Teacher in the South, 1862–1870* (Nashville: Vanderbilt Univ. Press, 1941), 36.

22. Rev. Samuel G. Wright to Rev. Geo. Whipple, January 29, 1864, AMA Papers (Miss.).

first to establish freedmen's schools in Vicksburg, for the United Brethren of Ohio were pioneers in the area. Other groups soon arrived, and by January of 1864 eight different societies were supporting teachers there.[23] Tuition charges ranged from nothing to $1 per month, according to family income, and although it is dangerous to generalize on the basis of the one month's records which are available, most students appear to have paid little or nothing for their education.[24]

The greatest problems encountered in teaching the refugees were caused by the lack of suitable schoolhouses, occasional interference of the military authorities, and the scarcity of books, especially primers. "Our school here is in the barn," wrote one teacher, "and the weather quite cool and damp,"[25] while another rejoiced at finally securing a tent in which to hold her classes.[26] Military authorities were in general favorably disposed toward the work of educating refugees, and U.S. Adj. Gen. Lorenzo Thomas even authorized rations, quarters, and transportation at Government expense for workers involved in the effort.[27] Vicksburg was especially fortunate in being governed by men like Maj. Gen. N. J. T. Dana, who was of much the same mind as Thomas.[28] But Natchez, her sister town to the south, was an example of the mischief an ill-disposed commander could cause.

23. *Vicksburg Daily Herald*, February 24, 1865; Rev. S. W. Magill to the "Secretaries," January 7, 1864, AMA Papers (Miss.).

24. Records for April 1865 indicate that of 461 pupils in one group of schools in Vicksburg, only 6 paid the full fee, while 222 were charged nothing at all and 115 contributed less than 25¢ each. *Pupils*, Vol. 289, RG 105 (Miss.), NA.

25. Rev. S. G. Wright to Rev. Geo. Whipple, November 25, 1863, AMA Papers (Miss.).

26. Fannie J. Scott to Rev. C. W. Fowler, February 1, 1864, AMA Papers (Miss.).

27. Special Orders # 63, September 29, 1863, Adj. Gen. Lorenzo Thomas, quoted in Eaton, *Grant, Lincoln, and the Freedmen*, 194.

28. Dana, for example, sent wagons and men to assist the Sisters of Mercy Convent in rebuilding their schoolrooms. Elder, *Civil War Diary*, 112.

The Freedmen of Vicksburg 41

The brigadier there, General Tuttle, was quoted by one prospective teacher as saying he wished "the missionaries and teachers would let the niggers alone that they were well enough off." A Union soldier stationed there also took note of the general's attitude, writing to his sister in Wisconsin, "I think there is some copper composition about him,"[29] meaning that he was a "copperhead," or Confederate sympathizer. As a result of General Tuttle's hostility, townspeople were more open in their opposition to the freedmen's schools, and guerrilla raiders felt free to come nearer town to prey upon schoolteachers and their charges.[30] Both General Tuttle and his subordinate, Colonel Kelly, were eventually relieved of their commands in Natchez, causing Samuel Wright to comment that, "the people all breathe easier."[31]

The lack of textbooks, however, was the most continuing problem in Vicksburg, with Fannie Campbell issuing in December 1864 an agonized plea for "200 Sanders Primary School Primers" and some "large alphabet cards."[32] Despite such difficulties, however, the freedmen school system in and around Vicksburg grew and prospered, reaching a fluctuating total of 1,500 to 1,800 scholars by April 1864, a number which was maintained for the next full year.[33]

The missionary-teachers usually held in high regard the academic ability of their pupils, with one pedagogue after another recording such comments as "the progress made was really astonishing," or "I . . . have *never* seen such zeal on the part of

29. Samuel G. Wright to Geo. Whipple, March 9, 1864, AMA Papers (Miss.); Samuel Glyde Swain to sister, April 12, 1864, Swain Papers, WSHS.
30. Wm. Thirds to Geo. Whipple, November 19, 1863, AMA Papers (Miss.); Samuel G. Swain to sister, April 12, 1864, Swain Papers, WSHS.
31. Samuel G. Wright to Geo. Whipple, May 23, 1864, AMA Papers (Miss.).
32. Fannie Campbell to Geo. Whipple, December 6, 1864, AMA Papers (Miss.).
33. Rev. Samuel F. Porter, "Statistics of the Freed People at Vicksburg, April 1864," AMA Papers (Miss.); *Pupils*, Vol. 289, RG 105 (Miss.), NA.

pupils nor such advancement as I see among these dusky sons and daughters of Ham."[34] Their students seldom left written opinions of the schools or teachers, but adult freedmen demonstrated their feelings by regular attendance and diligent study, even when they had to miss a few weeks on Army duty.[35]

The younger scholars in the group were not perhaps free agents in choosing school over hunting and fishing, for their attendance may well have been under some initial duress. At least a few of them, however, did develop affection for their teachers, if not for the subjects themselves. Hannah Williams, conducting lessons in the state capital of Jackson after the War, related to her daughter Sarah the details of a touching scene in which a student presented to her one of his most prized possessions — "a large fancifully ornamented candy heart." And a teacher in Vicksburg described, with some hint of amusement, how "last Sabbath as our scholars passed out of school, one bright little black girl from the infant class came up to me and put *fifteen cents* into my hand with the words, 'For the *heathen* across the water who don't know anything about God.'"[36]

The education provided at this great expenditure of time, money, and tireless labor was necessarily of a rudimentary sort, yet it did result in the creation of thousands of new literates. This fact alone, thought John Eaton, made all the effort worthwhile, for it made the freedmen "no longer creatures whom it would be safe to re-enslave."[37] Alice Shannon was not especially upset by the presence of black schools in her city, but she maintained a

34. James Peet to John Eaton, May 7, 1864, and Fannie J. Scott to Rev. C. W. Fowler, February 1, 1864, both in AMA Papers (Miss.).

35. Fannie Campbell to Geo. Whipple, January 9, 1865, AMA Papers (Miss.).

36. Hannah Williams to Sarah Williams, February 7, 1868, Stratton (Edward F.) Papers, Friends Historical Library, Swarthmore College; E. Louise Lyon to agent, the AMA, March 9, 1868, AMA Papers (Miss.).

37. Eaton, *Grant, Lincoln, and the Freedmen*, 204.

great dislike for the persons who taught in them. Alice did not speak out publicly, but poured out her feelings in a long epistle to her sister Emmie. "This evening," reported the young girl, "two women came to the gate and asked Ma if there were any negro children on the place. Ma told them yes, they said they only wanted to let her know because there was going to be a school in the corner house, and it would be convenient to send them if they wanted to go. Oh, the impudence of these Yankees, I hate them more every day."[38] The white population of the city reacted carefully to the presence of freedmen's schools in Vicksburg, though John Eaton did find some who were "bitter in denunciation" of the effort made.[39] For most people, however, having their former slaves learn to read was not the major irritant in the new relationship fostered by the Union presence in Vicksburg. Alice Shannon expressed the feelings of many of these people when she wrote, "I am getting to hate all the negros, every Sunday if I want to, I might see a regiment of negro soldiers marching so grand in their blue uniform commanded by white officers . . . making a fine show."[40] In the first months after capturing the city, though, black troops devoted most of their time to working on the fortifications, and the Sunday evening parades were the high point of the week for them. The policy of enlisting former slaves into the Army was still new in July 1863, and even General Grant's attitude as to the proper employment of such troops was yet in its infant stage, as is suggested in a communication to General McPherson on July 22: "No more details of white troops will be made to work on the fortifications in the vicinity of Vicksburg at present. Negro troops will be brought here for that purpose.

    38. Alice Shannon to Emma Crutcher, November 19, 1863, Crutcher-Shannon Papers, MDAH.
    39. Eaton, *Grant, Lincoln, and the Freedmen*, 204.
    40. Alice Shannon to Emmie Crutcher, November 19, 1863, Crutcher-Shannon Papers, MDAH.

During the present hot weather, it is necessary to save our men as much as possible from fatigue duty in the sun."[41] Grant revised his ideas in the months to come, but well into the next year, after he had gone east, some regiments of ex-slaves still did garrison and fatigue duty along the river to the virtual exclusion of all other activities.[42]

Black regiments, of course, demonstrated their military talent many times in the course of the War; and events like the heroic charge of the 54th Massachusetts at Fort Wagner, the seven assaults on Port Hudson, and the ferocious defense of Milliken's Bend are part of the valor of the Civil War.[43] Not so well publicized, however, were the actions of the "First Mississippi Cavalry of African Descent," which assisted in the defense of Vicksburg during the months after the city was captured.

This impressive-sounding group was "under the command of the venerable George Washington . . . mounted on a sprained horse, with his hat plumed with the ostrich feather, his full belly girt with a stout belt, from which hangs a terrible cleaver, and followed by his trusty orderly on foot." General Sherman brought this group to the attention of his fellow commander, McPherson, with the amused suggestion that this "army on your flank" would give "every assurance of safety from that exposed quarter." Opéra bouffe as it sounded, however, Adj. Gen. Lorenzo Thomas was able to report to Stanton in December 1863 that this band, riding mules, "have already proved their efficiency in that branch of the service, 150 having recently defeated 300 rebels in a conflict near Vicksburg."[44]

41. Grant to McPherson, July 22, 1863, *OR*, Ser. I, Vol. XXIV, pt. 3, 542.
42. Samuel Glyde Swain to sister, March 18, 1864, Swain Papers, WSHS.
43. Dudley Taylor Cornish, *The Sable Arm: Negro Troops in the Union Army, 1861–1865* (New York: Longmans, Green & Co., 1956), 142–45,153–55.
44. Sherman to McPherson, September 4, 1863, *OR*, Ser. I, Vol. XXX, pt. 3, 336–37; Thomas to Stanton, December 24, 1863, *OR*, Ser. 3, Vol. III, 1191.

First Mississippi Cavalry of African Descent — Bringing in Confederates captured at Haine's Bluff.

The black regiments at Vicksburg were only a small part of the area's total population, but their camps formed the core of a teeming, unnamed, and unofficial community, in which dwelled in many cases the wives, daughters, sons, and parents of the men stationed there. These squatting refugees were not willing to leave their relatives and go to the regular camps, where they would be among strangers, and as a consequence, the superintendent of freedmen refused to issue them rations.[45] It is entirely possible, therefore, that many of the thefts attributed to soldiers were committed by men who simply could not support families on their own meager pay.

The great majority of freedmen in Vicksburg, however, were not in any direct way connected with the military, but were free and in the city as a result of the War. The sudden coming of freedom necessarily evoked differing responses from those affected, for some slaves were more capable and desirous of assuming responsibility for their own subsistence than were others. As the former soon reached out and developed a black society in Vicksburg modeled after its white counterpart, the latter yet clung to the old ways and "looked unto Master at every decision."[46]

Many ex-slaves supported themselves as barbers, hack drivers, cooks, laundresses, fruit and vegetable vendors, blacksmiths, cobblers, or in any other way in which a little money might be earned,[47] but the presence of thousands of refugees in the city meant that even the most willing laborers often found no opportunities for employment, and some, like the Shannons' former slave Calvin, even offered to return and work for their old masters, "the same as . . . always."[48]

Although the Shannons were not necessarily typical of Vicksburg's slaveowning families, there was evidently more than or-

45. A. Eberhard to Rev. C. W. Fowler, February 1, 1864, AMA Papers (Miss.).
46. Henry Rountree to Cincinnati Contraband Relief Commission, March 1, 1864, *Henry Rountree Letter Book*, RG 105 (Miss.), NA; Rountree's observation of the more timid part of the freed population caused him, so he said, to favor not immediate, but "gradual emancipation."
47. Eaton, *Grant, Lincoln, and the Freedmen*, 132–133; Marmaduke Shannon to Emma Crutcher, May 18, 1864, Crutcher-Shannon Papers, MDAH; "Trade Permits in Effect in Vicksburg, 1864," Box 222A, RG 366, 2nd SA, NA.
48. Alice Shannon to Emma Crutcher, November 19, 1863, Crutcher-Shannon Papers, MDAH.

dinary affection—or perhaps it was just a mutual dependence—between the eight "servants," as they were called, and the sons, daughters, and parents of the household. "It is a little surprising," wrote Anne Shannon to her older sister Emmie two months after the surrender of Vicksburg, "that father's servants should stand by the family when almost everyone else's left."[49] Even the Shannons, however, soon found that their most able servants were anxious to develop their own lives separate from those of their former owners, and within a few months only "Harriet and her girl," who "would do nothing,"[50] remained in the household.

The Marmaduke Shannon family were among the fortunate ones in Vicksburg, for, reported Lavinia, "We are living very comfortably here. Our fences are all up and the garden looks beautiful though very much overgrown with weeds." The elder Shannon, no longer a newspaper editor, was completely capable of doing his own chores, so that his household ran quite well, even without outside help.[51] Many families in Vicksburg, however, were not so able to adapt to the loss of their slaves, and hiring replacements from among the newly-coined freedmen was not always satsifactory.

"The great multitude," wrote John Eaton of Vicksburg's black residents, "were unprepared to work beyond supplying their immediate necessities. As laborers, they came and went regardless of their agreements or the wishes of their employers. Housekeepers often had a new cook for each meal in the day."[52] Some persons, however, managed to find satisfactory replacements for their departed slaves, and these gems were often praised to an extreme.

49. Anne Shannon to Emma Crutcher, September 16, 1863, Crutcher-Shannon Papers, MDAH.
50. Alice Shannon to Emma Crutcher, November 19, 1863, Crutcher-Shannon Papers, MDAH.
51. Lavinia Shannon to Emma Crutcher, July 1, 1864, Crutcher-Shannon Papers, MDAH.
52. John Eaton to Levi Coffin, July 5, 1864, printed in Eaton, *Grant, Lincoln and the Freedmen*, 105.

48 *Enclave: Vicksburg & Her Plantations*

Marriage Ceremony — This black soldier at Vicksburg was one of thousands whose family tie was solemnized by Chaplain Warren of the Freedmen's Bureau.

A cook secured in Natchez, for example, was described as "perfect in every detail of her department — from snowy rolls and feathery pastry to the most substantial and recherche dinner, and so pleasant that I find myself making frequent unnecessary trips to the kitchen." Even a member of this family, though, was forced to describe another employee as "the plague of my life" who felt that "answering bells is played out."[53] Although the itinerant nature of many house servants released from bondage was quite an irritant for the employer, it was a predictable exercise of newly acquired prerogatives and served as an important confirmation of the fact that indeed they were free. Corroboration of this new

53. Amelia Mandeville to Rebecca Mandeville, January 4, 1864, Mandeville Papers, Louisiana St. Univ. Lib.

status could also be found in the creation of a legally recognized black family unit.

Missionaries and Army chaplains in the area performed over 3,000 marriage ceremonies during 1864 alone, despite a charge of 50¢ for each wedding solemnized. The half-dollar fee, so Col. Samuel Thomas explained in a special order, went "to pay for blanks, books, and other expense of keeping the records,"[54] and each couple joined together received a printed certificate similar to the one given after a Davis Bend wedding:[55]

I HAVE this day united in Matrimony, *Hamilton Oliver* of *Davis Bend*. Age of man *59* years; color, *Black*; do. of his father *Black*; of his mother *Black*; lived with another woman *12* years; separated from her by *Force*. Age of woman *24* years; color *Mulat.*; do. of her father *White*; do. of her mother, *Black*; lived with another man *4* years; separated from him by *Force.* They unitedly have — children; do. of the man by previous connection, *1*; do. of the woman by do. *2*.

WITNESS_____ MINISTER_____

Although there were in Vicksburg a few activities, like watching performances at the local theater, in which black and white citizens participated jointly, most freedmen demonstrated a desire to establish themselves in their own community, as in the founding of an African Methodist Episcopal Church in the city and the choosing of delegates in September 1864 to a freedmen's convention in New York. It is not known, however, whether anyone from Vicksburg actually went to the meeting.[56] The National Freedmen's

54. Benjamin Quarles, *The Negro in the Civil War* (Boston: Little, Brown, & Co., 1953), 289; Special Orders # 23, December 2, 1864, Col. Samuel Thomas, *Special Orders, Provost Marshal of Freedmen*, RG 105 (Miss.), NA.
55. Certificate of Marriage, June 8, 1865, in "Reports," *Mississippi Davis Bend, Letters Received*, RG 105 (Miss.), NA.
56. Revels A. Adams, *Cyclopedia of African Methodism in Mississippi*, 147, 204, cited in Ross H. Moore, "Social and Economic Conditions in

Relief Association cared for orphans in the city,[57] but an enterprising group at the AME Church took care of some of their own needs by founding the Daughters of Zion, a sort of mutual health insurance and income protection cooperative composed of "females of African descent. The subscription is only $1.00 enterence [sic] fee and fifty cents a month afterwards, securing to each member $2.00 [per month] while unable to provide for herself."[58]

Apparently, however, not all new residents of Vicksburg were as thrifty or as farsighted as was the group at the AME Church, for a report filed by the superintendent of freedmen for the city gloomily explained that, "having been provided with the necessities of life by their masters they [slaves] were accustomed to spend the little money they came in possession of, for some little luxury," and many were still demonstrating an appalling lack of thrift over a year after the coming of freedom to the area.[59] John Eaton, too, saw that many newly freed persons were having a difficult time, for "speculation, vice, and crime swarmed around young and old alike, stealing their little gold and silver, or decoying them away to abuse their ignorance."[60] And Colonel Eaton was in a good position from which to observe the freedmen of Vicksburg, for though all civilians necessarily had numerous contacts with the occupying forces, no people had their lives more touched by the men in U.S. uniforms than did the former slaves.

Though they were now nominally free, each black civilian had his wanderings closely watched by the local provost marshal and

---

Mississippi during Reconstruction" (unpublished Ph.D. Diss. Duke Univ., 1937), 286; *Vicksburg Daily Herald*, September 14, 1864. There may have been an AMA church in the city before the War, as one is shown on an early map of Vicksburg.

57. "Report of Edward Wilkes," June 27, 1865, Box 36, RG 105 (Miss.), NA.

58. *Vicksburg Daily Herald*, July 15, 1864.

59. Lt. A. M. Brobst to Col. John Eaton, July 16, 1864, Box 35, RG 105 (Miss.), NA.

60. Eaton, *Grant, Lincoln and the Freedmen*, 135.

was not permitted on the streets after 8:00 P.M. without written permission from the military authorities.[61] Local commanders, spurred by incessant grumblings from the white population, were continually attempting to remove from the city any idle or unruly freedmen; and after a complaint in the *Herald*, for example, in which "quarreling, fighting, throwing bricks, &c.&c." were specifically noted, a group of six unidentified black women was sent across the Mississippi and warned against returning.[62]

In addition to the occasional deportation of an unemployed black civilian—there are no records of whites being sent out except for disloyalty—both Col. John Eaton and his successor, Col. Samuel Thomas, attempted to bring additional order to the city by providing that only those freedmen with a letter of employment be allowed to remain and pass through the lines.[63] This system, though it may have had some slight effect, was generally ignored by the thousands who never attempted to cross the picket lines or leave the city of Vicksburg.

Col. Thomas' superior, Maj. Gen. C. C. Washburne, also took an interest in the refugee situation and issued orders requiring that a "large number of the Colored people of the city and vicinity, that were living in idleness and vagrancy . . . be removed." Thomas' attempts to carry out the charge, however, were frustrated by "the mistaken idea of philanthropy" of a civilian chaplain named Carruthers. The chaplain, said Colonel Thomas, was plac-

---

61. General Orders #1, printed in *Natchez Daily Courier*, September 18, 1863; this order was enforced even late in the War, as witnessed by the March 24, 1865, arrest of one "Major Cook," a "col'd Citizen" who was hauled before the provost marshal's court for "Being out after hours." Cook pled guilty to the charge and was released, "There being no evidence of any further misconduct." *Criminal Docket, Maj. T. S. Free* Vol. 279, RG 105 (Miss.), NA.
62. *Vicksburg Daily Herald*, September 7, 1864; September 8, 1864.
63. Passes issued James Roberts, "colored," by John Eaton, August 12, 1864, and by Samuel Thomas, June 22, 1865, both found in Roach-Eggleston Papers, SHC, Univ. of North Carolina.

Colonel Samuel Thomas — Young, vigorous and strong-willed administrator of freedman's programs in Mississippi. Courtesy: Library of Congress

ing obstructions in the way of sound administrative practice by continually questioning the legality of his methods.[64]

Thomas' acute awareness of the presence and potentially powerful influence of men like Carruthers was well illustrated in comments submitted in a report on the military's attempts to cope with the growing number of freedmen in the city. Because no funds were available in Vicksburg for the burial of destitute blacks, wrote Thomas, the civilian population of the city should be required to bear the expense. He had therefore issued an order establishing a "Permit to remain in the city," the cost being set at 20¢ per month. Exempted from the necessity of obtaining a permit were "Government employees, Officers' Servants, Laun-

---

64. Endorsement of Col. Samuel Thomas, January 31, 1865, *Endorsements, Provost Marshal, Vicksburg, Mississippi (1865)*, Vol. 73, RG 105 (Miss.), NA.

dresses of Regiments, &c., making the tax fall on those who ought to leave the city." Though everyone in the population was included within the scope of the order, Thomas was apparently aiming the regulation at vagrant freedmen. He had first submitted the order to Brig. Gen. Morgan L. Smith, who approved it, as did Maj. Gen. Washburne. It next received the sanction of U.S. Adj. Gen. Lorenzo Thomas; and now, said Colonel Thomas, "I hope it will . . . receive that of Mr. Carruthers, when the whole thing will certainly be settled."[65] Even this seemingly encompassing campaign against indolence, however, was doomed by events over which Thomas had no control and which could not be blamed on the ideas or actions of anyone.

The late winter months of 1865 were quite rainy over much of the Mississippi Valley, and this runoff, coupled with the normally large volume of water created by melting snow and ice, swelled the great river at Vicksburg's front and pushed it out of its normal bounds. "There being no levees," Marmaduke Shannon wrote, "the country is nearly all under water; this has driven thousands of negroes here, in addition to what we had before. Our population is very thick and dark."[66]

Colonel Thomas apparently resigned himself to the continued presence of thousands of freedmen in the city[67] for at least as long as the lands about were flooded, but Provost Marshal Maj. S. Cornwell recommended, "As a sanitary precaution that as soon as the river falls there be a general cleaning out of the colored population who have no honest means of support."[68]

65. *Ibid.*
66. Marmaduke Shannon to Emma Crutcher, May 2, 1865, Crutcher-Shannon Papers, MDAH.
67. The exact size of the black population of Vicksburg is undetermined, but Marmaduke Shannon estimated in April that there were still as many as 25,000 "loose negroes" in the immediate vicinity. Marmaduke Shannon to Emma Crutcher, April 9, 1865, Crutcher-Shannon Papers, MDAH.
68. Endorsement of Maj. S. Cornwell, April 21, 1865, *Endorsements, Provost Marshal, Vicksburg, Mississippi (1865)*, Vol. 73, RG 105 (Miss.), NA.

54 Enclave: Vicksburg & Her Plantations

Many of Vicksburg's leading white citizens had long since decided that something had to be done about the "countless thousands of former slaves" who now thronged the city's streets, and few were pleased by the ineffectiveness of Colonel Thomas' proposals. J. M. Swords, the fervently pro-Union editor of the *Daily Herald*, reflected much community sentiment in his column of March 8, 1865, when he enumerated facts and expressed opinions which he felt were indisputable. "Negro huts," he declared, "are crowded all over the city—within and without the fortifications, each little shanty of boards or tent containing from one to half a dozen families. . . . The inevitable result of such a crowded population," he explained, "must be disastrous to the health as well as to the safety of the city. The negro is not remarkable for his observance of the laws of cleanliness, and the atmosphere around their cabin is not always of the purest." Expressing fears of smallpox and yellow fever epidemics, Swords urged that all unemployed freedmen be resettled on plantations away from the city. He then described life in the country as it would be for those fortunate enough to be transported there. "The plantations which have been set apart for them," wrote the editor with more than a little exaggeration, "are so fertile that moderate labor will yield an ample remuneration. It will be no hardship, but an actual benefit to these people to send them to these farms."[69] Many blacks had, of course, already made the suggested move, and thousands more would do so within the next year, but whether they were better off than their city-dwelling cousins is quite open to debate.[70]

69. *Vicksburg Daily Herald*, March 8, 1865.
70. The number of freedmen who left the city proper after the War is reflected in census figures which reveal that in November 1866, only 3,793 blacks lived in Vicksburg. *Census Returns, 1866, Sunflower, Tallahatchie, Tippah, Warren, Washington, and Wayne Counties*, RG 28, Records of Secretary of State, MDAH.

Plantations without Slaves

JUST AS THE CITY OF VICKSBURG depended largely on the Mississippi River for its commercial importance, so the plantations around it owed their ultimate existence to the same source, for it was the river which had created their lands. Each spring for thousands of years before anyone entered the area known as Mississippi, the great, muddy river, gorged with waters of half a continent, backed up into the smaller rivers, creeks, and bayous which meandered over the flat lands on each side of its channel. These tributary streams thereupon spilled out over the countryside, and when they finally returned to their normal courses, they left behind a layer of silt which each succeeding year became thicker.[1] Early in the nineteenth century, planters moved into Mississippi and discovered its rich soils, and their agricultural efforts had by 1860 made the state the nation's leading cotton producer.[2] The coming of the Civil War, however, put an immediate halt to the expanding cotton production characteristic of the previous four decades, and during 1862 and early 1863 many planters along

---

1. Robert L. Brandfon, *Cotton Kingdom of the New South: A History of the Yazoo Mississippi Delta from Reconstruction to the Twentieth Century* (Cambridge: Harvard Univ. Press, 1967), 26–30.
2. United States Department of the Interior, Bureau of the Census, *Eighth Census of the United States: 1860. Agriculture*, 185.

the Mississippi River were forced to flee at the approach of Union troops.[3]

Slaves freed by the blueclad soldiers were generally ecstatic over the sudden turn in their lives. As one elderly ex-slave remembered the event some sixty years afterward, "De Yankees come 'roun' . . . and tol' us we's free an' we shouted an' sang, and had a big celebration fer a few days. Den we got to wonderin' 'bout what good it did us."[4] Indeed, this new freedom was not as unbridled as many anticipated it would be, for the Federal government quickly stepped in to impose a new order on the situation. The cotton crop of 1862 was still much in the fields when U. S. Grant arrived on the Mississippi early the next year; and to provide employment for refugees, he gave authority to gather this crop to a group of white businessmen. Those with whom Grant made the arrangement then employed the displaced blacks to gather the cotton at a rate of a penny a pound. Half of the cotton picked under this contract belonged to the Government, but the contractors received some 67¢ a pound for their share.[5]

In many cases, the newly freed slaves had little or no choice but to work for those with whom cotton arrangements were made, for the provost marshal at "every military post" was charged with seeing that "every negro within the jurisdiction of the military authority is employed by some white person, or is sent to the camps provided for freed people."[6] The Government soon expanded this system of employment for the refugees. An act passed in June of 1862 had given authority to the tax commissioners to lease "abandoned lands," and under its provisions the Treasury De-

3. Quarles, *The Negro in the Civil War*, 126–127.
4. Slave narrative of Clara Young, Slave Narrative Collection, Mississippi, Library of Congress.
5. Thomas W. Knox, *Camp-Fire and Cotton-Field* (Philadelphia: Jones Bros. & Co., 1865), 307; McNeily, "War and Reconstruction," 193; Livermore, *My Story of the War*, 351.
6. General Orders #51, August 10, 1863, *OR*, Ser. I, Vol. XXIV, pt. 3, 149.

partment opened for leasing an area that stretched along the Mississippi River from twenty miles south of Vicksburg to thirty-five miles north of the city.[7] The "primary objects" of the lease program, according to U.S. Adj. Gen. Lorenzo Thomas, were "to line the banks of the Mississippi River with a loyal population and to give aid in securing the uninterrupted navigation of the river, at the same time to give employment to the freed negroes whereby they may earn wages and become self-supporting."[8] Unfortunately — and perhaps unavoidably — in its desire to accomplish quickly the first of these objectives, the Government evidenced little concern over the character of those to whom leases were given. The results were quite predictable, and according to John Eaton, as soon as the leasing began into the valley swarmed "a distinct class whose interests were primarily commercial and involved patriotism or humanity only as secondary and incidental considerations."[9]

James Yeatman of the Western Sanitary Commission expressed a similar opinion, stating that "the parties leasing plantations and employing freedmen do it from no motives either of loyalty or humanity. The desire of gain alone prompts them, and they care not whether they make it out of the blood of those they employ or from the land."[10] Joseph Warren, who as superintendent of Freedmen at Natchez had plenty of dealings with lessees, felt that the group was largely composed of men "whose highest thought is a greenback, whose God is a cotton bale, and whose devil is a guerrilla."[11]

---

7. Eaton, *Grant, Lincoln and the Freedmen*, 49; "Plot of Vicksburg District for Leasing Abandoned Plantations, 1864," MDAH.
8. Circular, October 27, 1863, *OR* Ser. 3, Vol. III, 939–40.
9. Eaton, *Grant, Lincoln and the Freedmen*, 148.
10. James E. Yeatman, *A Report on the Condition of the Freedmen of the Mississippi presented to the Western Sanitary Commission, December 17, 1863* (St. Louis, 1864), 148.
11. Bell I. Wiley, "Vicissitudes of Early Reconstruction Farming in the Lower Mississippi Valley," *Journal of Southern History*, 5 (1937), 442.

A former overseer pointed out the hard-driving qualities of many non-Southern lessees when he stated, "I'm hiring now to a Northern man who gives me three thousand. A Northern man will want to get more out of the niggers than we do. Mine said to me last night, 'I want you to get the last drop of sweat and the last pound of cotton out of my niggers.'"[12]

Some lessees, to be sure, were quite interested in the treatment given their laborers, if only because they desired stability in the work force, but overseers were a constant problem for such men. Said one plantation lessee of the man who managed his workers, "He can't get the notion out of his head that they are still somehow slaves. When I see things going right badly, I take him and give him a good talking to. Then for about three days, he'll use 'em better, and everything goes smooth. But the first I know, there's more bullying and beating, and there's more niggers bound to quit."[13]

The character and motives of the lessees as a group apparently did not improve after the first year, and indeed Thomas Knox observed that the few "men of character" who were "not like the sharp-eyed speculators" were "outstripped in the struggle for good locations by their more unscrupulous competitors."[14] An American Missionary Association observer in the area reported in March of 1864 that "I fear from what I see that their days of oppression are not all past. Cotton growers and cotton speculators . . . have little conscience where the Negro's rights are concerned."[15] In some instances, however, men whose design was not that of cheating the freedman or abusing his interest contributed to this un-

---

12. John T. Trowbridge, *The South, a tour of its Battle Fields and Ruined Cities, a journey through the desolated States, and talks with the people, etc.* (Hartford: L. Stebbins, 1866), 386.
13. Wiley, "Vicissitudes," 368.
14. Knox, *Camp-Fire and Cotton-Field*, 319.
15. Samuel F. Porter to George Whipple, March 5, 1864, AMA Papers, (Miss.).

fortunate result more from ignorance than from cupidity. George C. Benham and his partner Dobson were two such men, as they were typical of the group whose knowledge of the South had come solely from hearing and reading romanticized tales of white-columned mansions with wide verandas.

"I fancied the grand sweep of an eleven-hundred-acre plantation, with a roll of laborers running up into the hundreds," wrote Benham, "riding on a fine horse, with a broad Panama hat, and a ringing spur, under a Southern sky." His partner Dobson was less the romantic, but he was equally uninformed about the condition of affairs in the lands they proposed to manage.[16]

"The Southern country needs the regenerating influences of the North," lectured Dobson. "The same element that swept across the Alleghenies, that felled the forests . . . , that tunneled mountains, that bridged rivers, that has spun a network of railroads throughout the country — that same element is needed in the South."[17] Dobson's proposal was to use improved agricultural implements, more fertilizer, and more mechanization to increase the cotton yield. Neither of these men, however, knew anything about cotton, army worms, floods, or freedmen, so that when the year was up their operation had failed completely.[18]

The first experimentation with free black labor and the leasing of plantations in the Mississippi Valley was quite confused, with various commanders promulgating their own interpretations of the Governmental will. Indeed, the Roman Catholic bishop of Natchez recorded in his diary after a journey through the Vicksburg area that he "had asked several Federal Officers what are the intentions or what is the policy of the government in regard to the negroes. Everyone whom I have asked has lamented that he thinks there is no policy in their regard . . . and their belief is that as far as

---

16. [George C. Benham], *A Year of Wreck: A True Story; By A Victim* (New York: Harper & Bros., 1880), 17.
17. *Ibid.*, 14.
18. *Ibid.*, 402.

the Federal Government and Army prevail, the race will die out like that of the Indians."[19]

Though Bishop Elder was in fact exaggerating the situation, it was not until the next year that the confusion of authority between War and Treasury Departments was eliminated, and even then there were signs of continued competition between the two departments. Lorenzo Thomas, U.S. Adjutant General, was the man who pushed the Army's interest in controlling the freedmen. Late in February 1864 he wrote to Secretary of War Edwin Stanton to urge the superiority of the military program. "The system adopted by Colonel Eaton," he stated on February 21, with some glossing over of the rough spots, "has now the result of experience, and works well. My system . . . has also worked well. Under these plans, with such modifications as experience has taught us, the Treasury agents and the military authorities would have worked in harmony."[20]

A week later he wrote again to Stanton, proclaiming that "If the Treasury agent should insist on carrying out his regulations . . . , none of the blacks can be provided for." Stanton, meanwhile, had apparently gotten Lincoln's ear, for on February 28 the president told the adjutant general "to go to the Mississippi River at once and take hold of and be master in the contraband and leasing business. You understand it better than any other man does," said Lincoln, adding that "Mr. Mellen's [the Treasury agent] system doubtless is well intended, but from what I hear, I fear that, if persisted in, it would fall dead within its own entangling details."[21]

Thomas, who was in Kentucky when he received the president's order, wasted little time in journeying to the Mississippi, where he found "all along the river great confusion; everything at odds

19. Elder, *Civil War Diary*, 57.
20. Lorenzo Thomas to Edwin Stanton, February 20, 1864, *OR*, Ser. 3, Vol. IV, 124.
21. Lorenzo Thomas to Edwin Stanton, February 27, 1864, *ibid.*, 138; Lincoln to Lorenzo Thomas, February 28, 1864, *ibid.*, 143.

and ends, and the opposers of the system for the proper employment of the poor blacks glad of it."[22] The adjutant general consulted immediately with William P. Mellen, the Treasury agent there, and with his agreement issued a lengthy general order which, with modification, regulated the lives of the freedmen at Vicksburg until the War had ended.[23] As it was finally arranged, the Treasury Department controlled leasing of plantations, while the Army was responsible for the freedmen.

Thomas' regulation, which he freely and admittedly modeled after one issued a month earlier by Maj. Gen. N. P. Banks of the Department of the Gulf at New Orleans, consisted of 25 paragraphs including some of a philosophic and pedagogical nature. Important provisions of the document forbade enlistment into the military of laborers on leased plantations and outlawed the whip and "other cruel and unusual punishments." All sick and disabled persons were to be provided for on the plantations on which they lived, except for those individuals who were received at the "home farms" to be established for the care of the ill and infirm.[24]

Working hours were fixed at ten per day in summer and nine in winter, "of respectful, honest, faithful labor," with minimum wages of $10 per month for men and $7 for women, with lesser amounts to children and the aged. Rations, clothing, quarters, fuel, medical care for everyone and schooling for the children were to be furnished in addition to the above amounts. All labor agreements were to be for one full year, and any who attempted to shirk their responsibilities would supposedly find themselves toiling without pay on the public works. To protect the interests of the freedmen, no commutation of wages was allowed "except"

22. Lorenzo Thomas to Col. E. D. Townsend, April 19, 1864, *ibid.*, 235.
23. Lorenzo Thomas to Edwin Stanton, March 14, 1864, *ibid.*, 176–177.
24. General Orders #9, March 11, 1864, Lorenzo Thomas, *ibid.*, 166–167.

$3 a month for clothing; and the crops were pledged as security for the promised wages, of which at least one-half had to be reserved until the end of the year.[25]

Overseers were regarded by Thomas as particularly recalcitrant and obtuse individuals, and they were forcefully warned of the consequences they would meet should they not accept the new order. "The last year's experience," he wrote in paragraph XIX, "shows that the planter and the negro comprehend the revolution. The overseer, having little interest in capital and less sympathy with labor, dislikes the trouble of thinking, and discredits the notion that anything new has occurred. He is a relic of the past and adheres to its customs. His stubborn refusal to comprehend the condition of things occasioned most of the troubles of the past year. Where such incomprehension is chronic, reduced wages, diminished rations, and the mild punishment imposed by the Army and Navy will do good."[26]

The document was basically a well-reasoned one, but John Eaton felt that "the scale of wages enforced . . . as a minimum rate was higher than . . . the situation could sustain." Because of the difficulties that confronted almost every planting attempt, many lessees simply went bankrupt, leaving nothing for the end-of-the-year payment to laborers.[27]

The problems encountered by particular lessees or planters varied from place to place, but most of those who attempted to raise a cotton crop in the Vicksburg area were troubled by guerrilla raids, insect pests, and confusing and sometimes contradictory Government trade regulations.

Confederate raiders began hitting the plantations along the Mississippi River almost as soon as the lessees occupied them, commencing their attacks with a raid on the Milliken's Bend area, fifteen miles north of Vicksburg, in June of 1863. Mules, cattle,

25. *Ibid.*, 167–68.
26. *Ibid.*, 168.
27. Eaton, *Grant, Lincoln and the Freedmen*, 153–54.

and horses were taken by the Rebel raiders, as were a number of refugee Negroes. No one was injured in this particular instance, though not every group of guerrillas was as considerate as these.[28] A raid several months later in the area near Baldwin's Ferry on the Big Black River resulted in the death of one of the black plantation workers and greatly roused Gen. William T. Sherman's ire. Taking his usual direct action, he ordered General Dennis, his subordinate, to "have the matter inquired into, and, if true, send a couple of regiments across and out a couple of miles, with orders to burn the house of some known secesh, and give notice it will be repeated as often as they please."[29]

Even this measure, however, produced no relief for the planters. The *Natchez Daily Courier* commented in mid-November that "The system of guerrilla warfare in Mississippi and Louisiana is rapidly arriving at some degree of perfection. For small parties, under ordinary circumstances, it is no safer to travel through those States than it would have been during their occupation by the organized armies of the rebellion. Every principal highway is the object of rigid surveillance. Every river crossing is controlled by the unerring sharpshooter."[30]

The new year brought no respite from the menace of guerrilla attack, for General Sherman found it necessary to withdraw many of the troops stationed in outlying areas and send them east where they were needed to reinforce other Union armies. "Guerrillas took advantage of this," reported Samuel G. Wright of the American Missionary Association, "and came within a few miles of us committing murders and robberies without let or hinderance [*sic*]."[31]

Missionaries representing the Friends Freedmen's Association

---

28. Knox, *Camp-Fire and Cotton-Field*, 313.
29. Sherman to Dennis, August 29, 1863, *OR*, Ser. I, Vol. XXX, pt. 3, 211.
30. *Natchez Daily Courier*, November 13, 1863.
31. Samuel G. Wright to George Whipple, January 29, 1864, AMA Papers (Miss.).

reported to their parent organization at the end of April 1864 that "Raids on camps and plantations are daily occurrences, and the poor blacks are carried off as trophies, and if resistance is shown, death is the portion." In a recent raid on Young's Point, the Friends stated, the colony lost "twenty-nine of our colored people, forty-six head of horses, Dr. Fahenstock of Indianapolis, and a lessee of a portion of land near Young's Point." Two other persons, both freedmen, were killed by the guerrillas; others were wounded by them; bodies of the doctor and the lessee were subsequently found and interred at Young's Point.[32]

Treasury Department records report in fair detail numerous raids on plantations near Vicksburg, from which the guerrillas carried off everything from mules to molasses, corn to castor oil (one case). Frequently, too, freedmen were the object of their attack, as was reflected in the terse notation where "Lucinda's" wages should have been recorded — "Rebels took her."[33]

The same plantation was sometimes hit two or three times in a single year, and Union authorities suspected something more than Rebel instigation in certain instances. "On the Buckner Place," reported Lt. Dougal McCall to Col. Samuel Thomas, "all the Negroes and mules were taken last night by the guerrillas. I fear that the Dr. connives with the enemy. . . . He has been raided the second time and I think it possible that he had an understanding with those that raided him. I only mention this because I am much opposed to his having more freedmen to be taken into bondage."[34]

Northern lessees were generally treated with greater harshness

---

32. Elkanah and Irene Beard to Samuel R. Shipley, April 30, 1864, in *The Freedmen's Friend*, I (Sixth Month, 1864), quoted in Qualls, "Friend and Freedmen," 116.
33. "Claims of Plantation Lessees for Losses due to Guerrilla Raids, April-December 1864," RG 366, NA.
34. Lieutenant McCall to Colonel Thomas, May 9, 1864, Box 36, RG 105 (Miss.), NA.

Plantations without Slaves 65

than were local planters who had simply remained on their plantations when Union forces arrived, but natives who cooperated too closely with the U.S. Government were in no way spared by the Confederate guerrillas. Writing to her husband from near Utica, Mississippi, Maria Swanson informed him that "our own cavalry [CSA] arrested Mr. N. for selling his cotton to the Federals, burned one hundred bales they found on the river bank — searched his house and carried him off."[35]

The situation grew progressively worse through 1864, and by the end of the year over a dozen lessees had lost their lives on plantations around Vicksburg alone. As a result of continued partisan activity, over one-third of the leased plantations in the vicinity of the city had been abandoned by the beginning of 1865. The military units stationed there tried to protect the lessees, but plantations were so scattered and troops so few that guerrillas could strike almost with impunity. Troops were sent whenever a raid occurred, but they invariably arrived too late to do anything except to confirm the damage. In an attempt to use the native population to exert pressure on the guerrilla bands, Union authorities in Vicksburg announced that any lessee whose property was stolen or destroyed by the marauders would be reimbursed with property taken from disloyal persons residing in the area. In addition, the commander at Vicksburg threatened in mid-year, if any lessee were killed by the guerrillas, "an assessment of ten thousand dollars will at once be levied upon the disloyal people residing within thirty miles of the place where the offense was committed. Property of any kind will be seized and sold for this purpose."[36]

Ultimately, however, the defensive responsibility was thrown

35. Knox, *Camp-Fire and Cotton-Field*, 313; Roland, *Louisiana Sugar Plantations*, 71–72; Maria Swanson to Alex B. Swanson, January 13, 1864, Swanson-Yates Papers, MDAH.
36. Wiley, "Vicissitudes," 446, General Orders #6, May 12, 1864, in *Vicksburg Daily Herald*, June 7, 1864.

on the planter himself. Across the Mississippi River in Madison and Carroll parishes, Louisiana, Maj. Gen. E. R. S. Canby gave permission for the lessees to organize a 600–man force to patrol and guard the plantations. Guns, ammunition, and rations for this group were furnished by the Government.[37] On the Mississippi side, however, the emphasis was placed on purely stationary defensive measures.

Guerrilla troubles continued into the next year, and in February 1865, General Dana issued General Orders #21, which required that "Owners or lessees of plantations . . . will immediately . . . without delay, construct stockades or other such temporary defense as may be necessary to secure their laborers, stock, and other property from the danger of being carried off by small raiding parties of the enemy; and any lessee who shall disregard or neglect this regulation will suffer the withdrawal of the approval from his lease and the forfeiture of his privileges, besides such further penalty as the case may render proper."[38]

There is no evidence that the authorities ever levied the assessment upon disloyal persons. Nor is there any indication as to the success of either the private militia forces in Louisiana or the stockade system in Mississippi. Guerrilla raids continued, even as the War drew to its close. In early April 1865, for example, the Bazinsky plantation, just six miles from town, was visited by raiders who ran off with all the mules on the place.[39]

Guerrillas, however, were only one of the major problems faced by most lessees, and in many respects they were the easiest with which to deal. Another "army" which could be even more disastrous to the planter was the army worm, so-called because of

---

37. Special Orders #213, December 14, 1864, Maj. Gen. E. R. S. Canby, in *Vicksburg Daily Herald*, December 24, 1864.

38. General Orders #21, February 16, 1865, Brig. Gen. N. J. T. Dana, in *Vicksburg Daily Herald*, February 21, 1865.

39. *Vicksburg Daily Herald*, April 2, 1865.

its behavior — like the Army officer, it took nine-tenths of the cotton it touched.

These voracious little caterpillars, which were the larvae of a species of moth, appeared in July and August of 1864 and moved slowly and steadily toward Vicksburg, devouring all the cotton in sight. First they were at Grand Caillou, then at Thibodeaux; not even the Mississippi River could stop them, and they swept across Davis Bend, destroying five-sixths of the crop there; finally they reached Vicksburg. The destruction there was unprecedented. The nearest previous disaster had occurred in 1849, but even that year did not equal 1864, when the *Daily Herald* reported that "every plantation in this neighborhood is laid waste, and many fields will not make five bales to the hundred acres." Altogether, the effect of the pernicious worm was devastating, reducing cotton production in the Vicksburg district from 40,000 bales to 8,000 bales.[40]

There was little the planter could do to combat the worm, though ingenuity of the time tried many tactics, including that of the man whose workforce was "organized as an executioners squad. Each one had two paddles, and there were two laborers to each cotton row. Walking along, each one kept a sharp lookout on his side, and whenever they espied an army worm lying on top of a cotton leaf, they crushed him with their paddles." Another scheme was that of setting out in the field plates of oil with lighted wicks in them. Theoretically, the moth would be attracted to the flame and perish therein. This idea failed, as did that of sprinkling the worms with dilute carbolic acid.[41]

Fortunately for the planter, some cotton was usually left after the worms ran their course, and with a bit of luck he could salvage

---

40. Knox, *Camp-Fire and Cotton-Field*, 449; McNeily, "War and Reconstruction," 189; *Vicksburg Daily Herald*, August 2 and October 5, 1864; Wiley, "Vicissitudes," 446, citing John Eaton.
41. [Benham], *A Year of Wreck*, 339, 346, 348.

enough to get himself through to the next season. The final problem, however, was shipping to market what cotton had gotten past the guerrillas and the army worm, and this in itself was no easy task.

Though attempts were made by the Union authorities to bring order to the commercial situation in the Mississippi Valley, the years there from 1863 to the end of the War were largely characterized by uninterrupted confusion both within the Treasury Department, which ostensibly controlled trade, and between it and the War Department, which was supposed to look after freedmen's interests. Though there were occasions, such as a brief period during the fall of 1863, when military and naval authorities created problems for the shipper of cotton, the more usual difficulties occurred because of the different trading areas through which the shipment had to pass on its way from the Mississippi Delta to the market in New Orleans.[42]

The apparent lack of coordination within the Treasury Department was so acute that one district, like New Orleans, often refused to respect the permits issued by another district, like Vicksburg or Natchez. "In consequence of the inharmony of these 'regulations,'" wrote lessee Thomas Knox, "the most careful shipper would frequently find his goods under seizure, from which they could generally be released on payment of liberal fees and fines. . . . The invariable result of these little quarrels was the plundering of the shippers. The officials never suffered."[43] Treasury agents were also frequently suspected of accepting bribes to expedite the passage of legitimate cotton to market or even to overlook the obliterated "C.S.A." markings on other bales.[44] Indeed, rumors of corruption in the cotton trade were so persistent that Congress established a "Commission on Corrupt Practices in the South," to interview witnesses and consider testimony on

42. *Natchez Daily Courier*, October 6, 1863.
43. Knox, *Camp-Fire and Cotton-Field*, 402.
44. *Ibid.*, 382.

the subject. The commission was headed by an Army officer, Maj. Gen. William F. Smith, and a civilian, James T. Brady, and spent time along the river at Vicksburg, Natchez, and New Orleans. In its report the Smith-Brady Commission made direct accusations against several individuals prominent in the cotton trade.

Col. Harrai Robinson at New Orleans, stated the commission, engaged regularly in bribery and extortion. In December of 1864, for example, 336 bales of cotton were shipped to New Orleans under permit. Robinson seized it for allegedly being in excess of the quantity allowed on the permit. For a payment of $5,000, however, he offered to release the cotton. He got the money, and the cotton was sent on its way.[45]

Up-river in Natchez, J. F. Richardson, Assistant Special Agent for the Treasury Department, and J. H. Stevens, another local Treasury agent, were accused by the committee of "outrageous violations of the Treasury Regulations in the matters of allowing supplies to go out and cotton to come in."[46] The extent of the problem could not be explored fully by the commission in the short time it had for investigation, but under-the-table payments of $1,400 – $1,500 were apparently quite common as a means of preventing unnecessary delays in shipping large quantities of cotton down the river.[47] A "former Wisconsin resident" described the situation to a home state newspaper:

Dear [*Wisconsin Daily*] Journal — Who hath woe, who hath sorrow? He that runneth a cotton crop on a government plantation! Who hath much greenbacks and expecteth more? The official that letteth the plantation, blocketh the game during its cultivation, and putteth an embargo on the crop when raised. Who hath honesty undefiled? He that hath hair growing in the palm of his hand![48]

    45. Commission on Corrupt Practices in the South, *Report*, 85, RG 94, NA.
    46. *Ibid.*, 159.
    47. *Ibid.*, testimony of George Lockwood.
    48. Quoted in the *Vicksburg Daily Herald*, November 3, 1864.

70 *Enclave: Vicksburg & Her Plantations*

The planters themselves, however, were by no means untainted by greed, and much of the cotton shipped through Vicksburg, especially during the spring of 1864 when as many as 500 bales a day cleared the city's wharves, was undoubtedly not raised by the planters.[49] Gen. N. J. T. Dana, commander of the post there, was well aware of the situation and issued in August of that year General Orders #35, which attempted to impose a degree of control on the area. "Owing to the dishonest, treasonable and corrupt traffic carried on heretofore by that class of small steamboats commonly known as 'cotton thieves,'" stated the order, the quartermaster for the district was authorized to furnish transportation for products of leased plantations.[50] The general shortly followed this order with another providing an additional and more restrictive regulation of shipping. "Hereafter," he stated, "no new cotton, raised by the labor of Freedmen . . . will be taken on board of Government or private transports without the permit of the proper agent of the Treasury Department for the District in which such cotton is raised."[51]

An additional restriction on the shipment of cotton was imposed on the lessee in an attempt to protect the interests of the freedmen who had labored on the crop. The new requirement was that each application for a permit to ship cotton had to be accompanied by certification from the provost marshal of freedmen that either the laborers had been paid or that sufficient security had been given to guarantee their payment.[52]

In addition, there were taxes to be paid on cotton shipped

---

49. John K. Bettersworth, *Confederate Mississippi: The People and Policies of a Cotton State in Wartime* (Baton Rouge: Louisiana St. Univ. Press, 1943), 180.

50. General Orders #35, August 30, 1864, Gen. N. J. T. Dana, AL Papers (microfilm), reel 80, #35731.

51. General Orders #46, September 19, 1864, Gen. N. J. T. Dana, AL Papers (microfilm), reel 82, #36463.

52. *Vicksburg Daily Herald*, September 8, 1864, quoted in McNeily, "War and Reconstruction," 187.

from the Vicksburg area and enough forms and papers to be filled out that a new type of business grew up: that of attending to all government documents. Alston Mygatt, who later served as a delegate to the 1868 Mississippi Constitutional Convention, established his office at 29 Washington Street in Vicksburg and offered to "attend to all such business, prepare plantation accounts, and obtain certificates for all who will entrust me with their business, and permit me to examine their books and papers, thereby saving the planter much trouble, and enable him to ship his cotton without delay."[53] Indeed, the quantity of paperwork which lay between the baling and the shipping of a cotton crop was such that a group of "Loyal Citizens of Vicksburg" printed a petition protesting the actions of the military commander there and sent it to President Lincoln.

"With a view to assist the Government in this development of the capacity of the freedmen for freedom," began the missive, "and also relieve it of the burdens for their support at this time when it required all the available means which ingenius financiers could provide for the payment of the actual war expenses, we came into the Valley of the Mississippi." The petition, occupying two closely printed pages, detailed the troubles encountered by this group which represented its efforts as nothing short of humanitarian and concluded by pleading for relief from the "petty annoyances and prohibitory orders persistently promulgated by the district commander at this post."[54]

Problems with shipping continued to the end of the War, however, with planter protests coming to no avail. "There has been," understated the *Daily Herald* in March of 1865, "no little perplexity and annoyance to the business men, and especially to the planters of this region concerning the apparent vacillation and

53. *Vicksburg Daily Herald*, October 14, 1864.
54. Petition to Abraham Lincoln, November 15, 1864, AL Papers (microfilm), reel 87, #38358.

unsteadiness of the government in respect of some of their interests."[55] The situation had been in a state of confusion for almost two years, and only the end of the War brought order out of the chaos. There were other problems, too, facing the would-be planter, such as the recruitment of his hands by the military;[56] but the major difficulties encountered in raising profitably a cotton crop along the Mississippi were neatly summed up by "Ben" in the *Daily Herald*.

"Ye Cotton Planters"
There came a sound upon the breeze
    Plaintive and sad in tone,
Like spirits ill at ease,
    Disconsolate and lone.

Behold a varied throng appear
    Of Yanks and German-Jews,
Quaking alike with fear
    Over the fearful news.

The army worm! The army worm!
    The cry they all repeat,
The first and only worm
    We ever failed to cheat.

Before them bend the cotton plant
    Our pockets and our pride,
In vain we strive and pant
    To stem this living tide.

Guerrillas next invade the soil,
    To fill their hungry maw,
To capture contrabands and spoil,
    Despite the higher law.

55. *Vicksburg Daily Herald*, March 4, 1865.
56. J. U. Green to T. J. Callicott, August 3, 1864, Box 222A, RG 366, NA; U. S. Grant to Brig. Gen. E. S. Dennis, July 11, 1863, *OR*, Ser. I, Vol. XXIV, 500–501; Wiley, "Vicissitudes," 445.

> Taxes, the bane of every land,
>   Fall heavy, thick and fast,
> While orders on every hand,
>   Deprive us of a pass.
>
> Mourning thus, the cotton band
>   Sigh over the ills of life,
> And desert the cotton land
>   Which gave them woe and strife.
>
> Moral: O ye who live in northern clime
>   Contented stay at home;
> In cotton ne'er invest a dime
>   On land you never own.[57]

Not all planters and lessees, of course, were "Yanks and German-Jews," as implied in the poem, for there were in the Vicksburg area native white Southerners who chose to remain and take the oath of allegiance, as well as a sizable minority of freedmen who themselves secured land and planted it.

Those former slaveowners who attempted to keep their agricultural establishment in operation frequently encountered problems they were ill-equipped to resolve. Their hands had most often left the plantation as Union troops grew near, but an occasional owner found an even worse problem—Negroes who refused to work and refused to leave. This situation developed on the Roach plantation between Vicksburg and Yazoo City in late July 1863. The owner did not know what to do, for they were "on the place doing no work, and eating up what the soldiers have left—the corn and fruit and cattle. They kill the cattle which they find in the woods—eat what they want, and sell the rest to the soldiers."[58] There was an occasional humorous side to events, such as the report from a plantation in the Eagle Lake area that

---

57. *Vicksburg Daily Herald*, December 6, 1864.
58. Elder, *Civil War Diary*, 53.

"The ladies actually had to get up and get breakfast. They said it was funny to see their first attempt at milking."[59] And there were more somber notes, such as the plaintive cry of James Allen of Nanechehaw plantation who had owned seventy-seven slaves in 1860: "Wife . . . sick no one to wait on her."[60] More often, however, the situation simply changed, as when A. M. Paxton returned to the Deer Creek area and directed Israel "that the cotton picked on Sunday be spread on scaffolds to dry. Israel looked at me and answered, 'Mr. Paxton, I want to tell you that that thing is played out.'"[61]

Even if the ex-slaveowner accepted the fact of slavery's being "played out," he faced the formidable task of convincing would-be workers that he felt this way. In addition to problems with guerrillas, army worms and government regulations, the Southern-born planter encountered substantial difficulty in securing labor, for at least in the beginning the freedmen preferred to work for someone who had not owned slaves.[62] One who had gained a prior reputation for kindness as a slaveowner usually managed to hire laborers, and according to a survey taken by the War Department in the area south of Vicksburg, "the men who are known as the 'old planters' of this country, so far as dealing fairly with the freedmen is concerned . . . have paid them more promptly, more justly, and apparently with more willingness than have the new lessees from other parts of the country."[63]

While not exactly contradicting the results of the survey, John Covode in an 1865 report to Edwin Stanton expressed the idea that there would be "difficulty in an old and cruel master employing his former Slaves. He cannot treat them different from what he

---

59. Anderson, *Brokenburn*, 173.
60. James Allen Plantation Book, January 1, 1860; May 1865, MDAH.
61. Paxton manuscript, MDAH.
62. Knox, *Camp-Fire and Cotton-Field*, 375.
63. *OR*, Ser. I, Vol. XLVIII, Part I, 707.

did and they will not stand it now they are free."[64] Records in the Treasury Department, Freedmen's Bureau, and War Department files cannot substantiate either position. Although there are few identifiable complaints from freedmen about Southern-born planters during the War, freedmen apparently did not raise an official complaint very often, but simply quit and moved to another plantation if a planter mistreated them.

The third group of lessees were the ex-slaves themselves, whose reasoning was disarmingly simple. "I always kept master and me," stated one man. "Guess I can keep me."[65] These black lessees were usually quite careful about the land they chose to cultivate, being sure that they were as safe from enemy activity as was possible and leasing in smaller tracts than did the Northern-born speculators. They did experience certain difficulties, for they were generally without capital or credit and had to accumulate stock, tools, and materials from nearby abandoned plantations. Food for themselves and their hands was sometimes advanced by the Government, but more frequently it came at usurious rates from Vicksburg merchants and businessmen.[66]

In the Vicksburg district in 1864 there were some 136 abandoned plantations, of which 113 were leased by Northern whites and 23 by blacks. There were, additionally, 29 instances in which the owners of the plantations had remained on their lands, claiming loyalty to the U.S. Government.[67] Many black land-users leased plots of from 2 to 20 acres each, and though holdings of this size

---

64. John Covode to Edwin Stanton, undated, Covode Papers, Library of Congress.
65. Oliver Otis Howard, *Autobiography of Oliver Otis Howard, Major General United States Army* (New York: The Baker and Taylor Company, 1907), I, 186.
66. Eaton, *Grant, Lincoln and the Freedmen*, 163–64.
67. William C. Harris, *Presidential Reconstruction in Mississippi* (Baton Rouge: Louisiana St. Univ. Press, 1967), 21; "Plot of Vicksburg District . . . ," MDAH.

were not included among the number of "plantations" leased, the families living on them were frequently able to clear a distinct profit at year's end, in contrast to those freedmen who merely hired-out their services.[68]

Other former slaves went into planting in a larger way, with Robert Miner, who tilled 120 acres on a plot opposite Milliken's Bend, ending the 1864 season with 40 bales of cotton and 40 acres of fine-looking corn.[69] James Yeatman of the Western Sanitary Commission listed 19 black lessees in his report for 1864, each of whom had made from 8 to 12 bales of cotton.[70] By limiting the size of their holdings to what they, their families, and perhaps a few close friends could cultivate, these lessees avoided the necessity of hiring laborers, while at the same time diminishing the need for reliance upon outside capital. "Give them anything like a fair chance," wrote the Rev. J. P. Bardwell, "and they will compete successfully with any other class of men under similar circumstances."[71]

Some former slaves went beyond the small family plots of cotton and corn, however, and set themselves up as full-scale plantation lessees, especially in the early months of 1865. Indeed, of 176 plantations leased by one Treasury agent during the first 8 months of that year, more than 40% were leased by blacks. These had a median size of 80 acres, though John Winn, a black lessee, took on the job of cultivating the 800-acre Palmetto plantation on Glasscock's Island in the Mississippi River. He wound up the year with a meager 9,600 pounds of cotton.[72]

68. "Report of Sgt. Proctor Moses at Young's Point," June 1864, Box 36, RG 105 (Miss.), NA.
69. Eaton, *Grant, Lincoln and the Freedmen*, 209.
70. Yeatman, *A Report on the Condition of the Freedmen of the Mississippi*, 10.
71. J. P. Bardwell to M. E. Strieby, December 24, 1864, AMA Papers (Miss.).
72. "Monthly Report of Captain J. H. Webber . . . of Abandoned and Confiscated Lands in His possession during the Month Ending August 31,

By far the greatest number of ex-slaves, however, were unable to secure even a small plot of ground to cultivate and were forced, either by the local provost marshal or by necessity, to enter into some sort of labor contract. Remuneration was extremely low during 1863, with able-bodied men receiving $10 per month, women $7 per month, and youths aged 12 to 15 getting $5. John Eaton recognized, however, that many lessees could not even afford this scale, and explained that "free Negro labor in the Valley was as yet unknown in quantity; it was still somewhat problematical how much the free Negro could earn, and wholly problematical how much the ex-slaveholder and the Northern speculator could be made to pay him."[73]

Though they were by military order forced to work and limited in their monetary demands, some ex-slaves insisted on certain conditions before agreeing to terms. Desiring to have as few reminders as possible of former bondage, they sometimes refused to live in the old slave quarters. The planters who acquiesced in this demand thereupon proceeded to tear down the old shacks and construct new ones, which, built from the old materials, were seldom superior as dwellings.[74] The typical freedmen might well refuse to work on a plantation where there was an overseer, but according to one report would "engage cheerfully to work under a 'superintendent,'" who likely as not was a former overseer with a refurbished title.[75]

1864," Box 54, RG 105, (Miss.), NA. "Articles of Agreement between John Winn and J. P. Richardson, Asst. Special Agent of the Treasury Department, March 6, 1865," Box 213A, RG 366; NA; Receipts, Samuel Glyde Swain Papers, WSHS; with seventeen hands, Winn probably cultivated less than 200 acres. His 24 bales of cotton would have brought over $4,000 at New York prices (43¢ per pound), less the eighth due the Treasury Department. Figuring 10 months' wages at $284 per month, Winn may have broken even on the deal.

73. Eaton, *Grant, Lincoln and the Freedmen*, 60.
74. Moore, "Social and Economic Conditions in Mississippi," 357.
75. Trowbridge, *The South*, 367.

78 *Enclave: Vicksburg & Her Plantations*

Assuming that the proper quarters and supervisory personnel could be provided, there was yet the question of the actual contract between the laborer and the planter. The conditions and terms of this contract were regulated in great detail, with standardized forms often used.

A contract similar in its provisions to many others found in the Treasury Department records is one executed on March 6, 1865, between John Winn, black lessee of the 800-acre Palmetto plantation on Glasscock's Island, John Richardson, the Treasury agent who approved the lease, and Winn's 17 laborers. Winn agreed to pay the Government one-eighth of the year's produce as rent on the plantation and to pay his hands — 5 male and 12 female — from $12 to $25 a month, the average being near $17. These wages, which seem to be fairly in line with those recorded for other plantations in 1865, were to be paid half in cash at the end of each month and half at the end of the year, the withheld wages to constitute a first lien upon the crops produced. In other provisions of the contract, Winn agreed to furnish his workers, who ranged in age from 12 to 70, "free of charge, good and sufficient quarters, a separate tenement for each family, fuel and medical attendance." The laborers were to work no more than 10 hours a day, 5½ days a week, with a holiday on July Fourth;[76] these working hours compared most favorably with those for slaves in Mississippi, for as historian Charles Sydnor commented, "The length of the [slave] field hand's working day depended mainly on the number of hours of daylight."[77] In addition, Winn was "to sell to the laborers at actual cost, on the plantation, a sufficient supply of wholesome food and proper clothing for themselves and their families." The entire contract was to be enforced by the superintendent of freedmen, with forfeitures visited upon the les-

76. "Articles of Agreement" between John Winn and J. F. Richardson, March 6, 1865, Box 213A, RG 366, NA.
77. Charles S. Sydnor, *Slavery in Mississippi* (Baton Rouge: Louisiana St. Univ. Press, 1966), 20.

see for nonperformance of his duties.[78] It was altogether an impressive agreement. Whether these laborers actually received the agreed-upon benefits, however, is indeterminable, but if they were like most who worked for another, the promises of the contract and the realities of the plantation were antithetical.

The major problem, of course, lay in the character and motives of the lessees, already discussed at some length earlier in this chapter. The most common method used by lessees to cheat the laborer was that of keeping a set of books which revealed at the end of the planting season that the freedman and his or her family had eaten or worn or broken more in goods than they had earned in wages. Col. Samuel Thomas guessed that nearly two-thirds of the freedmen on privately-run plantations had been defrauded of their wages in 1864, and lessee Thomas Knox confirmed his judgment.[79] This simple practice was continued by Mississippi Delta planters for many years after the Reconstruction period was over. Hortense Powdermaker, who studied the town of Indianola, Mississippi, during the early 1930s, stated, for example, that "It can be roughly estimated that not more than twenty-five or thirty per cent of the sharecroppers get an honest settlement at the end of their five months of labor."[80]

An even more insidious method of reducing labor costs and providing greater profit on a plantation was that of skimping on essential and agreed-upon benefits, like medical care. "The system for letting hands was an incentive," wrote Dr. D. O. McCord, Medical Director and Inspector of Freedmen for the Department of Mississippi, "to ill usage when sick. When the head of a family became an employee, the employer was forced to assume the support of the whole family. It often happened that the employer

78. "Articles of Agreement," Winn and Richardson.
79. Trowbridge, *The South*, 363; Knox, *Camp-Fire and Cotton-Field*, 315.
80. Hortense Powdermaker, *After Freedom: A Cultural Study in the Deep South* (New York: The Viking Press, 1939), 86.

would be thus obliged to feed more dependents than he worked; every dependent that died saved the planter one ration from the date of death to the end of the season."[81] This failure to provide a physician's services became so widespread in 1864 that Colonel Thomas was moved to issue a circular on the subject, reminding the planters that they were responsible for the freedmen during the entire term of the lease and that this responsibility included the furnishing of medical care.[82] This entire situation is quite thought-provoking, however, for the requirement that the lessee support the freedmen throughout the season, regardless of whether the laborer became sick, disabled or totally incapable of work, placed the freedmen in a paternalistic relationship not unlike that embodied in part in the former system of slavery.

Despite the interest in the welfare of the freedmen displayed by Samuel Thomas and others, a second major source of trouble for the ex-slave was found within the very military establishment that was charged with protecting him. Military personnel were by nature conservatively oriented individuals, and even Gen. Oliver O. Howard, first head of the Bureau of Refugees, Freedmen, and Abandoned Lands, recognized and admitted this fact. "The Commissioners themselves," wrote Howard, "seem to have done more for the lessees than for the laborers; and in fact the wages were from the beginning so fixed as to benefit and enrich the employer."[83]

Charles Roland, who studied Louisiana plantations during this same period, concluded that provost marshals in the area were quite frequently dominated by planters.[84] Closer to home, however,

---

81. "Report of D. O. McCord, Medical Director and Inspector of Freedmen, Department of Mississippi — Annual Report, July 1865," Box 36, RG 105 (Miss.), NA.
82. Circular, September 1, 1864, Col. Samuel Thomas, in *Vicksburg Daily Herald*, September 2, 1864.
83. Howard, *Autobiography*, I, 187.
84. Roland, *Louisiana Sugar Plantations*, 112.

Plantations without Slaves 81

were rules "To Govern Hands" issued by the authorities at Natchez, examination of which leaves little doubt as to the party favored by the contract enforcers in that area. Each hand two hours late to work, stated the rules, was to be docked one-half his daily wages, and an additional half-day's pay for each further two-hour absence. "No man shall be allowed to leave a plantation without a pass from the manager," stated another rule, the breaking of which required forfeiture of a full day's pay for each offense; while any hand out after 9:00 P.M. without a proper excuse was to lose half a day's pay. Furthermore, to reduce possibilities for theft, no hand was allowed to grow cotton or sugar cane on his garden plot; he had to produce corn or vegetables.[85]

Local military representatives, like Lt. Dougal McCall at Milliken's Bend, frequently stepped in to assure that freedmen lived up to their contracts. Lieutenant McCall, for example, informed Thomas in mid-1864 that he had fined a female laborer half her month's wages "for a stubborn refusal of duty."[86] Sometimes, though, the military force was exerted in the other direction, such as in November 1864 when Colonel Thomas ordered the seizure of "all the horses, mules, cattle, and Property of all kinds on the Bums and Maher Plantations, . . . to secure the Feeding and proper care of the Freedmen."[87]

The lot of the plantation laborer in the Vicksburg area was not an easy one, for most planters, especially those who were not experienced cotton growers, over-extended themselves in an attempt to garner quick riches. Whitelaw Reid on his tour in 1865 saw and recognized the problem and expressed the freedman's dilemma quite well. "Negroes were . . . ill-paid," he wrote. "Rations were likely to be of the cheapest and scantiest. If the

85. "To Govern Hands," Box 213A, RG 366, NA.
86. Lt. Dougal McCall to Col. Samuel Thomas, May 9, 1864, Box 36, RG 105 (Miss.), NA.
87. Special Orders #20, November 18, 1864, Col. Samuel Thomas, in *Special Orders, Provost Marshal of Freedmen*, RG 105 (Miss.), NA.

negro, dissatisfied with this specimen of the workings of free labor, broke his contract and ran away, it was a proof that 'free niggers would never make cotton without a system of peonage.'"[88] The example to disprove those who felt this, however, was close at hand, for when Reid made his observation, the all-black colony at Davis Bend was well into its second full year of operation.

88. Whitelaw Reid, *After the War: A Tour of the Southern States*, ed. C. Vann Woodward (New York: Harper & Row, Publishers, Harper Torchbooks, 1965), 290–291.

4

Davis Bend

U. S. GRANT learned of Davis Bend during his 1863 campaign against Vicksburg, and he was struck by the opportunity it presented him. This pear-shaped peninsula, called Palmyra on some maps, lay but eighteen miles below the city and contained, among other lands, the huge plantations of Jefferson Davis and his brother Joseph. Grant, in one of the supreme ironies of the Civil War, decided to seize the 10,000-acre peninsula and make of it a "Negro paradise," a refuge for slaves who escaped from Davis' own Confederacy.[1] It was an ambitious and idealistic plan that finally unfolded on Davis Bend, and, in a sort of double irony, a large part of the success achieved on the Palmyra soil must be attributed to the Davis brothers and their efforts of the previous forty years.

Joseph E. Davis was a full two decades older than his brother, and it was he who patented in 1818 the land on which the brothers developed their plantations. Jefferson did not even acquire an interest in the Bend until 1835, ten years after his brother had begun work on the Hurricane place, but in that year Joseph had induced his younger brother to abandon his Army career and to settle with him on the Mississippi. For doing so, as well as in payment of a longstanding family debt, Jefferson was given some

---

1. Eaton, *Grant, Lincoln and the Freedmen*, 85–86.

(Hand-drawn map)

Upper / North section:
- Bayou
- Holmes 1500
- McFarland
- Dawson
- Bennett
- Fisk 1500
- Sedgwick Smith
- Walnut ...
- Mrs. Hoggett
- Cypress Brake
- Sau Hastings
- Rusman 600
- Allen 600
- Sargeant 500
- White
- Killikranks 500

Center (Hurricane / Palmyra bend):
- Grove 1500
- Lion James 1000
- N. Vaughwood
- Tartan
- Turner
- Keyfarthay
- Palmer
- Baker
- MacGrow
- Calcox
- Perkins
- Hurricane Id.
- Palmyra Id.
- Palmyra 1000
- Banks 1200
- Hurricane Jos. L. Davis 2200
- Lake F. Woods 1600
- Brierfield Jeff Davis 1600
- R. F. Woods
- Hen...
- Cutoff
- Big Black Id.

Lower section:
- Smith
- Ogden
- Brown 800
- Dorsey 1000
- Buckner 1000 / 1200
- Lloyd 1000
- Turner
- Wilson 500
- Mason 600
- Tartan 1600
- Bush 500
- Hall
- Linwood
- Williams
- Ogden 500
- Winter Quarters 1200
- Coffees Point
- Thrasher
- Ballard
- Little Bayou
- Big Black Bk.
- Grand Gulf

2,300 acres of unimproved river land of such richness that goldenrod grew "large enough for a strong walking-stick."[2]

Davis called his place "Brierfield," after the profusion of trailing thorn bushes which covered much of the land, and he set out to make it a model plantation. It took three years of steady land clearing, with Jefferson's slave Jim Pemberton in charge, before the first sizable crop of cotton was raised, and by 1845 both Davis plantations were reaching their prime.[3] A visitor to Brierfield and Hurricane in that year was quite impressed by the area, for although crop prospects were not so good elsewhere in the state, cotton at the Bend was "so abundant" that the visitor doubted "very much whether the planters will be able to pick it all," despite the herculean efforts of such workers as "a boy of Mr. Joe Davis' who picked 468 pounds, and did not pick all day."[4]

The brothers erected houses on their land, each dwelling reflecting the desires and tastes of its owner. Jefferson and his second wife Varina designed their own home, and made it a long, rambling one-story structure with thick walls, much room, and an utter lack of outward pretension. Behind Brierfield were gardens of "rare roses and shrubs," while on the sides were "eight acres of peaches, figs, and apples." The furnishings were a bit more splendid and included two mantles of imported Carrara marble and a pair of magnificent chandeliers which hung impressively from the 16-foot ceilings. Auxiliary buildings were scattered around the main house, the largest of them a 32-stall stable. Brierfield was a large, comfortable, practical place, but it was not

---

2. Frank E. Everett, Jr., *Brierfield: Plantation Home of Jefferson Davis* (Hattiesburg, Miss.: University and College Press of Mississippi, 1971), 7, 22–24; Varina H. Davis, *Jefferson Davis, Ex-President of the Confederate States of America: A Memoir by His Wife* (New York: Belford Company, Publishers, 1880), I, 475–476.

3. Everett, *Brierfield*, 26–27; V. Davis, *Jefferson Davis*, I, 163.

4. Joseph Howell to William B. Howell, September 5, 1845, Howell Collection, MDAH.

Garden Cottage—Also called the Library, it was the only major building the Union soldiers left at Joe Davis' Hurricane Plantation after an 1862 raid. It is pictured here in 1865 with some of the former slaves on the place. Courtesy: J. Mack Moore Collection, Old Court House Museum, Vicksburg

in any way as impressive as was the mansion Joe Davis built.[5]

Hurricane, located about 1½ miles from Brierfield, was surrounded by oak trees and ornamental shrubs, with wide lawns reaching out toward the river. The house itself had three stories and was furnished, through the ingenuity of Davis' slaves, with piped-in running water. Southwest of the main house was the Garden Cottage, or Library, twenty-two feet on a side and made of brick, with handsome white columns all around. There were the usual other out-buildings, but east of the Hurricane mansion

---

5. Everett, *Brierfield*, 42–49; V. Davis, *Jefferson Davis*, I, 193.

was a truly unique structure: the Hall of Justice, where slave offenders were brought to trail before a jury of their peers.[6]

Although historian Charles Sydnor mentions one other antebellum Mississippi planter who used a system of jury trial before punishing his slaves, it is quite likely that the Davis brothers used the practice to a greater extent than did anyone else of that time.[7] Joseph Davis, a lawyer himself, first instituted the system of trials, and Jeff adopted an identical procedure at Brierfield. Other planters laughed at "Joe Davis' free negroes," but the system worked remarkably well.[8]

In each trial there were a slave judge and a jury; black sheriffs aided the court; and witnesses were examined and cross-examined as in the state courts. The only place where their owner participated in the legal procedure was at its end, where the pardoning power was sometimes used. "Aunt Florida" Hewitt, a former Davis slave, was interviewed in Vicksburg sixty years after the Civil War, and her recollection was that the brothers "would never let nobody touch one of their niggers. Ever' nigger done wrong dey tried him wid a jury odder niggers, and dey fixed de punishment."[9] Not even overseers were allowed to punish the Davises' slaves, and at least one man left their employ simply because he could not abide the system.[10]

Both Davis brothers encouraged enterprise among their servants and allowed ambitious slaves to develop their own businesses. One man, Benjamin Montgomery, kept a variety store at the Bend and bought and sold on his own account; others raised chickens

6. Everett, *Brierfield*, 9–13; V. Davis, *Jefferson Davis*, I 192–193; *Jefferson Davis v. J. H. D. Bowmar*, 55 Miss. 671.
7. Sydnor, *Slavery in Mississippi*, 76.
8. Walter L. Fleming, "Jefferson Davis, the Negroes and the Negro Problem," *Sewanee Review*, 16 (October 1908), 410.
9. Fleming, "Jefferson Davis," 410; V. Davis, *Jefferson Davis*, I, 174–75; Dennis Murphree, "Hurricane and Brierfield, the Davis Plantations," *Journal of Mississippi History*, 9 (April 1947), 106.
10. Fleming, "Jefferson Davis," 411.

and sold them to the white families, feeding their poultry from the open corncribs on the place. Jefferson Davis used Jim Pemberton, a slave, as his plantation manager for almost twenty years, and after Pemberton died the white overseers who replaced him were never completely satisfactory.[11]

Joseph gradually sold some of his holdings at Davis Bend, and by 1860 two other large plantations were there, one known as the Turner and Quitman place, on which were 308 slaves; the other belonged to R. Y. Wood, who owned 132 servants and field hands. Joe Davis, by comparison, owned 355 slaves, while Brierfield supported 113. There were other, smaller holdings, on the Bend, as well as people like Elias West, a white woodchopper, but it was the Davis slaves who had the most influence on later events at the peninsula.[12]

The Davis Bend plantations suffered much during a terrible flood in 1859, but the next year saw vast improvements in the crop, and it certainly appeared that fortunes were to be made in the rich alluvial soils. Then Lincoln was elected; the South began seceding; and by February 10, 1861, the owner of Brierfield had learned that he was to be leader of the Confederacy. Jefferson Davis left for Montgomery, Alabama, the next day, and within two weeks Brierfield was in the hands of the slaves who lived there, the remaining white members of the family having also departed.[13]

Although Joseph Davis and the other owners maintained their farming operations on the Bend, it was not long before the heretofore remote Civil War came sailing to their very doorsteps in the ships of Admiral Farragut's fleet. As the Union officer approached Vicksburg in June of 1862, he sent out raiding parties, one of which touched Davis Bend and burned the Hurricane

11. *Ibid.*, 410–11.
12. Everett, *Brierfield*, 8; "Eighth Census of the United States (1860)," manuscript, NA; Elias West to Gen. N. J. T. Dana, March 1865, Joseph Davis Papers, MDAH.
13. Everett, *Brierfield*, 60–68, 71–74.

Joseph E. Davis — Elder brother of Jefferson Davis who first settled on Davis Bend. Courtesy: Mississippi Department of Archives and History

mansion.[14] Shortly afterward, Joseph, seventy-eight years old, moved his family and many of his slaves to a plantation further inland, leaving Benjamin Montgomery in full command of the Davis brothers' farming operations on the Bend. Though only a few of the Davises' nearly 500 slaves remained with him, Montgomery did his best to raise a crop, reporting in January of 1863 that he had harvested over 300 bushels of corn.[15]

The next months were quiet ones at Davis Bend. The Mississippi rose, lapped at the protecting levees, then went down again. Willow trees showed their new yellow-green leaves and became deeper green as late spring approached. Montgomery and the other slaves, including his sons Isaiah and Thornton, kept up the grounds as well as they could and planted food crops for themselves and the stock that remained.[16] The tranquillity was suddenly broken, however, when Farragut's Union fleet again approached the Bend early in May 1863. When the ships reached Palmyra, wrote historian James W. Garner, the fleet "stopped long enough to destroy everything of value."[17] The invaders then departed a second time, leaving destruction behind them. Again, however, the Brierfield mansion was inexplicably spared the fiery treatment that had been given Hurricane.

Grant's army and Farragut's fleet struggled many days before Vicksburg was finally theirs, and the inhabitants of Davis Bend were undisturbed during that time and for some months thereafter. Finally, the time came to make Grant's dream into reality, and Col. Samuel Thomas was placed in command of the operation. "I received on the 18th of December, 1863," recounted Thomas, "from Gen. McFerson [sic] an order to take two companies of

14. Joseph Davis to Andrew Johnson, March 1, 1866, Joseph Davis Papers, MDAH.
15. Everett, *Brierfield*, 76–77.
16. Maurice Elizabeth Jackson, "Mound Bayou: A Study in Social Development" (unpublished M.A. thesis, University of Alabama, 1937), 39.
17. Garner, *Reconstruction in Mississippi*, 252.

U.S. colored infantry and take possession of Palmyra Bend. The order told me to take a Quarter Master with me who was to take possession of all property found on the Bend, except the cotton, which was to be returned to the Treasury Agent."[18] The condition among the slaves there, reported Thomas, "was about as usual where negroes are alone. They were in comfortable quarters, but lacked clothing and food. The first day I landed I issued rations to 900 people."[19]

Actually, the Davis Negroes seem to have been in a fairly enviable condition when Thomas arrived. Their slave quarters were intact, and Ben Montgomery had secured some $4,000 from Joseph Davis to enable them to raise crops for the year. Even their court system had survived the departure of the Davis brothers. Indeed, their legal system was still vital a year after Union troops took over, and a Northern officer, seeing its operation and supposing it to be of recent vintage, marveled at "how one year of freedom would elevate the blacks."[20] In some respects the coming of freedom to Davis Bend was a mixed blessing, for the owners had already fled and few whites were in residence at the time. Slavery in most particulars had ended some time before, and the only immediate result of the December 18 Union expedition was the eviction of many blacks from their homes so that Union soldiers could live in them. This action created hardship for numerous people, and even Colonel Thomas admitted that "many must have suffered."[21]

His particular property, said Joseph Davis later, had been selected for refugee use "on account of its security from disturbances by Confederate forces, being situated between the Mis-

---

18. Samuel Thomas memorandum (undated), Joseph Davis Papers, MDAH.
19. *Ibid*.
20. Benjamin T. Montgomery memorandum (undated), Joseph Davis Papers, MDAH; Fleming, "Jefferson Davis," 411.
21. Dennis Joice and Phillip Gaiter memoranda (undated), Joseph Davis Papers, MDAH; Samuel Thomas memorandum (undated), *ibid*.

sissippi & Big Black Rivers, of which the Federal forces had the entire control."[22] Union authorities, moreover, soon added to the natural defensive advantages enjoyed by the Bend by stationing eight companies of black troops there; by cutting a canal across the neck of the peninsula, making it an island at high water; and by positioning a gunboat in the Mississippi River at that point.[23] Thus guarded, the population of Davis Bend was never in danger of being molested by the Confederate guerrillas who lurked nearby, and in the early spring of 1864 the first positive steps were taken toward fulfilling General Grant's dream of a "Negro paradise" on the Bend.

It was in March of that year that U.S. Adj. Gen. Lorenzo Thomas delineated the status to be given Hurricane and Brierfield, whose lands were the heart of the peninsula. "All of the property in the Palmyra Bend, Miss.," he stated, "except the Turner and Quitman plantations, is hereby reserved for Military purposes, on which will be established a 'Home Farm,' and to furnish land for Freedmen, for their own cultivation."[24] A set of *"Rules and Regulations . . .* for the *Government* of the *Freedmen* at *Davis Bend, Miss."* was drawn up by the military authorities, and this document, consisting of thirteen numbered paragraphs, formed the basis of organization for the administrative system which functioned there.

Paragraph I of the "Rules and Regulations" provided that "The Bend with the exception of the *Jeff Plantation* will be leased to those who seem willing and able to work lands upon their own accounts." Subsequent paragraphs went on to explain that freedmen who desired to lease lands would have to form themselves

22. Joseph E. Davis to Bureau of Refugees, Freedmen and Abandoned Lands (undated), *ibid.*
23. *Vicksburg Daily Herald*, July 6, 1864; *OR*, Ser. 3, Vol. IV, 708, Lorenzo Thomas to Edwin Stanton, September 11, 1864.
24. Special Orders #15, March 28, 1864, Adj. Gen. Lorenzo Thomas, Box 35, RG 105 (Miss.), NA.

into "companies" of "from three to twenty-five hands that are able to do their share of the labor." Once organized, the members of each company would be registered "in a book kept for that purpose," and members would then select one of their own "who will be known as the head of the company and who will transact the business for the entire company and no account will be kept with any other partner."[25]

Company members were to be careful in joining a group, for once organized and registered, "no changes will be allowed except by consent of two-thirds of the members and the approval of the *Post Superintendent*." Even the hiring of extra hands was discouraged, and everyone who remained with the company through the season was expected to pay a portion of the expenses and share in the profits. Mules, horses, farming utensils, and food supplies were obtainable from the Government as available, but each company was required to pay for such as it received.[26]

For administrative purposes the companies were divided into "colonies," for which a "Superintendent" was appointed, whose duty was "to see that every company in his colony work their ground in the proper manner. He will have a general supervision over all the people in his colony," stated Paragraph VII, "and all companies and people living within his colony will be subject to his orders." The authority given superintendents of colonies was extensive, and included the power to punish whoever should "refuse or neglect to perform his share of the labor, (except in cases of actual sickness) or shall absent himself from the company without their consent" by forcing him to labor without pay until "willing to work for himself."[27] Strict control was placed on the issuing of rations, and unless a refugee received a "certificate of disability" from the surgeon, he was not to receive food supplies

25. "*Rules and Regulations* . . . for the *Government* of the *Freedmen* at *Davis Bend, Miss.*," RG 105 (Miss.), NA.
26. *Ibid.*
27. *Ibid.*

unless he was either in a company or on the Home Farm, which was Government operated.[28]

Every effort was made to rid the peninsula of certain undesirable characters who were "Stealing, plundering, killing stock, and living in idleness and vagrancy. Extensive measures," warned Paragraph XIII, "will be adopted and vigorously carried out," such as banishing to Big Black Island any proven to be thieves and robbers. Heads of companies were enlisted as part of a crime prevention campaign, for it was duly noted in the "Rules and Regulations" that any "who allow . . . their members to steal from one another or from the Government will be disposesed [sic] and sent from the Bend."[29]

Some 76 companies organized under the new system, and over 2,500 acres of land were parcelled out for their cultivation in plots ranging in size from 5 to 100 acres. Companies received their seeds, mules, and implements from the Government and began their plowing and planting. Henry Rountree, a Quaker missionary who visited the Bend, could, however, already see problems in the making. The mules, he observed, were of poor quality, and the shortage of hoes would be a definite hindrance once the cotton was up.[30]

A number of refugees had taken up residence at Davis Bend even before Union forces arrived there, and with the coming of 1864 their numbers increased every day. Soon over a thousand persons were occupying space at the Home Farm, which itself was only a small part of Davis Bend. Of the 1,015 persons recorded in a special census taken that year, approximately 25% each were boys and girls under the age of 15, while less than 4% of the total were males that age and older. The largest part of the refugee

28. *Ibid.*
29. *Ibid.*
30. Henry Rountree to Cincinnati Contraband Relief Committee, April 25, 1864, *Henry Rowntree Letter Book*, RG 105 (Miss.), NA; Quarles, *The Negro in the Civil War*, 285.

population — some 45% — was made up of females 15 and over. This largely dependent population had for the most part fled from nearby counties, with Adams County (Natchez) claimed as home by 300 persons. Most others came from counties along the Mississippi, but 6 persons had made the long trek across from Alabama. These included a mother with two small sons, a lone forty-year-old man, and a seventeen-year-old with her son.[31] Interestingly enough, only 19 persons, including several children, claimed to have been house servants, and only 1 man said he had a skilled occupation — that of shoemaker. There was 1 white refugee family in the group, headed by a forty-year-old woman with 2 children, ages 12 and 7. Altogether, 11 Mississippi counties were represented on the Home Farm at the time of the census, with persons from Louisiana, Alabama and Ohio also present.[32]

Missionaries, too, came to the Bend, following closely behind the Union soldiers. Indeed, by January 1864 the Rev. Samuel B. Wright reported that his organization, the American Missionary Association, had "about 250 scholars in schools and the religious interest in camp was increasing."[33] By October of that year 14 organizations were represented at Davis Bend, supporting a total of 31 teachers and missionaries.[34] The United Presbyterians were praised by an AMA official as having "large and promising" schools,[35] but the continuing rivalry among organizations and individuals was underscored by a soldier's account of the burial of one "Miss Mc . . . ," a missionary from Ohio. "She was not well taken care of," wrote Samuel D. Barnes. "Very poor prep-

31. *Record People, Home Colony Davis Bend, Miss.—1864*, RG 105, (Miss.), NA.
32. *Ibid.*
33. Samuel G. Wright to Rev. George Whipple, January 29, 1864, AMA Papers (Miss.).
34. "Report of Missionaries and Teachers, Vicksburg, October 28, 1864," Box 36, RG 105 (Miss.), NA.
35. J. P. Bardwell to Rev. M. E. Strieby, January 5, 1865, AMA Papers (Miss.).

eration were made for her burial. I assisted as much as I was able [;] I went to help bury her[.] As it was a negro had to help carry the coffin to the grave. She had no particular friend here, and a good many did not belong to her society, hence seemed to care little whether she lived or died."[36]

Spring of 1864 soon became summer, and as July approached, preparations were made for a grand Fourth of July celebration. It was exactly a year after the city of Vicksburg had fallen, and the residents of Davis Bend made quite a day of it. Brierfield was decorated for the occasion, and a sign across its front read "The House Jeff Built." A Miss Lee of Pennsylvania and a Miss Huddleson of Indiana, two missionaries, placed an "Exit traitor" sign across the rear entrance, and the missionaries prepared food to serve the large crowd expected at the Jeff Davis mansion.[37]

Dr. Warren, an AMA member, conducted the exercises, which began with Henry Rountree reading the Declaration of Independence. Dinner was served inside because of a slight drizzle, then the assembled guests offered toasts to the nation, the President, General Grant, Jeff's house, and other august personages and things. The festivities were finally climaxed by singing — twice — a song composed by a Mr. McConnell entitled "The House that Jeff Built," the first stanza of which was:

> How oft within these airy halls
>   The traiter [sic] of the day
> Has heard ambition's trumpet calls,
>   Or dreamed of war's array!
> Or of an Empire dreamed, whose base
>   Millions of blacks should be;
> Aha! before this day's sweet face
>   Where can his visions be?

36. Samuel D. Barnes Diary, September 19, 1864, Samuel D. Barnes Papers, Library of Congress.
37. *Vicksburg Daily Herald*, July 6, 1864.

Brierfield Plantation—Home of Jefferson Davis, inexplicably spared by Union troops. It is shown here as decorated by Northern missionaries in 1864. Courtesy: J. Mack Moore Collection, Old Court House Museum, Vicksburg

The final two verses of McConnell's composition were similar in spirit to the first, and the entire effect of his work, which was set to the tune of "Auld Lang Syne," so enthralled the crowd that copies were sent to both the *New York Tribune* and Jefferson Davis himself.[38] There is no record of what either recipient thought of the gift.

In addition to the cooperative companies of refugees who tilled the Davis Bend area, a private concern, J. H. Carter & Co., had leased the entire 2,900-acre Hurricane plantation, former home of Joseph Davis and certainly among the choicest land on the

38. *Ibid.*

Bend. Carter & Co. employed some 53 women and 27 men on the place, with 30 children present. Joe Davis, by comparison, had maintained 355 slaves on this same property in 1860.[39]

John Eaton and the Freedmen's Department, naturally enough, were interested in the treatment given the Hurricane hands and queried the company quite specifically about food, treatment of the sick, pay, subsistence goods furnished, working conditions, and views on the refugee in general.

Food, stated the company, generally consisted of bacon, flour, meal, fish, and molasses, the amount of each being "based upon the requirements of the receiver." Children, the infirm, and other dependents were supplied rations partly by Carter and in part by the Government. The company pointed out the uniqueness of their situation by noting that "we took the hands that were in the quarters at the time we came to the plantation, & in many cases the women workers were largely predominant." Any hands who became sick, said the company, were continued at full rations, provided with "whatever our private table stores contained," and were given medical treatment by the Government physicians at Davis Bend.[40]

Those employed by the Carter operation were paid according to the scale set down under "Orders No. 9" issued at Vicksburg in March of 1864. Under its provision, men fourteen and over received $10 per month; women received $7 per month; children, aged, and other workers received half pay.[41] According to Carter, hands received "whatever they required" in the way of dry goods, "at a profit or rather advance of 15 or 30 per cent from invoice

---

39. Everett, *Brierfield*, 24; Report, J. H. Carter & Co., October 6, 1864, Box 36A, RG 105 (Miss.), NA; "Eighth Census of the United States (1860)," manuscript, NA.

40. "Answers to Questions for Planters by J. H. Carter & Co. Lessees Joe Davis Plantation Davis Bend," Box 36, RG 105 (Miss.), NA.

41. "Answers to Questions"; Eaton, *Grant, Lincoln and the Freedmen*, 153–54.

cost," a sum which seems excessive until compared with contemporaries who charged $2.50 for $1 shoes or 75¢ per yard for 24-cent calico.[42]

The usual workday for their people, reported the Carter Company, was 9½ hours, and they confessed "a fair degree of success in the time worked." Middle-aged hands made the best laborers, the Company felt, while "the girls say from fourteen to twenty years old have been inclined to waste their time." Comparing their system with slavery, the lessees determined that with free laborers, "there is one-third less time labored & full one-third less daily labor performed now than under the slave system." Cotton, concluded the Company, "can never be raised as cheaply again as it has been."[43]

Both J. H. Carter & Co. and some of the missionaries on the Bend felt the need for moral uplift among both refugees and residents. "There may have been greater suffering," Henry Rountree had written of the inhabitants of the Davis lands, "but never greater need of the right kind of labour and influence being extended to them."[44] The businessmen opined that "One of the most revolting effects slavery has produced upon the negro is their almost utter want of chastity or morality, hence the marriage relation is as yet but a loose bond."[45] The missionaries preached and exhorted and performed impressive weddings on Davis Bend, but Carter felt that it would "take stringent laws rigidly enforced to break up the licentious habits of this generation." Above all, however, said Carter & Co., the freedpeople had to "be brought to understand that *liberty is not licence*. Every true friend of the negro must desire this," concluded the Company, "else the results

---

42. "Answers to Questions"; James E. Yeatman, *A Report on the Condition of the Freedmen*, 9.
43. "Answers to Questions."
44. Henry Rountree to Cincinnati Contraband Relief Committee, April 15, 1864, *Henry Rowntree Letter Book*, RG 105 (Miss.), NA.
45. "Answers to Questions."

can but be deplorable, and furnish the enemies of freedom much occasion to blaspheme."[46]

Prospects for the Davis Bend cotton crop had been good at the beginning of 1864, and the early months of the season had done nothing to dispel high hopes. The incomparably rich alluvial soil practically thrust the cotton stalks from the ground, and the Home Farm companies were expecting a crop of at least 1,500 bales. Even the weather was cooperating with the newly minted planters. Then the worm struck.

The dreaded army worm, forerunner of the boll weevil in the list of Southern agricultural nemeses, crossed over the wide Mississippi in the form of a small, rather plain looking moth, which laid eggs in the blooms of the cotton plant. Within a few short days the eggs hatched, and the larvae — the army worms — began to eat their way across the fields. Even the most advanced planters were helpless in their path, and before the worm had run its course on Davis Bend the 1,500-bale hopes of the Home Farm had been reduced to the stark reality of 130 bales.[47]

"Still," said one observer, "the experiment was a success." Thanks to the high price of cotton, which in 1864 was over $1 per pound, almost every company at the Home Farm recouped expenses, and some few cleared as much as $1,000 profit. This first planting season with freed workers had shown much of the ability of the ex-slave to care for himself, but it was only a prelude to what was to come.[48]

Federal authorities were pleased with the preliminary results of the Davis Bend Experiment, and in November 1864 Gen. N. J. T. Dana, commanding at Vicksburg, issued orders expanding the scope of the program. "The exceptions made in the order

46. Reid, *After the War*, 284–85; "Answers to Questions."
47. [Benham], *A Year of Wreck*.
48. J. S. McNeily, "War and Reconstruction in Mississippi, 1863–1890," *Publications of the Mississippi Historical Society, Centenary Series*, II (Jackson, 1918), 193; Reid, *After the War*, 285–86.

Davis Bend 101

above," he stated, referring to private leasing of land, "will no longer be regarded, and the whole peninsula known as Davis Bend . . . is reserved for military purposes and will be exclusively devoted to the colonization, residence, and support of Freedmen." Furthermore, he ordered, no whites would even be allowed to land at Davis Bend after January 1, 1865, without permission of the proper authorities.[49]

Almost at this same time, Benjamin Montgomery, Joseph Davis' talented and literate ex-slave, returned from self-imposed exile and once again assumed a leadership role on Davis Bend. This fortuitous combination of circumstances, together with what seems to have been genuine desire on the part of Federal authorities at Davis Bend to allow more refugee self-government, led to one of the most innovative aspects of the Union experiment.

Although the pre-War system of courts set up by the Davis brothers had survived the onset of Union occupation, the early months of 1865 saw the establishment of a more formalized administration of justice. On January 27 the machinery for a three-judge court was created by the post superintendent of freedmen. This tribunal, with authority "to try all cases that may be brought before it," was to meet each Saturday at the Jeff Davis mansion. The court was empowered to "Swear Witnesses, examine them and decide the case according to their Ideas of justice and the evidence produced." Cases were brought before it by sheriffs, one serving at each plantation; and in addition to deciding civil disputes, the court in criminal cases was empowered to levy punishments of up to $1,000 fine, forfeiture of crops, expulsion from the Bend, confinement in the guard house, or hard labor at the Home Farm. Interestingly enough, the order establishing the court provided that judges and sheriffs, all of whom were elected by the people, were subject to fine or other punishment if they failed

49. Special Orders #120, November 5, 1864, Gen. N. J. T. Dana, in *Vicksburg Daily Herald*, November 10, 1864.

102 *Enclave: Vicksburg & Her Plantations*

"to do their duty" or "perform their part." Provision was made for review of court decisions by the post superintendent of freedmen, but court records do not reveal a single instance where he overturned the findings of the freedmen court.[50]

The judges, all former slaves, were Simon Cable, Daniel Davenport, and J. A. Gla, among whom only Gla could write even his name. Col. John Eaton, however, was much impressed with the "shrewdness of the colored judges," and found their performance "very remarkable."[51]

Election of sheriffs and judges and full implementation of the court plan necessarily consumed several months, so that the first session of the "Court of Freedmen, Davis Bend, Miss." did not take place until June. According to extant records, the court met some 10 times between June 10 and December 2, 1865, considering a total of 21 cases. Of this number, 10 resulted in criminal convictions; 3 civil cases were resolved in favor of the plaintiff in the suit; 2 persons were fined for failure to appear in court; 1 defendant was acquitted; and 5 civil cases were thrown out for lack of evidence.[52]

Most of the charges were minor, such as stealing fruit or disturbing the peace, and in such cases the emphasis was usually placed upon reforming the convicted one. John T. Trowbridge, who toured the "battlefields and ruined cities of the South," stopped by Davis Bend on his trip upriver late in 1865 and recorded his version of the chastisement given by one of the judges to two persons accused of stealing some corn. "'Now listen, you!'" he began sternly. "'You and your mother are a couple of low-down darkies, trying to get a living without work. You are the cause that respectable colored people are slandered, and called thieving and lazy niggers. Now this is what I'll do with

---

50. *Record Court of Freedmen, Davis Bend, Miss.*, RG 105 (Miss.), NA.
51. *Ibid.*; Eaton, *Grant, Lincoln and the Freedmen*, 165.
52. *Record Court of Freedmen.*

you. If you and your mother will hire out today, and go work like honest people, I'll let you off on good behavior. If you won't, I'll send you to Captain Norton. That means you'll go up with a sentence. And I'll tell you what your sentence will be: three months hard labor on the home farm, and the ball and chain in case you attempt to run away. Now which will you do?'" Taking no time at all to weigh alternatives, they decided to "hire out," and a contract was signed on the spot.[53]

More serious charges, too, were brought before the court for decision. William Spencer, for example, was accused by his wife of "assault and battery with the intention of killing her and [of being] a man of a dangerous character." Spencer was convicted as charged and sentenced to "leave the Bend or go six months into the Block house," giving him the dubious distinction of receiving the stiffest penalty handed out by the court.[54] John Eaton thought the court system an unqualified success, and reported that "exposed property was as safe on Davis Bend as it would be anywhere."[55]

Eaton's analysis is all the more remarkable when the poverty of so many of the residents is taken into consideration. The cotton crop of the preceding year had been decimated by the army worm, and the vast majority of the population were beginning the new year with little to show for their efforts, though some few planters had managed a nice profit at the end of the previous year. Despite the benevolent work of Rountree and others, living conditions were poor and material possessions few. Housing was still in critically short supply, and one observer reported that "Some are living in old sheds, which are in a very dilapidated condition; some with only a covering overhead, exposed to the cold damp winds on every side; some in cabins without any floor, or anything to stop the spaces between the logs. Others again with only *bushes*

53. Trowbridge, *The South*, 201.
54. *Record Court of Freedmen*.
55. Eaton, *Grant, Lincoln and the Freedmen*, 165.

stuck into the ground around them to break off the wind, without any attempt at a covering overhead."[56]

It was exceedingly difficult, moreover, to effect any great improvements in refugee conditions, for throughout the spring and summer of the year the number of freedmen remained at around 4,000.[57] The number of missionaries and teachers serving this group was quite small, amounting at the end of April to but 12 individuals.[58] Upon the shoulders of these 12, together with 9 civilians in the medical service, 5 enlisted men, and 1 officer, more and more responsibility was placed as the War wound down along the Mississippi River.

Even before peace settled on the region, other refugee camps up and down the river were phased out, and all the "infirm and old people and children unable to labor" were removed to Davis Bend, where they were promised "all needful care."[59] This influx of dependent persons did not actually swell the total number there, because they simply replaced the more able-bodied who were leaving; but their presence prompted D. O. McCord, Medical Director of Freedmen for the area, to report that Davis Bend was a place where the "quality is as poor as the quantity is great."[60]

Lee's surrender in April of 1865 was cause for "quite a celebration . . . in the house of Old Jeff," but the end of the War seemed to be largely irrelevant to the pattern of existence on the peninsula.[61] Of more impact was the death only a week later of

56. J. P. Bardwell to M. E. Strieby, January 5, 1865, AMA Papers (Miss.).
57. Reports of Lt. Col. R. S. Donaldson, April 30, 1865; May 31, 1865; June 30, 1865; July 31, 1865; Box 36, RG 105 (Miss.), NA.
58. Report of Lt. Col. R. S. Donaldson, April 30, 1865, Box 36, RG 105 (Miss.), NA.
59. Special Orders #22, March 28, 1865, Col. Samuel Thomas, *Special Orders: Freedmen's Dept. (old organization) and Provost Marshal Genl. Freedmen May 3, 1864, to June 16, 1865*; RG 105 (Miss.), NA.
60. Report of D. O. McCord, Box 36, RG 105 (Miss.), NA.
61. Barnes Diary, April 16, 1865.

President Lincoln, who had been one of John Eaton's firmest supporters throughout the War.[62] The reaction to the President's death was immediate, and the jubilation of the previous week was replaced by universal sadness. "All the Colored people," recorded Samuel D. Barnes of the 64th U.S.C.I. in his diary, "have crape black strung or mourning of some kind for as their Uncle Sam, Massa Lincoln is dead."[63]

The death of the President and the ending of the War were ultimately of great consequence to the inhabitants of the old Davis lands, but in the spring and summer of 1865 the more immediate challenge was that of planting, cultivating, and harvesting a crop which — hopefully — would make up for the disappointment of the previous year.

The year had not begun auspiciously, for difficulties with the Federal authorities had initially hindered preparations necessary for putting in the crop. As Ben Montgomery had written to Joseph Davis in the middle of January, "I can only say that we are still in ignorance of the terms on which this place can be cultivated this year. The work on the levee has been stopped until something is known, M.E.S. Bedford is here as Col. Thomas agent, and for some reason, unknown to me, we are kept in suspense. We may learn something soon."[64]

Thomas soon decided to continue with much the same set-up as in 1864, but on a larger scale. Five thousand acres of land — compared with 2,500 the previous year — were turned over to a

---

62. Lincoln had written Eaton two months before the end of the War directing him to "continue your supervision of Freedmen over the same territory and on the same principles as in the past, making such improvements as experience may suggest, until legislation shall require some further change." Lincoln to Eaton, February 10, 1865; *Mississippi-Davis Bend Letters Received*, RG 105 (Miss.), NA.

63. Barnes Diary, April 23, 1865.

64. Benjamin Montgomery to Joseph E. Davis; January 15, 1865, Davis Papers, MDAH. Letters from Montgomery to Davis are hereinafter cited as "BM to JED." All such letters are in the Joseph Davis Papers, MDAH.

Joseph Davis' Slaves — As photographed in 1865 at an unidentified plantation on Davis Bend. Courtesy: J. Mack Moore Collection, Old Court House Museum, Vicksburg

total of 1,750 freedpeople, of whom 300 were adults. "These people," wrote Colonel Thomas in his year-end report, "were left free to manage their own affairs; not even officers of the Freedmen's bureau were allowed to meddle with the pecuniary or domestic affairs."[65] Actually, Thomas was guilty of exaggerating the degree of freedom accorded these planters, for the provost marshal of freedmen at Davis Bend issued a series of twelve very strict and explicit orders to the superintendents of colonies detailing their duties during the planting season. The first of these charges was indicative of the closeness with which the planting operations were to be observed. "Great exertions must be made on the part

65. Senate Executive Document No. 27, Thirty-ninth Congress, First Session, 38.

of Superintendents," it began, "to have every foot of tillable land within their colony properly cultivated. You are expected to make yourself familiar with the affairs and condition of each company in your charge, and to be at all times ready to report the condition of their crops."[66]

Other paragraphs noted that "As a general rule you must require the companies to plant two thirds their land in cotton," a larger portion if the freedmen wished to do so. Also, "You are expected to exercise a complete supervision over all the people in your charge. Listen to their complaints and do all in your power to get along peaceably with them."[67]

Numerous problems were associated with the successful cultivation of the Palmyra peninsula, one of which was the recurrence of flooding, a plague which had often striken the Davis brothers in earlier years. The spring of 1865 did not see the highest mark ever reached by the Mississippi, but the river did rise considerably above flood stage, and the weakened levees protecting Davis Bend were unable to resist its force. Not all of the land was flooded, but for much of April and May about one-third of the Bend lay unproductive under the gradually vanishing water.[68]

Another problem confronting planters was a shortage of mules, plows, and other agricultural supplies, part of the reason for which was their removal by Federal authorities early in the year. According to a petition furnished by a group of planters on the Bend, they had been "deprived of horses, mules, and oxen as well as farming utensils of every description; very much of which had been captured and brought into the Union lines by many of the undersigned."[69]

66. "To superintendents of Colonies, Davis Bend, Miss." April 17, 1865, *Henry Rowntree Letter Book*, RG 105 (Miss.), NA.
67. *Ibid.*
68. Endorsement, Lt. Stuart Eldridge, April 25, 1865, *Endorsements, Provost Marshal, Vicksburg, Mississippi*, Vol. 73, RG 105 (Miss.), NA.
69. Petition from J. A. Gla, *et al*, to Col. Samuel Thomas, July 15, 1865, Joseph Davis Papers, MDAH.

At least one planter from Port Gibson, Mississippi, however, disputed the refugees' claim to livestock in their possession. In a strong letter, he stated "on oath" that "the colored people from the Davis, Woods, and Palmyras [sic] plantations about the month of March 1864, made a raid on his plantation on the Miss. River above the mouth of the Big Black, and with force of arms carried of . . . one hundred & seven head of horned cattle, consisting of milch cows and calves, heifers, steers, and work oxen. . . . Also about thirty work mules . . . and one iron axeltree ox wagon." Thrasher went on to report that he had recently visited the Bend and had found many of his cattle and mules, still marked with his brand "JBT." He had his pardon and now wanted his property returned. A month later he had it back.[70]

Despite confiscation by Union authorities, however, some mules remained in the colonists' hands, and every effort was made to encourage their use by as many planters as possible. Part of the instruction issued to the superintendents of colonies touched on this point, urging that arrangements be made "with those having more teams than they require for their own use to plow for those having no team. This agreement can be made by the acre; or to be repaid in labor; or to be paid at the end of the season — in this case the agreement should be made in writing, signed by both parties and witnessed and approved by the Superintendent of the Colony."[71]

There were not, however, enough draft animals to serve the farmers' needs, and some were forced to turn to white financiers like "Mr. Hawley," who wrote frantically to Colonel Thomas in May when he learned of flooding on the Bend. Some of "his men," he reported to Thomas, "are drowned out," and he was greatly

---

70. J. B. Thrasher to Capt. Weber [sic], October 6, 1865, with endorsement, Col. Samuel Thomas to Capt. Norton, Nov. 7, 1865, *Mississippi-Davis Bend, Letters Received*, RG 105 (Miss.), NA.

71. "To Superintendents of Colonies," *Henry Rowntree Letter Book*, RG 105 (Miss.), NA.

concerned about losing his investment in their efforts. Hawley had already supplied "mules and provisions," but he was certainly not going "to furnish supplies to the people who have no land to work." Thomas wrote Lieutenant Colonel Donaldson suggesting that an adjustment be made to insure Hawley's continued support, and it is quite probable that new land was given to those who were dependent on Hawley for supplies.[72]

The flood waters had seeped into the soil by early June, and the level fields inside the levee were covered with young cotton plants struggling with weeds for mastery of the land.[73] A continuing shortage of hoes made agricultural excellence difficult, while the heat and humidity combined to drain energy from all creatures except the smallest. Insects, however, seemed to thrive on the summer climate at Davis Bend, and swarms of gnats and other winged nuisances made life miserable for all who lived there.[74]

In spite of flood waters, late planting, heat, humidity, and insects, the cotton crop was in excellent shape by mid-July, and the "Colored Planters of the Hurricane Plantation" decided it was time to approach Colonel Thomas with the idea that they should be allowed to run the gin at Davis Bend this year, unlike 1864 when a Government agent had been in charge. As far as the "Colored Planters" were concerned, arrangements for the previous year had fallen "far short of giving satisfaction," and they believed that a cooperative agreement among the users of the gin would be much better.[75] Fifty-six planters endorsed the petition, which stated: "Now that we have been kindly permitted to till the said plantation, numbering near 2000 acres land, unaided by an agent

---

72. Col. Samuel Thomas to Lt. Col. R. S. Donaldson, May 9, 1865, *Mississippi-Davis Bend, Letters Received*, RG 105 (Miss.), NA.
73. Reid, *After the War*, 280.
74. Barnes Diary, May 18, 1865.
75. Petition from the "Colored Planters of the Hurricane Plantation" to Col. Samuel Thomas, July 15, 1865; letter, "Colored Planters" to Thomas, July 31, 1865, both in Joseph Davis Papers, MDAH.

of any kind except the military protection, for which with the privilege of tilling the land we are grateful, and will most cheerfully submit to all legal charges for both land and machinery."[76]

Thomas, however, had begun much earlier making plans for the gin, stating in May that many people had already applied for the concession. "I propose," he wrote Lieutenant Colonel Donaldson, "to give them out to somebody who will spend five thousand dollars repairing them up, and then gin the cotton at a certain tax that we will impose. The gins are all in bad condition," he stated, "and must be repaired if they do the work at the Bend as it should be done."[77] Thomas did not immediately respond to the petition, prompting a letter from the "Committee of Five Appointed by the Planters." Ben Montgomery composed the missive, which told the Colonel: "it would be a source of pride to be able to demonstrate to the world our capacity to manage our own affairs, not only in raising, but also in preparing and carrying our products to market."[78]

The Freedmen's Bureau representative was evidently stirred by this letter, for he answered the Committee very promptly that he had no intention of letting any group of freedmen run the gin in 1865. "I am sorry to make this charge," he stated, "yet it is true, that you failed in running the saw mill placed under your charge last spring. If you conducted the ginning business in the same style it would be a complete failure."[79]

Thomas in the same letter moralized about the opportunities given to the Davis Bend population "to support themselves and develope [sic] their latent powers"; he assured the Committee that he really had their best interests at heart, for "Next after the

76. Petition from the "Colored Planters," July 15, 1865.
77. Col. Samuel Thomas to Lt. Col. R. S. Donaldson, May 19, 1865, *Mississippi-Davis Bend, Letters Received*, RG 105 (Miss.), NA.
78. Letter, "Committee of Five Appointed by the Planters," to Col. Samuel Thomas, July 31, 1865, Joseph Davis Papers, MDAH.
79. Col. Samuel Thomas to "Committee of Five," August 3, 1865, Joseph Davis Papers, MDAH.

interest of the Government, is that of the Colored people under my charge on the Bend"; and finally, he charged that some planters who had signed the petition were whiskey sellers and black speculators "who have located there for the purpose of making money off of the ignorance of their former fellow servants." In short, Thomas said "No."[80]

Cotton meanwhile was coming along quite well, and the Davis Bend colony was attracting attention in the newspapers of the state. The *Meridian Daily Clarion*, for example, reprinted with favorable comment an item from a Vicksburg paper which mentioned that "under many discouraging circumstances — the high water in the Spring, limited means, sickness, etc — the result thus far has been very satisfactory." Cotton was beginning to open "on a few of the dryest plantations," stated the *Daily Clarion*, and picking was expected to begin by the first of September.[81]

The commencement of picking brought one last try from the planters, who reported to Thomas that his agent had disparaged their abilities by asserting that they "had not the brains to manage such affairs." The Committee of Five replied to this allegation by requesting once again to be allowed to run the gin, offering to do the job of baling and ginning for $7.50 per bale, furnishing all necessary supplies.[82] Thomas did not reply to their correspondence, but merely ordered his agent, M. E. S. Bedford, to prepare the gin for the season's work. Bedford thereupon hired a white engineer and a gin superintendent to tend the machinery, paying each $100 a month.[83]

Cotton began coming into the gin in large quantities by early October, but the freedmen who had worked so hard on their crop were often disappointed when their accounts were figured. Be-

80. *Ibid.*
81. *Meridian Daily Clarion*, August 8, 1865.
82. Committee of Five to Col. Samuel Thomas, September 13, 1865, Davis Papers, MDAH.
83. BM to JED, November 10, 1865.

cause Thomas had taken from the planters the hoes, plows, spades, axes and all implements necessary to till the land, most planters had been forced to mortgage their crop to the commissary stores on Davis Bend in order to secure necessary agricultural supplies, not to mention foodstuffs for their families.[84]

Thomas had clamped strict controls on the cotton traffic, ordering that "not a pound of cotton must be shipped from the Bend till it is ginned and then only on permit." It was necessary, too, he stated, "to secure all claims we may have against the Freedmen."[85] These requirements were ripe for exploitation by unscrupulous persons, and if the testimony of several of the planters can be believed, Thomas' agent, Bedford, was one who took unfair and illegal advantage of the situation.

In what could only be described as the worst possible conflict of interest, Bedford, who controlled both ginning and shipping on Davis Bend, set himself up in the cotton business and bought from the poorer freedmen at 7¢ per pound. He was able to buy at this absurdly low price — cotton brought about 50¢ per pound in New Orleans — by allowing the larger planters to monopolize the gin for several months at the height of ginning. This action reduced those with smaller quantities of cotton to the necessity of selling to him, or in some cases to the larger planters, in order to get money to pay their bills and obtain additional supplies.[86]

The store where planters obtained supplies also got into the cotton act, buying all it could at 7¢ per pound, then charging the seller $2.50 a wagon load for hauling it to the landing.[87] As a result of dealings such as this, some of the smaller planters barely broke even on their year's work, despite the fact that the

84. BM to JED, October 14, 1865.
85. Col. Samuel Thomas to Capt. Gaylord B. Norton, August 29, 1865, *Mississippi-Davis Bend, Letters Received*, RG 105 (Miss.), NA.
86. BM to JED, October 14, 1865.
87. Joseph E. Davis to President Andrew Johnson, October 30, 1865, Joseph Davis Papers, MDAH.

cotton season had been relatively free from the troubles which had plagued the previous year. William Lewis, for example, raised 3 bales of cotton, but he received only $8.85 for his efforts. Philip Gaiter, one of the old Joseph Davis hands, raised some 1,340 pounds of cotton and was paid only $8.90.[88] Based upon contemporary and later patterns of the cost of "furnish" for sharecroppers in the Mississippi Delta region, figuring a bale of cotton at $200, and deducting the Davis Bend average of $183 paid by each adult freedmen for supplies that year, it is possible that Lewis and Gaiter were cheated out of about $400 each.

Thomas responded to the freedmen's complaints by sending an investigative committee, but according to Ben Montgomery, "they proved to be nothing more than members of the same clan and may approve of the acts of those here."[89] Joseph Davis had meanwhile applied to President Johnson for a pardon and for the return of his land and had then written a scathing letter to the President detailing charges of ineptness and unfairness in the conduct of affairs on the Bend. Samuel Thomas was a special target of his wrath. Wrote Davis, "I know nothing of the Freedmen's Bureau, but from what I have seen here, if Colonel Thomas is to be taken as a specimin [sic] there are few evils that can be more intolerable."[90] No illegalities were ever proven on anyone operating at Davis Bend, but as late as March 1866 Joseph Davis reported to President Johnson that "I was told last November by a person whose position enabled him to know that I could have my property restored, by paying Colonel Thomas a thousand dollars. This I could not do."[91] As nearly as can be determined, Davis' allegations were never investigated.

    88. Testimony given at Davis Bend, November 1865, *ibid*.
    89. BM to JED, November 10, 1865.
    90. *Natchez Democrat*, October 24, 1865, 4; Joseph E. Davis to President Andrew Johnson, October 30, 1865, Joseph Davis Papers, MDAH.
    91. Joseph E. Davis to President Andrew Johnson, March 1, 1866, Joseph Davis Papers, MDAH.

114 *Enclave: Vicksburg & Her Plantations*

Even as the year was drawing to a close, official operations at Davis Bend were diminishing, and it soon became obvious that 1865 would be the last year that the military forces would exercise their presence upon the inhabitants there. Early in October Captain Norton, in charge of the Home Farm there, rounded up all the Government horses and mules and advertised them for sale to private citizens.[92] Then on the twenty-fourth of the month the simple official statement that "the Post at Davis Bend is hereby discontinued" brought to an end over two years of military involvement there, going back to the early months of 1863 when U.S. Grant had expressed his desire to make a "Negro paradise" of the peninsula.[93] The Government hospital, however, continued its work on the Bend, and almost as the post there was closing, the medical facilities were augmented by the addition of a surgeon and two buildings.[94]

When Colonel Thomas made his report to Congress in December of 1865, there was every reason to believe the Davis Bend colony a success. In spite of individual complaints and the almost certain peculation of certain officials there, the balance sheet for the Bend as a whole was quite favorable. Not counting the Home Farm, which netted $25,929.80, the summary of receipts and expenditures was as follows:

RECEIPTS

12,000 bushels corn @ $1.00	$12,000
Vegetables sold (potatoes, melons)	38,500
1736 bales cotton @ $200	347,200
Total receipts	$397,700

---

92. *Meridian Daily Clarion*, October 10, 1865.
93. Special Orders #117, October 24, 1865, Maj. Gen. N. F. Force, *Mississippi-Davis Bend, Letters Received*, RG 105 (Miss.), NA.
94. Special Orders #43, Col. Samuel Thomas, *ibid*.

EXPENDITURES

to the Govt. for supplies	$160,000
to white partners for supplies	60,000
to BFRAL stores for rations	18,500
	$238,500

The net profit for the year was $159,200, which meant that each of the 1,300 adults — except for those who were cheated out of their share — received an average of slightly more than $120 for his year's work, a figure much better than that attained by freedmen who worked for white lessees in the area.[95]

This second year of the colony at Davis Bend had demonstrated once again the fertility of the Palmyra acreage and had whetted the desires of Benjamin Montgomery and others to remain on these lands where so much of their lives had been passed. The larger Government experiment at Davis Bend, however, was ended after 1865, for all the owners except the Davis brothers were pardoned at that time and had their land returned to them.[96] Joseph Davis had applied for a pardon in October 1865, but as of the close of the year his case had not been acted upon. The Government therefore kept possession of Brierfield and Hurricane into 1866, with Colonel Thomas reporting to Congress that he would "retain the Davis plantations and lease them this year at a moderate rent."[97]

Thomas, however, was not so prompt in telling the freedmen of his plans for the year. He visited the Bend in January 1866 and informed the assembled residents "of the disposition of the other part of the Bend," but did not mention the fate of the Davis

---

95. Senate Executive Document No. 27, Thirty-ninth Congress, First Session, 30, 38.
96. *Ibid.*, 39.
97. *Ibid.*, 30.

lands. "We are now filling up a couple of large cuts made in the levee to let out the water," wrote Ben Montgomery, who was by 1866 the de facto manager of Hurricane and Brierfield. "Also making rails. We need at least 10,000 or 15,000. It is rumored," he informed Joseph Davis, "that this land will be retained by the Government, but we shall go on with our work unless ordered to discontinue. Should like to commence dividing the land as early as possible so that the cleaning may be commenced."[98]

Montgomery went ahead anyway and divided the land among 107 lessees, who paid rent to "Montgomery & Sons" ranging from $20 to $1,050, the total for rent coming to $13,624. Montgomery was apparently acting as agent for the Government in collecting rent on the land, for he was himself paying $9 per acre for that part of Brierfield which his family worked.[99] Montgomery was evidently viewed as a threat by some of the Freedmen's Bureau officials, and a rumor circulated that he was not going to be allowed to remain on the Bend. This challenge, however, only served to create in Montomgery "a determination to test their power to drive me off."[100]

It was perhaps not surprising that certain less than scrupulous Bureau officials should want to be rid of Montgomery, for his position of leadership among the freedmen made him a very definite threat to Government influence. Moreover, if Montgomery's analysis was accurate, nine of the twelve Bureau men there were "cotton hunters," and the last thing they wished to contend with was a man like Benjamin Montgomery.[101]

Montgomery would have been recognized as a remarkable individual in any community, but his accomplishments are even

98. BM to JED, January 6, 1866.
99. "Names of Lessees on Davis Bend, Miss., for whom Montgomery & Sons have Land rent for the Year 1866," *ibid*; BM to JED, February 5, 1866.
100. BM to JED, January 22, 1866.
101. BM to JED, October 30, 1866.

Davis Bend 117

more notable in light of his background. Born a slave in Loudoun County, Virginia, about 1815, he was taken to Natchez, Mississippi, sometime before 1840, and it was there that Joseph Davis purchased him.[102] The elder Davis allowed Montgomery access to the Hurricane library, and there he learned to read and write.[103] It was Davis' feeling that his workers should develop their talents and abilities in whatever area they showed most promise, and Benjamin Montgomery displayed an aptitude for business. Davis encouraged Montgomery along this line, and soon the slave was placed in charge of shipping the extensive Hurricane plantation cotton crop. As Montgomery's experience grew, he began his own business venture — a dry goods and variety store which he maintained on Davis Bend for almost forty years.[104]

Montgomery was given an initial line of credit through Joseph Davis' guarantee, but thereafter he bought goods from both Natchez and New Orleans merchants in his own name. According to Jefferson Davis' wife Varina, "He shipped, and indeed sometimes purchased, the fruit crops of the Davis families, and also of other people in 'The Bend'; and in one instance, credited one of us with $2000 on his account. . . . He many times borrowed from his master, but was equally as exact in his dealings with his creditors."[105]

The business field was not Montgomery's only area of excellence, for according to historian John Hope Franklin he invented a boat propeller which Jefferson Davis attempted to have patented in Montgomery's name. Davis failed in his efforts, U.S. law at the time apparently not allowing a slave to be issued a patent. Franklin feels that this incident "perhaps accounts for the passage of a law

102. Jackson, "Mound Bayou," 38.
103. Everett, *Brierfield*, 86.
104. V. Davis, *Jefferson Davis*, I, 174–75; Mahala P. H. Roach Memorandum, August 22, 1897, MDAH; BM to JED, June 27, 1866; Jackson, "Mound Bayou," 38.
105. Roach Memorandum; V. Davis, *Jefferson Davis*, I, 174–75.

118 *Enclave: Vicksburg & Her Plantations*

by the Confederate Congress in 1861 providing that if the owner took an oath that his slave had actually invented a device, the patent would be issued to him."[106]

Throughout the pre-War years Montgomery demonstrated his abilities as a manager and leader, and when Joseph Davis packed his family and left Hurricane plantation in 1862, he left the trusted slave in charge.[107] Montgomery himself, together with his wife Mary and sons Isaiah and Thornton, left Davis Bend after Federal troops arrived in 1863, and went to Ohio. Isaiah then joined Adm. David Porter's gunboat fleet and served for several months in 1863.[108] The Montgomerys remained in the Midwest until 1865, when they returned and once again assumed strong positions of leadership among the freedmen on the Bend. They were indeed a family to be reckoned with by the Freedmen's Bureau officials who were supposedly in charge, and those individuals who talked of eliminating the Montgomerys from the Bend were eventually forced to concede defeat and accept their great influence as an established fact.[109]

Even as this conflict was resolving itself, the United States Army withdrew its physical presence from Davis Bend by removing the last few enlisted men who were stationed there.[110] Then in mid-April the hospital which had been treating as many as eighty freedmen a month finally closed its doors.[111] The only U.S. officials remaining on the Bend after April were the twelve employees of

106. John Hope Franklin, *From Slavery to Freedom: A History of Negro Americans*, 3rd ed. (New York: Vintage Books, 1969), 197.
107. Everett, *Brierfield*, 76–77.
108. Jackson, "Mound Bayou," 38.
109. Benjamin Montgomery wrote to Joseph Davis that "I think we shall have no further trouble with those controlling matters here." February 5, 1866.
110. Special Orders #24, February 27, 1866, Col. Samuel Thomas, *Mississippi-Davis Bend, Letters Received*, RG 105 (Miss.), NA.
111. "Report of Attendants Employed," January, February, April 1866, ibid.

the Freedmen's Bureau, who interfered little in the internal workings of the colony.

The Federal commander at Vicksburg maintained a watch over activities down the river, but he, too, apparently found little reason to disturb the residents of the Davis lands. Even the administration of justice remained a function of the freedmen, for Maj. Gen. Thomas J. Wood, commanding at Vicksburg, readily gave his sanction to "the Committee of Arbitration for the settlement of disputes and difficulties on the Davis' Bend and associate plantations, between colored people, the said committee being composed of colored men," approving the "decisions of said committee, when in conformity with well known principles of justice."[112]

The freedmen of Davis Bend were faring well in mid-year 1866, with Ben Montgomery exulting that "the present prospect and the general appearance of everything is fully as favorable as could be expected," adding however, that this did not "destroy a recollection of the evils of the past two years' transactions here."[113] July was hot and dry, and as a result the cotton bolls began to open early in August.

There was more than a hint of disgust in Montgomery's words as he informed Joe Davis that a number of merchants had suddenly decided to descend upon the Bend. "In the commencement of the season," he wrote, "when the prospects were gloomy they were not to be seen. Now we have more than is necessary."[114] Most of the credit extended to the colonists, however, had come from New Orleans merchants, some of whom had done business with Montgomery before the War.[115]

---

112. Endorsement of Maj. Gen. Thomas J. Wood, June 1, 1866, on letter, W. T. Montgomery to J. D. Nicholson, May 22, 1866, Davis MSS, MDAH.
113. BM to JED, June 27, 1866.
114. BM to JED, August 6, 1866.
115. BM to JED, September 10, 1866.

The end of August brought increased numbers of open bolls on the head-high cotton stalks, but it also signalled the appearance of the dreaded army worm, the scourge that had so decimated the crop two years earlier.[116] A week later Montgomery informed Joe Davis that "the weather being favorable to the increase of the worm they are spreading rapidly doing their accustomed damage as they proceed."[117] Picking had begun about the last of August, by which time sufficient bolls were opening each day to keep everyone busy from sun-up until too dark to pick. As the worms moved across the Davis lands, however, it became evident that the crop would be nowhere near the size previously expected, and by October 3, only 234 bales had been shipped from the Bend.[118] The crop of 1866 was not good, but the year itself was to prove a notable one for those on the Davis plantation lands.

Benjamin Montgomery had been corresponding regularly with his former master since the beginning of 1865, when the Montgomery family returned from Ohio. Out of either deference or habit, the ex-bondsman began his letters to Davis with the salutation "Dear Master," a practice which continued through the entirety of 1865. As the second year began, however, Montgomery addressed Davis as "Kind Sir," a change of format which signalled the establishment of a more nearly equal relationship between the two men.

This new arrangement was evidently acceptable to Davis, and subsequent letters during the year are those which one white Southern planter might well have written to another during the period. Then on October 7, 1866, Montgomery asked Davis to name the terms under which he would lease the land to him. "The repairs necessary are extensive," wrote Montgomery. "Fences are mere makeshift. Rain sheds all gone. Cisterns out of order.

116. BM to JED, August 31, 1866.
117. BM to JED, September 6, 1866.
118. BM to JED, October 3, 1866.

Davis Bend 121

Merely frame and roof of stables remaining — ditching and work on the levee necessary, besides the work required on the Quarters." He would prefer renting to sharecropping, explained Montgomery, "if renting does not conflict with the laws of the state." But his real desire was outright purchase of the Davis plantations, a move which, as he expressed it, "would I fear involve me for life."[119]

One problem blocked such a deal, however, for Joseph Davis was not yet in possession of his lands. He finally received on September 8, 1866, the pardon which President Johnson had granted over five months earlier,[120] and by the end of October the problem had been resolved. Davis was to be restored to full use and enjoyment of his property effective January 1, 1867, with rent paid to him from the effective date of his pardon — March 20, 1866.[121]

The idea of selling the plantations to Benjamin Montgomery and his family was attractive to Joseph Davis for several reasons. First, Davis was past the age of eighty, and he was not physically capable of supervising even a portion of the Palmyra acreage. Second, Jefferson Davis was still lodged in Fort Monroe, Virginia, and there was no indication that he would be released in the near future. Third, there was yet the possibility that Congress, displeased with the pardon given the brother of the Confederate President, might attempt to revoke Johnson's action. If the land belonged to a black family, however, this revocation might be less likely, so Davis reasoned. He therefore decided to offer the Brierfield and Hurricane plantations to Benjamin Montgomery, and in mid-November the contract was signed.

The price of the 4,000 acres on Davis Bend was set at $300,000, with interest of 5% per year in gold or 7% in paper

119. BM to JED, October 7, 1866.
120. Joseph E. Davis to Maj. Gen. Thomas J. Wood, September 8, 1866, Joseph Davis Papers, MDAH.
121. Maj. Gen. Thomas J. Wood to Gen. Oliver O. Howard, October 31, 1866, in Senate Executive Document #6.

currency.[122] Payments on the principal were due the first of each year, but Davis was resigned, for the near future at least, to receiving only the interest, which would in itself provide enough for his family's existence.

Benjamin Montgomery was in the unique and unenviable position of owing more money than any other ex-slave in the state and perhaps in the South. He was, however, elated over his purchase, for he had in mind for the Palmyra lands a great enterprise which he hoped would be of lasting benefit not only to himself and his family but to as many other ex-slaves as the land would accommodate and support. To explain his design he placed "on the part of the Association" an advertisement in the November 21 issue of the Vicksburg *Daily Times*:

The undersigned having secured for a term of years the "Hurricane" and "Brierfield" plantations in Warren County, in this State, from Joseph E. Davis, Esq., the proprietor thereof, proposes on the 1st day of January, 1867, to organize a community composed exclusively of colored people, to occupy and cultivate said plantations, and invites the cooperation of such as are recommended by honesty, industry, sobriety, and intelligence, in the enterprise.

He hopes by the pursuit of agriculture, horticulture, and manufacturing and mechanical arts, as well as the raising of stock, to attain as much prosperity and happiness as are consistent with human nature.[123]

The Association, he stated, would be governed by a council, "selected by the community," which would have the duty of providing "such rules and regulations as experience shall show to be necessary for its welfare." Meanwhile, however, he wanted it understood that a basic annual tax of 50¢ per acre would be

---

122. Deed, November 15, 1866, Joseph Davis Papers, MDAH.
123. *Vicksburg Daily Times*, November 21, 1866.

Davis Bend 123

collected, "in advance," from those who took land for cultivation. This sum would be "strictly applied to the building of levees to guard against overflows." Similarly, a tax on persons and property would be used to educate the young and maintain the "aged and helpless."[124]

Then in an expression of attitude presaging that of Booker T. Washington — upon whom he may well have exerted considerable influence — Montgomery made it clear that his colony was not at all interested in achieving political power or equality, but intended to be as apolitical as possible. "Regarding the suffrage question as of doubtful and remote utility," he stated, "the discussion of it and other political topics as more likely to produce contention and idleness than harmony in the community, such discussions will be discouraged."[125] This same philosophy, interestingly enough, was expressed some years later by his son Isaiah, who as the only black, only Republican delegate to the 1890 Mississippi Constitutional Convention spoke in favor of and voted for the poll tax, residency requirements, and literacy tests which swiftly disfranchised virtually every black voter in the state.[126]

Montgomery concluded the lengthy piece with a declaration that the governing body of the colony would not tolerate "drunken, idle, and evil-disposed persons," then appealed for white support and forbearance in the enterprise by assuring that "in their dealings the members of the community will aim to be strictly just, and hope their humble efforts will be regarded with charity and generosity by those of superior knowledge and position, whose good opinion it will be their honest endeavor to deserve."[127] He signed the announcement simply "B. T. Montgomery," describing himself as "Colored, formerly a slave and one of the business

124. *Ibid*.
125. *Ibid*.
126. Vernon L. Wharton, *The Negro in Mississippi, 1865–1890*, Harper Torchbooks (New York: Harper & Row, Publishers, 1965), 211–12.
127. *Vicksburg Daily Times*, November 21, 1866.

124 *Enclave: Vicksburg & Her Plantations*

managers of Joseph E. Davis, Esq. (the owner of the Hurricane and Brierfield plantations)."[128]

Newspaper recognition of the announcement was almost immediate, with the *Hinds County Gazette*, a leading conservative journal in the next county, reporting in November 1866 that "the scheme has the approval of Gen. Wood, the military commandant at Vicksburg, who also guarantees full protection to Montgomery and his colonists."[129]

Montgomery, however, largely devoted his next letter to Joseph Davis to such items as progress made in ditching and clearing the land, pausing only briefly in the middle of the letter to philosophize a bit. "For my part," he wrote, "I cannot see into the future but am forced to believe that cotton is bound to be lower in price and the only hope is to try and get everything in good working order and then work industriously and systematically to make the most we can."[130]

The end of November brought further comment from the *Hinds County Gazette*, which editorialized that the Montgomery idea had "suggested a similar arrangement to holders of large tracts of land in other parts of the state. We should not be surprised," guessed the *Gazette*, "if a like experiment were tried in our own county. All we have to say on the subject," concluded the writer, "is that we would prefer not to be a planter adjoining or adjacent to one of these colonies."[131]

Although 1866 had not been a successful year for the planters on Davis Bend, Montgomery and his Association looked toward the coming season with the greatest possible anticipation. The number of freedmen on the Bend had decreased greatly by mid-December, "owing to the demand for labor and the desire of those leaving to take advantage of the prices offered those who contract

128. *Ibid.*
129. *Hinds County Gazette*, November 23, 1866.
130. BM to JED, November 25, 1866.
131. *Hinds County Gazette*, November 30, 1866.

now," but persons who remained on the Montgomery-owned lands felt that with a bit of good fortune they might yet raise the bumper cotton crop that had eluded them so far.[132]

Joseph Davis was still an important influence on Palmyra, for many of the people there, such as Henderson Newton and Warren Watt, depended upon their former owner for loans with which to pursue their agricultural endeavors. Ben Montgomery continued to write to Davis, informing him on a near-weekly basis of the status of crops, army worms, and the Mississippi River.[133]

The winter of 1866–67 was a bad one throughout much of the area drained by the river which flowed past the Hurricane and Brierfield plantations, and the snow of that season melted in the spring and joined the rains of the lower valley to swell the Mississippi to record proportions.[134] The levees which surrounded and protected Davis Bend had been weakened considerably by seven years of neglect, and by late February 1867 the Mississippi was within three feet of reaching their top.[135] Montgomery worked ceaselessly to repair the threatened levees, which he described as "a den of crawfish & filled with rotten wood which allows a free passage of water through it," having at the peak a total of 250 laborers at work on the task.[136] Ultimately, however, the river prevailed, for early in March the churning brown waters broke through the feeble barrier and began flowing across the narrow neck of Davis Bend, just as they had done in 1859 and again in 1862.[137]

132. "Report on Affairs at Davis Bend," December 10, 1866, Vol. 18, RG 105 (Miss.), NA.
133. Henderson Newton to "Dear Master" (Joseph Davis), January 24, 1867, and Warren Watt to "My Dear old Master" (Joseph Davis), May 19, 1867, both in Joseph Davis Papers, MDAH. Montgomery sent Davis almost a hundred letters from mid-1867 to mid-1869.
134. Everett, *Brierfield*, 91.
135. BM to JED, February 28, 1867.
136. BM to JED, March 28, 1867.
137. *Ibid.*; Everett, *Brierfield*, 91.

This year was different from similar situations in the past, however, for the Mississippi had always before returned to its old channel as the flooding went down. In 1867, though, the volume of water which rushed across the 300 yards by which Davis Bend was joined to the mainland was such that a completely new channel was scoured. Davis Bend quite suddenly became Davis Island, its inhabitants now separated from the rest of Mississippi by the greatest river in the country.[138]

Some water, of course, continued to flow the long way around, in the old river bed, but, wrote Montgomery, "the cut-off . . . is enlarging rapidly and all boats except the packets are passing through it both up and down."[139] The ultimate implications of the new channel were undoubtedly not lost on Montgomery, but for the present he was more concerned by the continued flooding of his farm lands and the effects it would have on the cotton crop.

The waters continued their rise into April, reaching such a height by the first of that month that the gauges used to measure flood depth had all been swept away.[140] By mid-month the waters had begun to recede slightly, but Montgomery was brought to the realization that he could not hope to clear enough profit to meet his financial obligation to Davis.[141]

His first year as a landowner and planter could not have presented greater problems. There were levees to repair and fences to build. Cotton prices were down. Livestock was either gone or near starvation. The Association had not had time to become fully effective before the flood hit, and the members were unsettled. Recruiters from both sides of the river were constantly tempting the workforce with more promising offers. And much of the best land remained under water until the middle of May — long after

138. BM to JED, March 21, 1867.
139. *Ibid.*
140. Brig. Gen. M. D. McAlister to Gov. B. G. Humphreys, April 1, 1867, RG 27, MDAH.
141. BM to JED, April 15, 1867.

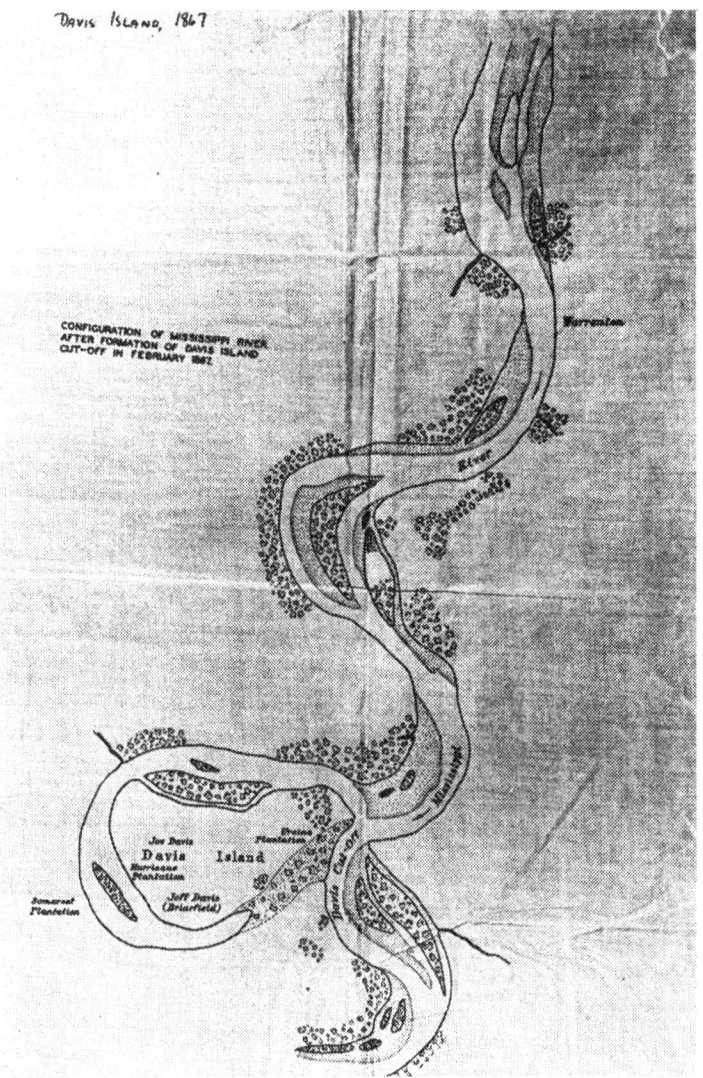

Davis Island, 1867—The mighty Mississippi River cut through the neck of Davis Bend in the spring of 1867, putting it on the Louisiana side. Courtesy: Mississippi Department of Archives and History

the normal time for planting cotton.[142] These last two problems were the greatest and most difficult to solve, but Montgomery pressed forward with the planting efforts as rapidly as the ground dried, and informed Davis that "if so fortunate as to even get organized I shall propose the dismemberment of any who may leave to work elsewhere when their services are needed here,"[143] meaning the offender would be expelled from the Association.

The next six months were a constant agricultural struggle, for though Montgomery's persuasion retained enough laborers to work the land, there was little he could do about the late start, or the weather, or the worms — which he feared most of all. "The weather has been excessively showery," he wrote on the Fourth of July. "Locusts still doing injury to the cotton. An early visit of the army worm can hardly prove otherwise than ruinous." He then provided an observation which he felt might offer some relief. "As I have before said," he stated "the abundance of destructive insects may be attributed to the scacity [sic] of birds. . . . I do hope that some step may be taken to extend some protection to them [the birds] which when more abundant the Insects were less troublesome. Even now the small portion of the fields that are subject to the range of chickens, are not troubled by the insects."[144]

A few army worms had been discovered by the final week of July, and Montgomery was "very much disturbed." He intended, he said, to use "every exertion to prevent their spread," but feared that "many parties will not make expenses."[145] Two weeks later the worm had established itself in force, and Montgomery employed the children on the Bend to collect the larvae, paying a bounty of 25¢ a pint for them.[146] In early September the battle between

---

142. BM to JED, April 15, 1867; April 18, 1867; May 6, 1867; and June 3, 1867.
143. BM to JED, May 6, 1867 and June 13, 1867.
144. BM to JED, July 4, 1867.
145. BM to JED, July 23, 1867.
146. BM to JED, August 8, 1867.

man and worm was still raging, but by the end of the month the planters had won out, and Montgomery could report that "the worms are doing no injury worth mentioning at present."[147]

Picking and ginning had commenced by mid-September, and the weather held favorable through October and most of November, by which time Montgomery was again having problems keeping labor in the fields. "We have shipped to date," he wrote on November 14, "from Hurricane and Brierfield only 314 bales. . . . By the acts of those planters on the other side of the river we have suffered considerable loss say at least 300 bales." He was not discouraged, however, for he was "inclined to think the community system will work well after becoming properly systematized, which will require time."[148]

It was by this time apparent to Montgomery that he would never be able to meet the terms required by the sale of property. "Double the time will be necessary," he wrote, "without an increase of the amt."[149] He sent Davis a draft for $1,000 early in December, promised an equal sum "as soon as possible," expressed his deep concern for Davis' well-being, and thanked him for his patience. "We cannot make or save anything this year," he confessed, "but shall meet liability as far as in our power."[150]

It had been a very difficult year for the Davis Bend Association, for the forces of nature had simply been too much against them. The total crop from Hurricane and Brierfield was in excess of 600 bales, a quantity quite remarkable under the circumstances, but one that left even many of the old-time residents of the Bend dissatisfied with arrangements there.[151] "The present is a severe trial for the working classes," admitted Montgomery, "but to all

147. BM to JED, September 9, 1867, and September 26, 1867.
148. BM to JED, September 24, 1867; October 14, 1867; and November 14, 1867.
149. BM to JED, November 14, 1867.
150. BM to JED, December 11, 1867.
151. BM to JED, December 30, 1867 and January 6, 1868.

130 *Enclave: Vicksburg & Her Plantations*

who escape starvation it may teach valuable lessons of economy that could be learned in no other way."[152]

Conditions on Davis Bend were not of course unique, for throughout the states of Louisiana, Arkansas, and Mississippi were many for whom the crop of 1867 had been disastrous.[153] Indeed the residents of Hurricane and Brierfield, though isolated to a large degree by the new river channel, were yet very much a part of Mississippi and even became involved in the political process of Reconstruction when registrars visited the Bend in June and enrolled more than 300 of them as voters.[154] Though Montgomery had professed a desire to curtail political discussions on the Bend—and in fact there is little evidence that much political activity ever did take place there—it was Davis Bend that produced the first black officeholders in the state's history.

As early as January 1867 some 1,500 residents of the Bend had signed a petition asking that a post office be established there and requesting that Thornton Montgomery be appointed postmaster.[155] This particular plan apparently failed, but some seven months later Maj. Gen. E. O. C. Ord, Commander of the Fourth Military District, appointed him constable for the Bend, naming C. P. Huntington, a white resident, as justice of the peace.[156] Huntington, however, refused the appointment and recommended that it be given to Ben Montgomery. Though pronouncing himself "quite unfit for the position," Montgomery nevertheless deemed

---

152. BM to JED, January 6, 1868.
153. Brig. Gen. Alvan C. Gillem to B.B. Eggleston, February 15, 1868, *Fourth Military District, Letters Sent, Civil Affairs*, Vol. 26, RG 98 (Miss.), NA.
154. BM to JED, June 13, 1867.
155. BM to JED, January 24, 1867, and February 16, 1867; Petition (undated), Joseph Davis Papers.
156. Special Orders #117, August 27, 1867, Maj. Gen. Ord, "Records of the War Department, U.S. Army Commands, Fourth Military District (Miss. & Ark.), 1867–1870," microfilm, MDAH.

it "prudent under existing circumstances to accept."[157] Huntington's suggestion was followed by the military commander, and on September 19, 1867, Benjamin Montgomery joined his son Thornton in office.[158] These actions antedated by over eighteen months the April 1869 appointment of John R. Lynch as justice of the peace in Natchez, Mississippi, though Lynch claimed in his autobiography that excepting only delegates to the 1868 Constitutional Convention, he was the first black officeholder in the state.[159] Moreover, the Montgomerys were not only the first of their race to hold office in Mississippi, but may well have been the first blacks to hold office anywhere in the South. Officeholding and politics, however, were the primary concern neither of the Montgomerys nor of the other Davis Bend residents, for agricultural success was still the primary goal of those who lived there. The first step toward that end was to rebuild the levees, for a repeat of the 1867 flooding simply could not be tolerated.

Montgomery was greatly disturbed by the attitude of those on the Wood plantation, for they seemed not at all concerned about the condition of the levee along their part of the river. "We have waited for the movement of the Wood colony about as long as it seems safe to do so," wrote Montgomery on January 23. Joseph Lovell, a white man who had leased one of the other plantations, was willing to cooperate in rebuilding the worst places, and Montgomery yet hoped for help from the "delinquent colony."[160] Teams from Brierfield and Hurricane worked on the Wood levee for many weeks, though, said Montgomery, "we can illy afford it as all our team is needed at the plow."[161]

157. BM to JED, September 16, 1867.
158. BM to JED, September 26, 1867.
159. John Roy Lynch, *Reminiscences of an Active Life: The Autobiography of John Roy Lynch*, ed. John Hope Franklin, Negro American Biographies and Autobiographies (Chicago: Univ. of Chicago Press, 1970).
160. BM to JED, January 23, 1868.
161. BM to JED, February 11, 1868.

132 *Enclave: Vicksburg & Her Plantations*

Fortunately for everyone on the Bend, the Mississippi did not rise enough to challenge unduly the strength of even the weakest levees, and the peril of flooding was averted until the next year. The river had, however, made its year-old cut-off both deeper and wider than before, and a bar was forming across the entrance to its old route around the Bend.[162] This development posed no particular problem for the present, but if the bar should prevent the boats from coming into the old channel to pick up cotton at the Hurricane and Brierfield docks, it would be necessary to haul the cotton bales across the island to another landing. This prospect, however, was on few people's minds at the time, for everyone was concerned first of all with producing the cotton crop.

Montgomery planned on working "several hundred acres by hired labor, while renting to others at $4-$5 an acre." He had in addition planted a quantity of potatoes, corn, and oats and sought Davis' advice on the feasibility of putting in some barley.[163] The first five months of 1868 were comparatively kind to the planters' needs, though the area was experiencing a shortage of rain. Corn suffered somewhat from the drought, but into June the cotton was described as "looking well."[164]

July brought an end to the dry spell, the rains coming with such violence that many of the open bolls were knocked from the plants. The month continued rainy, and Montgomery feared that the army worm, which seemed to thrive on dampness, would arrive to damage the crop. Without the worm, he said, this year could be a profitable one.[165]

By the first week in August, however, the worm had made its appearance, though not as yet in great numbers. Picking had already begun, and before the month ended almost 100 bales had

    162. BM to JED, December 30, 1867.
    163. BM to JED, February 11, 1868; January 23, 1868.
    164. BM to JED, April 30, 1868; May 11, 1868; June 8, 1868; June 29, 1868.
    165. BM to JED, July 23, 1868; July 30, 1868.

been ginned and shipped.[166] Joseph Davis was very much dependent for support on the profits made by Montgomery, and the former slave felt a deep sense of obligation toward his old master. Even before any of the cotton was sold, Montgomery secured an advance from the New Orleans merchants who handled his crop and sent to Davis drafts totalling some $4,000. This sum, Montgomery told Davis, would hopefully keep him "entirely free from want in pecuniary matters."[167] Ten days later Montgomery wrote to Davis that about half the crop had been destroyed by the worms. "It exceeds anything of the kind I have ever seen," he said. "We shall only have to try again."[168]

Picking had about ended by the first of November, the crop for the year coming to 790 bales, a somewhat larger total than had been anticipated after the worm struck.[169] Montgomery had discussed with Davis the possibility of purchasing Balmoral plantation near Lake St. Joseph, Louisiana, but decided against a new enterprise for the present.[170] Montgomery was yet quite full of hope that his idea of an association would ultimately succeed, but he expressed his great frustration at not being able to transmit his fervor to others. His philosophy was one of "associating ourselves together and exercising industry and economy with a due regard for law and order." He was hopeful that those freedmen who were wandering about in search of easy riches would realize the impossibility of their desires and settle down to work.[171] The difficulties facing him, however, were related to Joseph Davis in a sorrowful letter of November 30.

Some of the oldest residents on the Bend, he said, had broken

166. BM to JED, August 6, 1868; September 13, 1868.
167. BM to JED, September 13, 1868.
168. BM to JED, September 24, 1868.
169. BM to JED, November 2, 1868; December 17, 1868.
170. BM to JED, October 15, 1868; October 22, 1868; October 26, 1868.
171. BM to JED, November 9, 1868.

into the gin house, probably to steal cotton stored there. The watchman, however, was hiding in the gin under a pile of seed sacks, and he yelled at them to halt and fired a shot in their general direction. All the culprits escaped, but Matilda left behind her shoes, and it was little trouble, à la Cinderella, to identify her and thence the others. Events were somewhat comical up to this point, but the would-be thieves decided to eliminate the watchman by means of a "general assault" with an axe. Their felonious attempt was fortunately thwarted, and they were all turned over to the "proper authority" for trial. The leaders in the caper were eventually fined, but Montgomery, who had hoped to allow "the most thinking men of the place" to handle the matter, was distressed that he had been forced to turn outside the community for a resolution of difficulties.[172]

Montgomery felt the year had been "generally disastrous," but except for the few weeks during which he had considered purchasing Balmoral plantation, he had maintained his determination to make the success of Hurricane and Brierfield his primary interest. Joseph Davis was quite sympathetic with Montgomery and extended to him all possible patience and understanding. Jefferson Davis, however, was much less willing to allow for the natural disasters which had befallen the freedmen, maintaining instead that "the property is too large for the administrative capacity of a negro, and he must ultimately fail." The ex-Confederate President's advice was that Montgomery "retire with the means he has acquired" and "engage in small trade."[173] The decision, however, was not Jeff Davis' to make, and 1869 found Montgomery still at Davis Bend, laboring against the same problems as before: recruitment of hands by other planters and lack of progress on the Wood levee.

   172. BM to JED, November 30, 1868; December 17, 1868.
   173. *Davis* v. *Bowmar*, 55 Miss. 718; Bowmar was the chief executor of Joseph Davis' will.

Benjamin Montgomery was doubly concerned that many families were considering leaving Davis Bend. First, he feared that a shortage of labor would hinder agricultural efforts during the year; and second, Montgomery expressed his distrust at the "flattering terms" being offered to laborers. "Parties on the other side of the river," he wrote, "are offering $15.00 per month for 5 days work per week, and rations, with from 2 to 4 acres land and team to plow the same in addition to their wages." It was his feeling, he told Joseph Davis, that "the great probability of a non-compliance with those extravagant offers" was not even entering the minds of persons who agreed to the terms.[174]

The exodus from the Bend was fortunately not as large as Montgomery had feared it would be, with only a few of the most discontented actually packing their possessions and leaving. Most of the families on Hurricane and Brierfield seemed by this time to regard the land as their home, and quickly fell into the yearly routine of planting corn and preparing the ground for cotton seed.[175]

Montgomery felt that in most respects the colony was progressing well in this, the third year after its purchase from Joseph Davis. "Time —" he wrote, "if nothing else — will force a more perfect union in the way of industry, economy &c."[176] The Wood levee, however, was still greatly disturbing him, for no work at all was being done upon it by the white lessees who occupied the plantation. Indeed, the men who were running the Wood place were apparently quite content to sit back and wait for the other planters to do the necessary repairs on levees, roads, and bridges, confident that the conscientious freedmen would perform the upkeep necessary to protect their own holdings on the Bend.[177] These men were on firm ground, too, for not only was a uniform levee

---

174. BM to JED, January 25, 1869.
175. BM to JED, February 15, 1869; March 4, 1869.
176. BM to JED. March 4, 1869.
177. BM to JED, February 4, 1869.

necessary for flood control, but as a result of the bar that had formed across the entrance to the old channel, all the planters on the Bend were forced to ship their cotton from the Wood landing,[178] a situation which gave them considerable leverage in any discussion of requirements and responsibilities. For the time, at least, Montgomery was trapped by the circumstances. The proprietors of the adjoining plantation, he said, "lack energy," but he added, "I do not know how they can be forced."[179]

As mentioned above, Joseph Davis understood the problems that his former bondsman was having and sympathized greatly with him. Paying for a large plantation was no easy task, even for one who had built up his financial means over a period of years, and Montgomery had assumed the $300,000 debt with nothing more than his own good reputation with some New Orleans cotton factors[180] and Davis' forbearance.

Times had been difficult for Davis, too, for he had been counting on the interest from the note to provide a full measure of comfort for himself and his family. Nevertheless, Davis showed once again the close ties which existed between himself and those whom he had once owned when in March of 1869 he revised his will. "It is my will and desire," wrote the eighty-four-year-old planter, "that my executors should extend a liberal indulgence to B. T. Montgomery, or their survivors . . . , by extending the time for the payment, so long as they pay the interest thereon, or show a disposition to act fairly, by making the proper exertions to meet their engagements." Additionally, Davis arranged that the

178. BM to JED, July 23, 1868.
179. BM to JED, December 17, 1868.
180. "We deem it not improper," wrote the firm of Payne, Huntington & Co., "to remark that Ben [Montgomery] has from our return to the present kept a very good account & has shown more ability to manage his business & has taken better care of his credit than almost any country merchant who ships to us." J. V. Payne to Joseph E. Davis, December 7, 1867, Joseph Davis Papers, MDAH.

sum of $200 per year would be provided to Ben Montgomery "for the benefit of the aged and infirm on the plantation."[181]

Although the generous terms of Davis' will suggest his belief that the freedmen's difficulties would continue, Montgomery's letters of that time reveal an optimism tempered by experiences of the previous seasons. "We are trying to make proper use of the favorable weather," he wrote on March 22, while admitting that "but little cotton will be planted before the 1st of Apl." Two weeks later he informed Davis that "much of the corn is up, and cotton planting is going reasonable [sic] rapid." Though cotton was still seen as the primary crop, Montgomery was seeking diversification and mentioned to Davis that he was going to put in 25 to 30 acres of broom straw, for which a New Orleans firm was willing to pay $220 per ton.[182]

Four months later Montgomery was still filled with hope and enthusiasm, though the army worms had "made their appearance in some places." He felt, however, that "the crop prospect [was] as good as could reasonable be expected;" even the broom straw was doing well.[183] Cotton began opening on the higher and drier land by mid-August, so that by the first week in September 115 bales had been shipped from the Bend.[184]

Montgomery was more certain now that this season would prove his abilities as a planter, and his correspondence reveals the emergence of greater confidence in himself and in his enterprise. In addition, his letter of September 9, which could easily have been written by a white Southern Democrat, is further indication that Montgomery was a presager of the Booker T. Washington philosophy. "You need have no fears," he assured Davis, "of much time being lost in political affairs, for it seems to be

181. *Davis v. Bowmar*, 55 Miss. 718.
182. BM to JED, March 22, 1869; April 5, 1869.
183. BM to JED, August 9, 1869.
184. BM to JED, September 9, 1869.

the aim of the different squads of this community to make as loud speeches as possible in the shape of cotton bales." Furthermore, he stated, "Several persons who have been slothful and shiftless heretofore are now making creditable efforts to do something." The letter closed with Montgomery's statement that "Mary and the children ask to be remember [sic] to yourself, Miss Liza & Miss Mary Jane & family."[185]

Two months later Montgomery was less enthusiastic about the work of some of his hands, but over one thousand bales of cotton had been ginned so far, and the gin was "still crowded to its utmost capacity." There was difficulty in shipping the cotton, however, for the landings at both Hurricane and Brierfield had been rendered useless by the gradual silting of the old channel. "Our chute has become to [sic] shallow for Boats," wrote Montgomery, and though the roads were bad it was necessary to haul the finished bales to the far side of the island for shipment.[186]

The next few months found Montgomery busy ginning, baling, and shipping the crop, which by mid-February amounted to nearly 2,000 bales.[187] By this time, too, preparations had already begun for the coming year's crop, though it would be worked without the services of "Ben Ousley and his followers," consisting of thirteen families "who had been prosperous and with himself rendered restless thereby. Should they be so fortunate as to succeed as well elsewhere as they have here," opined Montgomery, "they will have no cause to complain."[188]

Joseph Davis was by this time eighty-six years old, and the

---

185. *Ibid.* A careful search of the Booker T. Washington Papers in the Library of Congress does not reveal any correspondence between these two men. Washington's early correspondence, however, is incomplete. There are letters between Washington and Isaiah Montgomery after the turn of the century.

186. BM to JED, November 4, 1869; November 29, 1869.

187. BM to JED, February 17, 1870.

188. BM to JED, February 3, 1870; February 10, 1870; February 17, 1870.

Steamboat *Katie Robbins* — Loaded to the gunwales with cotton bales from Brierfield plantation, which can be seen in the upper right of the photo. Courtesy: J. Mack Moore Collection, Old Court House Museum, Vicksburg

decades were telling deeply on his body, though his mind remained clear and alert. He and Montgomery still discussed the relative merit of "Dixon's seed of Georgia" versus "Holmes Early Prolific," but Davis realized that this year might well be his last, and he therefore had Montgomery begin preparation of the spot at Hur-

140 *Enclave: Vicksburg & Her Plantations*

ricane where he wished his body laid. Although Davis had not lived at Hurricane for almost eight years, it was still an object of his greatest affection.[189] The old planter died on September 18, 1870, and was buried at the Hurricane plantation in the small family cemetery, which had not been included in the sale to Montgomery.[190] Though Davis' death was mourned by those at the Bend, it had an immediate impact only upon Ben Montgomery, who had turned so often to his former master for advice. Unbeknownst to those living there, however, the demise of Davis left the ownership of Brierfield open to question, thus beginning the final phase of Montgomery's tenancy on the Bend.

Montgomery continued his planting efforts at Davis Bend for some years after the death of Joseph Davis, and, according to Thomas Dabney, a prominent white planter, he was in time accepted as one of the leading agriculturists in the state.[191] Meanwhile, a controversy had arisen over the validity of Davis' will, which had not specifically mentioned Brierfield. Jefferson Davis had by 1870 been released from imprisonment, and, though he was one of his brother's executors, he sought to gain possession of his old lands on Davis Bend by breaking his brother's will and voiding the sale of Brierfield.[192] The problem arose because Joseph Davis had never in all the years that his brother worked Brierfield given him a deed to the property. This peculiarity was seized upon successfully by the Davis brothers after the Civil War as a means of circumventing attempts to confiscate the Confederate President's property, but his ploy had now returned to haunt the younger Davis.[193]

Not until June of 1874 did Jefferson Davis finally file suit to

189. BM to JED, March 27, 1870; April 7, 1870.
190. Everett, *Brierfield*, 98.
191. Susan Dabney Smedes, *Memorials of a Southern Planter*, ed. Fletcher M. Green (New York: Alfred A. Knopf, 1965), 313–14.
192. 55 Miss. 671–814.
193. *Ibid.*, 708–709.

gain title to Brierfield, and after some eighteen months of extensive litigation, Chancery Judge Edwin Hill of Vicksburg, a man whose sympathies did not lie with Davis, dismissed the suit. Fortunately for Davis the composition of the Mississippi Supreme Court changed at this time, and the three Republicans on the Court gave way to two Democrats — both former Confederate officers — and one Republican.[194] Davis felt his chances enhanced for successful appeal, and his attorneys filed for a hearing before the high tribunal. Finally, in April 1878, the Court by a two to one vote carried by the ex-Confederate justices, granted Davis legal possession of Brierfield.[195]

Davis thereupon secured from the Warren County Chancery Court a foreclosure on the Brierfield mortgage on the grounds that Montgomery was in arrears on his payments. Montgomery and his sons appealed the decree, and its execution was delayed until 1881.[196]

Montgomery had meanwhile been making partial payments on the $15,000 yearly interest, though he found it impossible to reduce the $300,000 principal on the sale. Losing Brierfield was really not a great blow to the Montgomerys, for they retained possession of Hurricane plantation. Montgomery continued to work these lands until his death in 1885. For the next two years his eldest son Isaiah assumed colony leadership,[197] but the Mississippi River would cooperate no more with him than with his father. In 1886 a disastrous flood swept over the Bend,[198] and in 1887 Isaiah led the colony up-river to Bolivar County, Mississippi, where they were joined by some former residents who had left Davis Bend and migrated to Kansas. There, on lands well removed

194. Everett, *Brierfield*, 103.
195. 55 Miss. 779.
196. Everett, *Brierfield*, 105.
197. Brochure, *Mound Bayou Bolivar County Mississippi*, in Benjamin Montgomery Papers, Library of Congress.
198. Everett, *Brierfield*, 107.

from the possibility of floods, they founded the town of Mound Bayou. Isaiah Montgomery served as the first mayor and emulated his father in displaying, according to one who interviewed during the 1930s many of Mound Bayou's original settlers, "a paternalistic attitude toward the members of his colony."[199]

The all-black town of Mound Bayou (1970 population: 2,134)[200] is today virtually the only memorial to the Montgomerys' years on Davis Bend, for the plantations there ultimately failed. Although the Davis family and others tried to raise crops there until the third decade of the twentieth century, the forces which had defeated the Montgomery colony ultimately won out over those whose only advantage was the possession of more capital. The lack of a steady and dependable labor source, the fluctuating price of cotton, and especially the capricious and uncontrollable Mississippi River all combined to defeat the best agricultural efforts.[201]

The Davis plantations themselves are now fairly deserted, with the entire area which once was Davis Bend now functioning as a game preserve owned by a group of Louisiana lawyers. Indeed, except for a few crumbling chimneys and the ill-kept Davis family cemetery, the lands which now form Davis Island look much as they did in 1818, when Joseph Davis first took possession.[202]

The experiment at Davis Bend so grandly conceived by U. S. Grant was not, however, a failure. The first two years there proved, said John Eaton, "the capacity of the Negro to take care of himself and exercise under honest and competent direction the functions of self-government."[203] The next few years saw the virtual elimination of any Governmental direction, yet the colony proved able

199. Brochure, *Mound Bayou Bolivar County Mississippi*; Jackson, "Mound Bayou," 88.
200. U.S. Department of Commerce, Bureau of the Census, *1970 Census of the Population: Mississippi*, Table 2.
201. Everett, *Brierfield*, 113.
202. *Ibid.*, 6, 14–15, 118–19. Someone has begun raising beef cattle there in the last few years.
203. Eaton, *Grant, Lincoln and the Freedmen*, 166.

Isaiah Montgomery — Eldest son of Benjamin and Mary Montgomery. He served with the Union Navy and later was the only black delegate to Mississippi's 1890 Constitutional Convention. Courtesy: Mississippi Department of Archives and History

to handle its own affairs. It was at Davis Bend that the first black man held office in the state of Mississippi; and the remarkable Benjamin Montgomery demonstrated to all who knew of him that blacks were not inferior and incapable individuals. The Davis Bend experiment was important, too, for the blueprint that it might have been. Vernon Wharton, one of the first historians to relate part of its story, summarized its value thusly: "A wiser and more benevolent government might well have seen in Davis Bend the suggestion of a long-time program for making the Negro a self-reliant, prosperous, and enterprising element of the population. It would have cost a great deal of money for the purchase of lands, or would have involved an attack on the sacredness of property rights in their confiscation, but it would certainly have altered the future of the South, and it might have made of her a much happier and more prosperous section."[204]

Had this blueprint been followed, the credit would have belonged to three men: a Union general with foresight, an ex-slave with vision, and an ex-slaveowner with compassion. The place, the people, and the potential were right. The time was unfortunately wrong.

---

204. Wharton, *The Negro in Mississippi*, 41.

Post-War Agriculture

THE WORKINGS OF THE COLONY at Davis Bend, both during the War and after, were not characteristic of the course of agricultural adjustment wrought by the conflict. Problems encountered by the Montgomerys and others were in many ways similar to those experienced by other planters and freedmen in the Vicksburg area, but the isolation of Davis Bend and the uniqueness of the arrangement between Benjamin Montgomery and Joseph Davis afforded its colonists an autonomy not enjoyed elsewhere.

The ferocity of guerrilla attacks and the problems encountered by novice Yankee planters even in the Vicksburg area meant that while many plantations were cultivated all during the War, others simply lay abandoned and unused during 1864 and 1865. When the Confederate owners of these places came home — if they came home — they were greeted, as was Thomas J. Hudson, by "Plantations laid waste, houses and fences burned and stock of every description all gone." Hudson had entered Confederate service "at the commencement" and was paroled at Enterprise, Alabama, in May 1865 "without one cent of good money in the world." With help from some of his friends, however, he had begun putting his property back into order and hoped once again to make a living from his plantation.[1]

---

1. Thomas J. Hudson to Gov. Benjamin G. Humphreys, March 13, 1866, RG 27, MDAH.

It was not possible, however, to come back and pick up where things had been in 1860 and 1861, for the entire order was changed. Those planters who had remained on their land in the Vicksburg area had fairly well accepted the idea that slavery was no more and would not be resurrected, but others were slower in admitting this fact. Slavery had, after all, been a thriving institution in most areas of the state well into 1865, for only where Union troops entered and remained had slaves been freed. Indeed, blacks in the interior portions of the state were frequently subjected to even more close supervision as the War entered its last few months, as is indicated in the $500 fine given Elisha Bodford by the Lauderdale County Circuit Court for "permitting his slave boy, Ike, to go at large and trade as a free man."[2]

Even after the 1865 Reconstruction Convention had put the state on record as admitting that slavery was finished, many plantation owners who returned from a four-year absence were unable to view freedmen as other than slaves who did not belong to someone at the present; and many of these planters persisted in attempts to manage their hired hands just as they had their slaves. I. Pierce, for example, wrote to Gov. William L. Sharkey from his plantation in the Delta to say that he planned "to work 100 Free Laborers" on his place, but that "it will be absolutely necessary to have some mode of punishment and [I] do not know how to get at that, unless every plantation were declared a town, with the Planter as Judge of Police."[3]

The Freedmen's Bureau was well aware of problems inherent in the situation and warned its agents to be on the alert for planters who "continue their control over their former slaves, with the hope that some change will be made, by which they will be allowed the work of these people free of charge." Officers of the Bureau were ordered to "take immediate steps for the arrest, and trial

2. G. C. Chandler to Gov. Charles Clark, January 16, 1865, RG 27, MDAH.
3. I. Pierce to Gov. William Sharkey, July 15, 1865, RG 27, MDAH.

by military commission, of all parties who are accused of committing . . . abuses."[4]

Owners who returned from the War and secured a pardon were not allowed to move in and evict freedmen who were raising a crop on the place, even if there was no contract allowing them to be there. The Freedmen's Bureau was quite explicit in stating that "in all cases where freedmen have assisted in planting a crop this year, they are entitled to a full compensation for their labor." When Mrs. E. Green, a white citizen of Vicksburg, sued in the provost marshal's court to regain her property, she was informed that only after she gave fair payment to those living and working there would the property be returned to her.[5]

The return of Confederate veterans brought instant conflict, too, between owners of plantations and Northern lessees who had been occupying them under Government auspices. One such case occurred in Warren County when Dr. R. B. Scott brought suit under the law of "Forcible Entry and Detainer" against J. D. Collier, who had a lease from the Treasury Department. Scott claimed the plantation had never been an "abandoned place" according to the law and sought recovery of his property and revocation of the lease. Scott took the case into the Warren County court, where a judge and jury found in his favor; Collier, the lessee, was not even present, but he learned of the proceeding and went immediately to Col. Samuel Thomas for relief.[6]

---

4. General Orders #5, Col. Samuel Thomas, July 29, 1865, in House Executive Document #70, 39th Congress, 1st Session. There were many abuses, too. W. P. Atkins of Greenwood, according to a Bureau agent, beat one of his former slaves and tied her up by her thumbs "for her attempting to leave on a boat for Vicksburg." Capt. W. F. Griffin to Lt. Stuart Eldridge, August 21, 1865, microfilm roll #30, Records of the Assistant Commissioner for the State of Mississippi, BRFAL.
5. Circular #1, July 3, 1865, Bureau of Refugees, Freedmen, and Abandoned Lands, in House Executive Document #70, 39th Congress, 1st Session; Endorsement of Major Free, September 1865, Vol. 280, p. 43, RG 105 (Miss.), NA.
6. R. S. Buck to Gov. William Sharkey, July 27, 1865, RG 27, MDAH.

Thomas responded immediately, informing Collier, "You will be sustained in your rights and privileges as guaranteed by your lease, if it takes all the armies of the United States to support you."[7] Thomas immediately ordered the arrest and confinement of Judge Birchett, who had presided, and of R. S. Buck, Scott's lawyer. The order, stated Buck, "was duly and with alacrity executed by two negro soldiers, who came to my house while at table with my family, and compelled my immediate appearance before this [illegible] Colonel."[8]

Buck, the plaintiff's attorney, appealed for help to Governor Sharkey, who in turn recited the facts to Gen. Henry W. Slocum. "I regret to be compelled to say," stated the governor, "that Colonel Thomas has acted in this matter in a very unbecoming spirit of defiance."[9] When Slocum questioned Thomas about the incident the colonel remained firm in his convictions, maintaining that he had arrested Birchett and Buck only as ordinary civilians who were "interfering with him in the proper exercise of his powers, as guaranteed by the lease." Major General Slocum, it was noted in an endorsement on the letter, "declines to interfere."[10]

Some freedmen, too, had trouble accepting the responsibilities which freedom thrust upon them. Those who were raising crops on their own simply continued at their work, but some who had not tasted freedom before — and one did not have to go twenty miles from Vicksburg to find such — were inclined to test its limits and sometimes to mistake emancipation for license.

Clarisse Young complained to Governor Sharkey on several occasions that she wanted to evict "some negroes once servants,

7. Col. Samuel Thomas to J. D. Collier, July 22, 1865, copy in RG 27, MDAH.
8. R. S. Buck to Gov. William Sharkey, July 27, 1865, RG 27, MDAH.
9. Gov. William Sharkey to Gen. Henry W. Slocum, July 31, 1865, RG 27, MDAH.
10. Col. Samuel Thomas to Gen. Henry W. Slocum, August 21, 1865, RG 27, MDAH.

they have been annoying me in various ways." They had "annoyed and vexed" her, stated Mrs. Young, and "they think the place belongs to them."[11] Samuel G. Swain, who as a Freedmen's Bureau agent was constantly involved with ex-slaves and their former masters, wrote his sister that "it is very difficult to impress upon the minds of the colored people, who were slaves but a short time since, . . . the responsibility that rests upon them of working industriously and faithfully in order to fulfill their contract."[12] One of the ex-slaves confirmed the misunderstanding that existed among many freedmen as to what the ending of slavery meant for them. "De slaves spected a heap from freedon [sic] dey didn' git," recalled Isaac Stier to a Works Progress Administration interviewer in the 1930s. "Dey was led to b'lieve dey would have a easy time — go places widout passes — and have plenty o' spending money. But dey sho' got fooled. Mos' of 'em didn' fin' deyse'ves no better off."[13]

There was also a misunderstanding among the freedmen that land would be distributed to them at the end of the year, and as a result of this and the harsh treatment many received from white planters, there was much reluctance to enter into a labor contract for 1866. This intransigence infuriated the planters and led to demands that the state legislature take steps to force the freedmen to work. The result of these demands was a series of laws, collectively known as the Black Code, which among other things made possession of a regular job a legal requirement for all black males age eighteen and up.[14]

11. Clarisse Young to Gov. William Sharkey, July 28 and August 27, 1865, RG 27, MDAH.
12. Samuel G. Swain to sister, September 9, 1865, Samuel Glyde Swain Papers, WSHS.
13. Narrative of Isaac Stier, Slave Narrative Collection (Miss.), Library of Congress.
14. Will J. Martin to Maj. E. D. Reynolds, November 18, 1865, RG 27, MDAH; Wharton, *The Negro in Mississippi*, 85.

Land, of course, was not given to the freedmen, and the Bureau of Refugees, Freedmen, and Abandoned Lands itself began to pressure the ex-slaves to sign work agreements. Circular #2, issued by Col. Samuel Thomas on January 2, 1866, was directed to this goal: "The time has arrived for you to contract for another year's labor. I wish to impress upon you the importance of doing this at once. You know that if a crop is raised, the work must be begun soon, and the hands employed for the year. If you do not contract with the men who wish to employ you, what do you propose to do? You cannot live without work of some kind. Your houses and lands belong to the white people; and you cannot expect that they will allow you to live on them in idleness. . . . If you stay on the plantations where you are, you must agree to work for the owners of them. If not, move out of the way, and give place to more faithful laborers."[15]

Most freedmen soon agreed to contracts for 1866, aided in part by the Government, which furnished transportation for them to go anywhere they wished to work.[16] Terms generally offered by planters for this first year after the War were $150/year salary, payable at the end of the year, medical care, 200 pounds of pork for the year, and a peck of meal per week.[17] The laborers, however, held out for better offers. "Their pretensions were pretty considerable," reported the *Hinds County Gazette*, "and they were very generally realized, the demand being greater than the supply in markets."[18] Indeed, the scarcity of labor was such that George W. Humphreys was obliged to pay $20 to someone who secured two freedmen who were willing to contract with him.[19] As a result of

15. Circular #2, January 2, 1866, Bureau of Refugees, Freedmen, and Abandoned Lands, quoted in Eaton, *Grant, Lincoln, and the Freedmen*, 242–243.
16. Samuel G. Swain to father, January 11, 1866, Swain Papers, WSHS.
17. Trowbridge, *The South*, 366.
18. *Hinds County Gazette*, January 6, 1866.
19. Humphreys Papers, March 22, 1866, MDAH.

the scarcity of willing laborers, those who did contract usually secured terms of $15 per month salary, all their food, including flour, sugar, and molasses, a garden patch to cultivate for themselves, and Saturday afternoon off. There had been some sharecropping up to this time, but at least in Warren County the system of wage labor was predominant in 1866.[20]

Despite the problems inherent in successful cotton cultivation, the ending of the War brought with it an influx of would-be nabobs from the North, just as the opening of the Vicksburg area in 1863 and 1864 had done. Most of the first group had given up planting and had either gone home or turned to other pursuits, but the new ones took their places "with exalted ideas of the ease in which they should live and accumulate property."[21] Samuel G. Swain, who had been in the South long enough to see both its limits and his, did not recommend the area for immigration, since it was "too unsettled and will be for some time." He did, however, recognize "one inducement for young men of the north. . . . There is the finest opportunities for marrying plantations with nice young widows on them that I ever know of. They have the impression that Yankee boys can manage better than any other."[22]

Some of these "Yankee boys" may have known what they were doing, but many were totally unprepared for the difficulties inherent in a successful planting venture. The capital necessary for cultivating a large plantation was substantial at any time, but with all the repairs made necessary by deterioration and the War's destruction, even the most affluent among the newcomers soon felt the pinch. The influx of Northerners did have two definite effects, however. First, the price of land rose substantially, es-

20. Trowbridge, *The South*, 366; labor contracts, microfilm roll #49, Records of the Assistant Commissioner for the State of Mississippi, BRFAL.
21. Henry Musgrove, quoted in Robert F. Futrell, "Efforts of Mississippians to Encourage Immigration, 1865–1880," *Journal of Mississippi History*, 20 (April 1958), 64.
22. Samuel G. Swain to George Swain, July 26, 1865, Swain Papers, WSHS.

pecially on plantations near the Mississippi River; and second, the money they brought in gave a needed boost to the economy of the area.[23]

The expense of cultivating a cotton plantation varied according to its location, but an estimate by the "Southern Land Agency" in early 1866 was as follows:

rent of 500 acres @ $10	$5000
25 mules @ $150	$3750
wages of 60 hands for 10 months @ $15/hand	$9000
supplies (incl. food for hands)	$4800
TOTAL (incl. misc. expenses)	$20,907

"or about $42/acre."[24] The problem with this estimate is that the itemized expenses alone add up to $22,550, not even counting miscellaneous costs such as interest on money, salary of an overseer or "superintendent," and the cost of ginning, baling, and shipping cotton to market. Even the cost of plows, hoes, and other farming utensils may not have been included in the amount for supplies, but if they were, the estimate for that item is far too low. Such propaganda as this only encouraged unsuspecting Northerners to descend upon the cotton country like the army worms they all soon encountered, and the only ones to profit from the exercise were those who sold or rented land and furnished supplies.

The presence of Northerners was resented by many local planters, not only because they drove up the price of everything connected with planting, but also because Southerners feared the deleterious influences their presence might have upon the freedmen. After a hunting trip north of Vicksburg, Samuel G. Swain informed his brother Chester that "anyone who thinks that the war

---

23. Futrell, "Efforts of Mississippians," 62; Harris, *Presidential Reconstruction in Mississippi*, 166.
24. Trowbridge, *The South*, 380–81.

is over should go through the country between the Yazoo and Miss. rivers. The southern people are determined to drive northern people out of the country. . . . All the northern men planting in that part of the country bar thier [sic] doors night and have thier firearms where they can lay thier hands on them at any moment."[25]

Everyone involved in raising cotton was having a hard time of it this first full year after the War. Freedmen were barred by the Black Code from renting or leasing lands except within a municipality, and although the Freedmen's Bureau declared this portion of the legislation null and void, those individuals who did lease to blacks found themselves under constant verbal attack from their neighbors.[26] As a result, most of those cultivating lands on their own in 1866 were white, and it is hardly surprising that freedmen who had been more nearly their own bosses in 1865 should resent the pressure which had been exerted upon them by the state, the Freedmen's Bureau, and the white planters.

The planters grumbled about the worthlessness of free black labor, but they could do little about it. Some planters attempted to placate their hands by furnishing schools for the children, a move which the American Missionary Association ardently promoted. We should "lead the colored people decidedly to prefer those places," wrote Joseph Warren, "where they may enjoy educational advantage. When planters see this, their desire for schools will be wonderfully quickened."[27] Northern-born planters adopted this idea more quickly than did the natives. A man from Ohio, for example, offered $15 per month plus room and board for a teacher who would live on his plantation on the Yazoo River.[28]

---

25. Samuel Glyde Swain to Chester Swain, January 4, 1866, Swain Papers, WSHS.
26. *Natchez Democrat*, December 7, 1865.
27. Joseph Warren to Samuel G. Wright, March 12, 1866, AMA Papers (Miss.).
28. J. P. Bardwell to George Whipple, April 20, 1866, AMA Papers (Miss.).

Blakely Plantation—Built in 1843, this home was some seven miles from Vicksburg and was the residence of Mary Blake. Courtesy: Mississippi Department of Archives and History

Southern planters were generally opposed to freedmen's education, but by the end of 1866 Major General Wood was pleased to report to Gen. Oliver O. Howard that "planters are beginning to apply to me to aid them in getting teachers. They generally express a preference for male teachers, but doubtless I will be able in a short time to find employment for female teachers also."[29]

Positive reinforcement, however, was not the most prevalent way of convincing the freedmen to work. The Bureau itself was often involved in the enforcement of contracts, and agents spent much of their time discussing with freedmen the meaning of the papers they had signed earlier in the year. Lt. G. W. Corliss, for example, was directed to "go tomorrow to the plantation of Mr.

29. Maj. Gen. Thomas Wood to Gen. Oliver O. Howard, December 13, 1866, AMA Papers (Miss.).

B. Blake . . . explain to the Freedmen there employed the obligations and privileges of their contract, and the consequence of their violation."[30]

The consequences of breaking a contract, however, were not evident to most freedmen, because after passage of the Civil Rights Act in April 1866 over the veto of President Andrew Johnson, the only way in which planter could enforce a contract against a freedman was by a civil action. State law had previously allowed criminal arrest and prosecution of those who left a plantation before their time was up, and this possibly had been a deterrent to contract-breaking. General Wood, military commander of the state in 1866, explained the problem to Gen. Oliver O. Howard, national head of the Freedmen's Bureau: "The poverty of the Freedmen renders the civil action useless, as nothing can be recovered from the defendant on execution. The increasing summer heat is already acting to augment this difficulty — as the numbers of complaints show. Officers of the Bureau have been sent to speak to and advise the Freedmen when possible, but there are so few officers who have sufficient tact to perform this duty, that the little temporary good this action may have had will not be sufficiently felt."[31]

No longer able to secure adequate legal aid in enforcing contracts, some planters simply reverted to the old practice of slave times. Capt. H. Sweeney, a Freedmen's Bureau Agent in the upper Delta, reported to Major General Wood that "it is the practice of planters in Coahoma and Bolivar Counties Miss. to Systematically tie up and whip the hands [freedmen] employed by them for any, and all causes. . . . Numbers of them have reported that they are worse off now than when they were slaves."[32]

30. Lt. Stuart Eldridge to Lt. George W. Corliss, April 12, 1866, Box 54A, RG 105 (Miss.), NA.
31. Maj. Gen. Thomas Wood to Gen. Oliver O. Howard, June 20, 1866, RG 27, MDAH.
32. Capt. H. Sweeney to Maj. Gen. Thomas Wood, September 3, 1866, Box 54A, RG 105 (Miss.), NA.

Closer to Vicksburg, a "full Southerner and Secessionist" who simply wanted "those darkeys to have the ordinary justice" reported to General Wood that one Austin McNutt, who owned a place on the road to Utica, "has said frequently he would not pay them a dm cent and he is the man that will not do so if he can possible help it the most of them is destitute of common working cloths his contracts are all written and worded very differently to the contract or agreement made with them and they can not and will not get a cent from him without the intervention of your Beaurou."[33]

Other problems, too, confronted the planter in his quest for agricultural success, not the least of which were the army worms. These pests had been the one plague of the wartime planter which had remained unchanged since hostilities ceased, and 1866 saw them appear in great numbers. As Benjamin Montgomery and the planters on Davis Bend had discovered, there was no defense against the ubiquitous larvae as they moved in a leisurely fashion across the entire cotton-producing part of the state, diminishing the crop by at least five-sixths.[34]

As a result of the army worm and the wet autumn, which ruined some cotton which the worm did not get, most planters were discouraged after the 1866 season. The Northerner who came to Mississippi in late 1865 was more likely to have been cleaned out than not, with one man and his partner making only 65 bales on an 1,100-acre plantation on which they had hoped for 900 bales.[35] One of this type was Henry Musgrove, who made an attempt at planting, failed, then went into business and politics. Others, like Albert T. Morgan, found politics a more easily exploited commodity than were cotton plantations. His book *Yazoo: Or, On the Picket Line of Freedom in the South* describes his

33. S. G. Rowan to Maj. Gen. Thomas Wood, October 26, 1866, Box 54A, RG 105 (Miss.), NA.
34. *Hinds County Gazette*, September 21, 1866.
35. [Benham], *A Year of Wreck*, v, 459.

failures as a cotton planter and successes as a politician, and many like him remained in the area to provide leadership in the days of Congressional Reconstruction which followed.[36] Others who went north after a disastrous planting season were prone to "inveigh against the Southern section," thereby helping set the mood for passage of Reconstruction legislation in the Congress.[37]

"If Providence had smiled on this region in 1866 by giving it a reasonable crop," suggested George Benham with some exaggeration, "sectional politics, injustice to the negro and the newcomer, bitterness of heart, and hatred of the government would all have disappeared. In the absence of a good crop, the result was that these were all intensified."[38] The failure of the crop in 1866 produced several other unmistakable effects. The first of these was that the freedmen, whose year's work had been entered into so reluctantly, went largely unrewarded, for most contracts called for the cash payment of wages to be made at the end of the year, after the crop had been sold. With little or no crop, few wages were paid. This outcome led not to a total refusal to contract for the next year but to much choosiness about where and with whom the contract was signed.[39] For the 1867 season some individuals offered to supply the local need for laborers by promising to bring in "firstrate hands from Georgia, and deliver them on plantations,"[40] though the number of agricultural workers procured from this source is unknown.

One immediate result of the crop failure and the difficulty in hiring labor was a series of newspaper listings of plantations for sale or lease in the vicinity of Vicksburg. The issue of the *Daily*

36. Futrell, "Efforts of Mississippians," 64; A. T. Morgan, *Yazoo; Or, On the Picket Line of Freedom in the South* (N.p.: By the author, 1884).
37. *Ibid.*
38. [Benham], *A Year of Wreck*, 403.
39. Thomas Wood to Oliver O. Howard, October 31, 1866, in Senate Executive Document #6, pp. 97–98, 39th Congress, 2nd Session.
40. *Vicksburg Daily Times*, December 28, 1866.

Times of November 14, carried four such offers, in contrast to the previous year when none at all was listed. Three of these plantations, stated the advertisement, were within eight miles of town and had over 500 acres each of cleared land. "Prices," stated the agent, "Not only Moderate, but Cheap." Another plantation on the Big Black River, eighteen miles from the city, had 400 acres open and would be leased for a period of one to three years.[41]

A later newspaper carried an advertisement for a 1230-acre plantation, with 800 acres open, within two miles of the Mississippi, but "safe from overflow." There was a new dwelling on the place, and the owner was asking $40,000−$7,500 in twelve months, $25,000 at 8%.[42] The price of this plantation comes to about $40 per acre for the improved land and $20 per acre for the unimproved, assuming that the pre-War ratio of the value of improved to unimproved land remained true. Good cotton land in 1860, according to Charles Sydnor, was worth $18-$20 per acre, with uncleared land at half that.[43] The fact that some 300,000 acres in the Mississippi Delta remained flooded until well into the 1866−67 season was undoubtedly one cause of the rise in land prices,[44] while proximity to the city of Vicksburg was probably a factor in the asking price for this particular plantation.

Other plantations were also listed for sale or lease before the end of 1866. One was the William C. Smedes place, three miles below Vicksburg on the Mississippi River, with 1,000 acres total and 700 acres in cultivation. No asking price was listed, but one-third cash was demanded, with terms offered on the remainder. Another, a "Small and Valuable Plantation" of 360 acres was offered for sale some thirteen miles from the city. This plantation,

---

41. *Ibid.*, November 14, 1866.
42. *Ibid.*, December 4, 1866.
43. Sydnor, *Slavery in Mississippi*, 191−92.
44. Senate Report #126, "Levees along the Mississippi River," p. 2, 39th Congress, 1st Session.

Post-War Agriculture 159

so the advertisement stated, would produce from three-fourths to a full bale to the acre.[45]

If one wished to live out in the Yazoo country, the "Liverpool Plantation" was for sale four miles above Satartia.[46] An even more inviting place, however, was for rent ten miles below Yazoo City on the Yazoo River. This plantation consisted of 1,200 acres with a frame dwelling, but more important, "the old set of hands are on it, and everything is ready to commence work." These sixty individuals, stated the offering, were former slaves on the plantation "who are unwilling to leave their old home."[47]

George W. Humphreys leased his 609-acre "Sligo" plantation for the 1867 season in return for six bales of cotton, "weighing 450 pounds each, of the first picking and of average quality of said picking." The lessee, according to the agreement made with Humphreys, was to "only use the timber thereon for fencing, firewood, and improvements on said plantation."[48]

One arrangement which attracted attention in the *Hinds County Gazette* because it seemed to offer a solution to the eternal problem with the freedmen was the purchase by eight or ten German families of lands near the Big Black River. These settlers intended, so the writer stated, to divide the land into small farms and "to engage solely in agricultural pursuits." The settlement had much to recommend it, according to the *Gazette*, for the persons there were "sober, industrious, and thrifty."[49] There were numerous efforts to entice white immigrants to move into the area and displace the freedmen, but with few exceptions they resulted in little actual settlement.[50]

Benjamin Montgomery had announced in November 1866 his

45. *Vicksburg Daily Times*, December 28, 1866.
46. *Ibid.*
47. *Ibid.*
48. Lease, December 11, 1866, Humphreys Papers, MDAH.
49. *Hinds County Gazette*, November 23, 1866.
50. For a discussion of the entire scope of efforts along these lines see Chapter VI of Wharton's *The Negro in Mississippi*.

intention of forming an all-black colony at Davis Bend, and before long some white planters began to entertain ideas that this type of scheme might offer possibilities for them, also. A. T. Bowie of Franklin, Louisiana, near Lake Joseph, was one man who expressed an interest in establishing an arrangement similar to the one between Benjamin Montgomery and Joseph Davis, but he soon let the matter drop.[51]

Planters were largely at a loss to know what to do for the coming year, for the Civil Rights Act allowed little possibility of enforcing contracts signed with freedmen. Former Gov. William McWillie of Vicksburg wrote to Governor Humphreys at the end of December 1866 and suggested giving "to persons who may furnish capital for agricultural purposes a first lien on the crops made by the use of such capital." McWillie also proposed that the law needed to be rewritten to encourage keeping of contracts by allowing criminal sanctions against those who violated their agreement.[52]

McWillie's second suggestion was too similar to the recently discredited Black Code to receive serious consideration at the time. The idea of an agricultural lien, however, though certainly not original with the former governor, had great appeal to the legislature which met in Jackson in January 1867.

Pledging one's crops in return for credit advances was nothing new, for the antebellum cotton production system had rested on such a foundation. Most planters had a particular cotton factor with whom they did business, and through him the necessary credit was obtained. The lender knew the person to whom he gave the advance, and he knew the assets which could be used to support the loan, though this is not to imply that no paper changed hands or that everything was always done on a handshake. The antebellum system was, however, characterized by a very personal

51. *Vicksburg Daily Times*, December 15, 1866.
52. William McWillie to Gov. Benjamin G. Humphreys, December 31, 1866, RG 27, MDAH.

Post-War Agriculture 161

relationship in which the factor who advanced money to a reputable planter was not likely to be financially surprised.[53]

The Civil War and emancipation destroyed the planters' wealth in slaves, made his Confederate currency worthless, and left him with only the land, which in itself was not enough to justify the level of financial support enjoyed during the pre-War years, even if the old factor were still in business. The planter was therefore compelled to search elsewhere for a way to place his land into production. The crop lien seemed to offer such a possibility, and Mississippi was apparently the first state to offer this specialized type of mortgage.

Entitled "An Act for the Encouragement of Agriculture," Mississippi's agricultural lien law provided that "all debts hereafter contracted for advance of money, purchase of supplies, farming utensils, working stock, or other things necessary for the cultivation of a farm or plantation, shall constitute a prior lien upon the crop of cotton, corn and other produce of such farm or plantation." Copies of all contracts or liens executed under this law were to be filed with the circuit clerk of the county in which the farm was located, and the clerk was ordered to record these liens so that notice would be given to prospective lenders.[54]

The crop lien system has been called, among other things, "a curse to the soil," and to it has been ascribed almost every ill of the agricultural South, from the cash-crop system to financial peonage to the depletion of soil fertility.[55] Many of these charges may indeed be true, but the records of crop liens recorded in Warren County from 1867 to 1873 simply do not bear out these charges, at least in this one geographical area.

53. The best discussion of this system is found in Harold D. Woodman, *King Cotton and His Retainers: Financing & Marketing the Cotton Crop of the South, 1800–1925* (Lexington: Univ. of Kentucky Press, 1968).
54. Laws of Mississippi, 1867, Ch. CCCCLXV.
55. C. Vann Woodward, *Origins of the New South, 1877–1913*, 2nd ed. (Baton Rouge: Louisiana St. Univ. Press, 1971), 180–83.

162 *Enclave: Vicksburg & Her Plantations*

Mississippi's law went into effect on February 18, 1867, and within two weeks the first liens were entered on the books at Vicksburg. A total of only 110 Warren County agriculturists pledged their crops this first year, and the average advance of over $1,300 suggests that it was mostly the larger planters who benefited from this new source of credit. There was a total of 18 lienholders in 1867, with each supplying the needs of from 1 to 17 farmers or planters. Amounts furnished ranged from $93 to $7,000, the largest sum going to I. C. Pettit, who cultivated 700 acres near the city. The nine largest lienholders, all old-line mercantile houses in Vicksburg, supplied over 95% of the total advanced.

Nature, however, did not cooperate in 1867, and the crop was poor in quality while being lower in price than in the preceding year.[56] It is doubtful that many of the planters in the Vicksburg area were able to repay the generous sums advanced to them by the merchants, but few of them were taken to court as a result. An example of one lienholder who did take court action, however, was the firm of Goodrum & Stout, which had advanced some $12,450 to 13 planters, including $3,000 to William Whitaker for use in cultivating his 160-acre Villa Rosa Plantation. Whitaker produced only 30 bales of cotton and a few bushels of corn on the place and defaulted on his note to the lienholder. G & S thereupon secured a judgment against him and had the crops seized.[57] At the 1867 price of 25¢ per pound in New York, the lender lost on the deal even though he won the case,[58] and this experience was undoubtedly an eye-opener for those who were considering the supply and furnishing business.

56. Alvan Gillem to Oliver Howard, November 28, 1867, Vol. 20, RG 105 (Miss.), NA.
57. *Goodrum & Stout v. Wm. Whitaker et al*, November 1867, Chancery Court, Warren Co., Miss., microfilm, MDAH.
58. All cotton prices in this chapter are taken from James L. Watkins, *King Cotton: A Historical and Statistical Review, 1790 to 1908* (New York: James L. Watkins & Sons, 1909), 30.

It is quite evident that the lenders in 1867, perhaps enthused with the new system, were entirely too free with their credit and that many of them consequently made bad investments. Perhaps as a result, there were in Warren County only 11 lenders in 1868, compared with 18 the year before, and 8 of these were new to the business. Indeed, of the 3 lienholders from 1867 who came back for a second try, only one — Manlove & Hobart — had been one of the leaders the year before, with $6,000 advanced to 2 planters. In 1868 this firm particpated in name only, giving but one advance of $250.

As is evident in the following table, those who were involved in the business of supplying credit to the cotton farmer quickly became less free with their assets. Indeed, 1867 can be seen as definite watershed for the system, for never again were large amounts of credit given out to the average planter. As suggested later in this chapter, the response of the planters of Warren County was simply to go into business for themselves.

Not every lien had a monetary amount listed, for many of them simply indicated "Supplies" or "Rent" or some such. The figure in parentheses is the number of liens for which the value in dollars

TABLE 1
Enrolled Crop Liens[59]
Warren County, Mississippi

Year	Total liens	Approximate % of farms w/liens	Average Value	No. of Lienholders
1867	110 (83)	4.1	$1310.15	18
1868	73 (31)	2.3	336.61	11
1869	229 (198)	8.6	189.41	44
1870	607 (324)	22.9	275.93	98
1871	165 (59)	6.2	161.94	70
1872	249	9.4	—	53
1873	50	1.9	—	3

59. Ledger Book, OCHM, Vicksburg, Miss.

was given. The percentage with liens is figured on the 2,654 holdings recorded in 1869. It would vary slightly from year to year.

The average size of the holdings in 1867 is hard to determine, but an estimate can be made by using the records of those debtors whose cases wound up in the Warren County chancery court. This sample is biased toward those who were over-furnished for the year, in terms of the cotton actually produced, but the general average was $10-$12 per acre. These figures indicate an average holding of around 120 acres in cotton, though the actual size varied from 5 acres to 700 acres. A 120-acre place is not a large plantation, but proper cultivation would have required from 12 to 15 hands, and obviously the number of small family-type farms furnished through the crop lien system in its first year of operation was quite limited.

To be legally enforceable, a crop lien had to be recorded by the circuit clerk, and it is these legal contracts that represent the lien system in operation. Table 1, however, shows that the crop lien system never came close to dominating the Warren County area from 1867 through 1873, for only a small fraction of the farm operators ever gave a lien on their crops.[60]

The agricultural census of 1870, for example, revealed a total of 2,654 farms or agricultural units in Warren County. It is evident from this that only a very small proportion of farm operators, ranging from about 2% in 1873 to 23% in 1870, directly encountered the crop lien in a given year.[61] Neither were Warren

---

60. For the latest and most exhaustive treatment of the economic structure of the postbellum South, see Roger L. Ransom and Richard Sutch, *One Kind of Freedom: The Economic Consequences of Emancipation* (Cambridge: Cambridge Univ. Press, 1977). It is obvious in their discussion of the crop lien system (p. 123) that Ransom and Sutch are talking about a legally-enforceable debt, and not some extralegal arrangement.

61. 1870 Census of Agriculture (manuscript). These 2,654 farms averaged 55 acres of improved land each and produced a total of 28,208 bales of cotton, together with substantial amounts of corn and sweet potatoes. Ten

County's farmers bound to the lienholder year after year for failure to discharge their debts. Indeed, the number of farmers who renewed their financial arrangement with the same lienholder is surprisingly small, as is shown in Table 2:

TABLE 2   Crop Lien Continuity

Year	Total liens	# Renewed	% Renewed
1867	110	—	—
1868	73	2	1.8
1869	229	16	21.9
1870	607	40	17.5
1871	165	31	5.1
1872	249	30	18.2
1873	50	1	0.4

There is no indication, moreover, that even those who signed new liens with the same person did so because they had failed to pay the debt from the preceding year. As a test of this idea, an analysis was made of the 229 persons who gave liens on their crops in 1869. Careful search of the 1870 Census of Agriculture, which recorded the cotton production for the preceding year, enabled identification of 203 of the 229 lien-givers and furnished the total of cotton produced by each. Of the 203 located, the average size of the holding was 66.7 acres of improved land, or about 12 acres larger than the 55-acre mean for the county and a drop of nearly half from 1867. The average amount furnished per acre — $2.85 — was down considerably even from 1868, while compared with 1867 the decline was precipitous. In addition to

---

years earlier, by comparison, the 1860 agricultural census had recorded only 405 farms, averaging 273 improved acres each, which produced 33,733 bales of cotton. The actual amount of improved land in Warren County rose from 110,534.5 acres to 146,151 acres, a 32% increase, while cotton production fell by 16% from 1859 to 1869. One limitation in 1869 may have been the number of draft animals, for the census recorded only 2,795 mules and 478 work oxen for the entire county.

the monetary amounts, however, there were in 1869, and in succeeding years, unspecified additional liens for such items as "mules, horses, wagons, &c," so the exact dollar amount of the lien cannot be determined.

Of the 203 individuals who could be found in the 1870 Census of Agriculture, all but 11 (95%) raised enough cotton to have discharged the recorded lien, with some farmers perhaps clearing as much as $1,200 or $1,300, at New York prices. Even the 11 who fell short of their goal did not miss it by much, and 7 of them returned the next season to try again. Five of the 7, however, received their advances from another source in 1870. By contrast, 38 of those farmers whose cotton production was probably sufficient to have paid their lien renewed their furnishing arrangements with the same firm or individual while 48 secured a new source of operating capital for the coming year. The other 136 farmers did not give liens on their crops in 1870, and it is impossible to determine what happened to them. Perhaps they had accumulated enough resources to farm on their own for a time, for these were, by and large, the most successful of the cotton farmers of 1869, with a gross average of $1,123.14 above the amount of the lien, figuring cotton at its 1869–70 price of 24¢.

Only 15 of the 93 farmers who took out a lien in both 1869 and 1870 carried over to 1871, and 14 of these men changed lienholders from the previous year. Of these 15, only 1 individual took out a lien again in 1872. Characteristic of the lien system as it operated in Warren County during this seven-year period was that farmers dropped in and out of the system almost at will. Few people gave a lien on their crops for more than two years of the seven, and only a handful of farmers even did that. Warren County's farmers were apparently more successful in discharging their liens than were people in other parts of the cotton South, and the number of recovery actions in chancery court during this time — fewer than a dozen — suggests that the typical debtor came

Post-War Agriculture 167

so close to the amount of his debt that legal action was more costly than it was worth.

Some other observations can be made from study of this county's crop lien records. First, a surprising number of the advances made to farmers — as many as 15% in 1871 — specify that "money" or "cash" was given in return for the lien. Most liens, as might be expected, provide for "supplies to amt. of x dollars," though in 1867 the specificity under the column "Amt. of Indebtedness" leads one to believe that many, if not most, of the advances that year were in cash. Furthermore, a considerable number of liens were apparently granted not to merchants but to large planters who were subdividing their holdings. This is not the case in 1867 — when it was the planters who were giving liens — and it is unclear in 1868 and 1869, but by 1870 some 16% of the liens (100 of 607) included land use (lease), and this proportion rose from 33% in 1871 (55 of 165), to 55% in 1872 (137 of 249), to 92% (46 of 50) in 1873. Most of these liens did include supplies in addition to land rental, a phenomenon that suggests that planters in Warren County were able to resist the encroachment of the local merchants better than were most others. The reason may lie in the fact that this area was occupied territory during half of the Civil War and the planters there were able to preserve more of their assets — or maybe it was just to lose less — than was possible elsewhere.

Warren County may well have been atypical of the cotton South after the War, for obviously the crop lien system did not operate there as it is thought to have operated in other areas. Indeed, one of the other unique characteristics of the Vicksburg area is an indication that the wage system of labor continued longer there than elsewhere, perhaps because of the impetus given it during the War. At the very least, the Warren County experience with the crop lien is a curious one, suggesting that a detailed examination of the local records of other counties might be profitable.

The number of freedmen working for wages in Warren County, as contrasted with the sharecrop arrangement which predominated throughout much of the South, is uncertain, but substantial.[62] Eliza Ann Lanier's husband, for example, owned land in Warren County for which he hired men and women to work at $6 and $4 per month, respectively. The circumstances which allowed so low a payment are not recorded. Even so, recalled Mrs. Lanier, "My husband staid in the field with them most of the time."[63]

Charles Hill, who owned Glen Mary plantation on the Mississippi River near Vicksburg, expressed the uncertainties of the situation in a letter to Governor Humphreys midway through the 1867 season: "I hardly know what to say about the negroes, sometimes I think they work very well, at other times, I think they don't work so well. Those employed for a share of the Crop, and working in Small Squads made up by themselves do much better than those hired for wages, but taking all things into consideration, I reckon they do about as well, if not better, then we white folks would do under the same circumstances. I see no prospect of Cotton growers ever being able to pay their old debts at the present low price of cotton and the high price of everything we have to buy. A poor living is all that is to be made."[64]

The year 1867 was notable for the new lien law, and it was also characterized by substantial changes on the economic and political scene. Because of pressure he received from landowners, Gen. E. O. C. Ord, who had replaced General Wood as head of military forces in the state, issued on June 12 an order suspending all proceedings "for the sale of land under cultivation, or of the crops, stock, implements, or other material used in tilling such

62. As late as 1880, Warren County was one of the lowest in the South in percentage of sharecropping. See Ransom and Sutch, *One Kind of Freedom*, 93.
63. Recollections of Eliza Ann Lanier, Timberlake Papers, MDAH.
64. Charles Hill to Gov. Benjamin Humphreys, May 21, 1867, RG 27, MDAH.

land, in pursuance of any execution or writ, where the debt was contracted prior to January 1, 1866." This order, which was to be in effect until the end of the year, gave a breathing spell to impoverished planters who owed money from their days of pre-War affluence, and it was largely applauded by the citizens.[65]

The year closed, however, on a sour note, for rumors of a black insurrection were rampant during the last few months. General Ord was determined to prevent any such uprising and took what he considered all necessary precautions. On November 8, for example, he wrote to Gen. Alvan C. Gillem asking him for the "name or names of any official or other person who has been making or may make inflamatory [sic] speeches to Freedmen or endanger the public peace by exciting one class or color against the other."[66] During the month he took specific actions in various places throughout the state where trouble was rumored, but there were no attempts at insurrection or rebellion by freedmen or black agricultural workers anywhere in the state.

The ex-slaves themselves were quite upset that such a rumor had ever been started, though many of them did believe they might get free land this year. A meeting of freedmen in Columbus, Mississippi, investigated the charges that seizure of lands had been plotted by their people and found it "so absurd to our minds that we hardly know how to treat it." John Hinton, Secretary of the Committee, was directed to draw up a resolution to be sent to Governor Humphreys, who was a source of rumors of insurrection. In addition to requesting publication of the "names of the Gentlemen of high Official and Social position in different parts of the State, from whom he gets his information," the committee had the following statement to make: "We are unwilling

65. Garner, *Reconstruction in Mississippi*, 165.
66. Gen. E. O. C. Ord to Gen. Alvan C. Gillem, November 8, 1867, Fourth Military District, *Letters Sent, Volume 25, Civil Affairs*, 342, RG 98, NA.

to believe that the Governor of the State of Mississippi would willfully charge our people with such high crimes and misdemeanors as are set forth in said Proclamation with the view and for the purpose of blasting hope we have for the future and to raise a prejudice against us at home, and amongst our friends abroad, we therefore ask for names and localities as above indicated."[67]

There was no conspiracy on the part of the freedmen to rise up and seize the lands they worked, but once again few agricultural laborers were willing to sign contracts for the coming year. By the middle of December General Ord had become sufficiently concerned about the freedmen's intransigence to send a telegram to Gillem telling him to "Direct all your agents and Post Commanders to notify the leading Colored men that they will be required to go to work during the coming year—on the best terms they can get—if they do not, they will be liable to punishment as vagrants by the Sheriffs and deputies."[68]

Under this prodding, and when it became evident that land was not to be given to them this year, most freedmen contracted for the next year, with a sharecropping arrangement assuming primacy in most sections of the state.[69] According to the *Hinds County Gazette* there were three proportions in which shares were fixed, depending upon who paid or furnished what. In the first of these the landowner furnished the land and stock, and provisions for the freedman and the stock. The cropper would receive one-fourth for his labor. In the second arrangement the owner would

67. John Hinton to Gov. Benjamin G. Humphreys, December 21, 1867, RG 27, MDAH.

68. Ord to Gillem, December 14, 1867, Fourth Military District, *Letters Sent, Volume 25, Civil Affairs*, RG 98, NA; an identical letter was sent to Bvt. Brig. Gen. C. H. Smith, sub-district commander in Arkansas.

69. Moore, "Social and Economic Conditions in Mississippi," 61. As mentioned previously, Warren County was not part of this trend, which was bucked by Issaquena, Washington, Bolivar, and other Delta counties.

furnish land, stock, and provisions for the stock, but the freedman supplied his own food and clothing. The worker would get one-third of the crop under this set-up. In the final way the contract could be concluded, the landowner would supply the land and stock and one-half the food for the stock and all the food for himself; in return he was to get one-half the crop.[70] Although the *Gazette* did not indicate which of the three arrangements was most frequent, the third agreement seems to have been the most common in Warren County, in the instances where sharecropping was practiced.

Despite the military pressure, however, substantial numbers of freedmen ignored Ord's warning and by mid-January had not signed yearly contracts. William McCardle, editor of the *Vicksburg Daily Times*, thought the Loyal Leagues were behind the refusal,[71] though this appears to have been nothing more than speculation on the editor's part. At least one landowner took the situation in stride, and when he could not hire laborers on a regular contract he set them to work clearing land, promising to "give them all they make on the ground they clear."[72]

Some few laborers were still concerned about fair payment for their previous year's work, such as a group on the "Prince Plantation" which claimed that forty-one bales of cotton raised on the place in 1867 were rightfully theirs. The Freedmen's Bureau representative set up a three-member arbitration board to settle the dispute, with the laborers choosing one man, the planter one, and then these two men picking the third member. The process was quite orderly and dignified, and the decision rendered was that half the cotton belonged to the freedman, "subject to amt of supplies furnished laborers and further subject to amt of one

70. *Hinds County Gazette*, December 6, 1867.
71. *Vicksburg Daily Times*, January 10, 1868.
72. Anonymous to Mrs. M. L. Swanson, January 5, 1868, Swanson-Yates Papers, MDAH.

half of necessary expenditure of the Employer for the proper culture and gathering of the crop."[73]

Not all planters and landowners were willing to negotiate with their hands as Dr. McRae had done over the forty-one bales of cotton, an example of the "hard-liners" being the Washington County "Deer Creek Planters Assn," whose meeting was reported in the *Daily Times* on January 8. "It is apparent," began the rules and resolutions of the Association, "that the present great and increasing distress prevailing all over our country, proceeds from one great cause, namely: indisposition on the part of freedmen to discharge their duties as laborers in the fields." The contract system had failed, stated the Deer Creek group, and as a result they were issuing a series of twelve rules which would be followed and adhered to by any laborers who worked their land. These regulations, designed "to protect themselves from loss, and promote the welfare of the freedmen in whom they feel a deep interest," included a basic wage of $6 per month for a "No. 1 man" and $4 per month for a "No. 1 woman," plus provisions in each case. An alternate arrangement was to supply rations and a dwelling for each laborer, in return for the production of three bales of cotton. No money was involved unless more than three bales were produced, in which case a bonus of $10 per bale was promised to the laborer. Working hours, stated the planters, would be daylight to dark, six days a week, and any persons refusing to perform the required tasks would be "discharged from the plantation without any compensation for past services, or share of crops." Sunday was a day of rest, though the planters did "deprecate the practice of negro meetings for the ostensible object of divine services, believing them calculated to inculcate error rather than truth."[74]

---

73. Capt. E. E. Platt to Parties Concerned, January 6, 1868, Box 54A, RG 105 (Miss.), NA.

74. *Vicksburg Daily Times*, January 8, 1868.

Planters in the Deer Creek area, which was located midway up the Delta, "would in general discourage the renting of land to freedmen," though it was considered acceptable in "exceptional cases." Those who rented land rather than signing contracts were, however, charged $3 a month for their dwellings. Finally, the planter's association agreed to establish a "blacklist" of undesirable laborers and pledged not to employ freedmen who had been discharged by any of the members.[75]

It is unknown whether the "Deer Creek Planters Assn." was able to find workers who would accede to their rather stringent demands, for those in the Delta area could in 1868, as in the previous year, obtain free Government transportation to any place where they wished to work.[76] Even as late as the end of the first quarter of 1868, General Gillem reported to Gen. Oliver O. Howard that "the demand for labor is greater than the supply, there being applications in this office for several thousand more laborers than can possibly be procured."[77] Three and a half months later the demand for agricultural workers still far exceeded the supply,[78] so it is entirely conceivable that the group on Deer Creek were forced by the exigencies of the situation to moderate their demands.

The 1868 season was fairly uneventful until the army worm made its appearance in August, but by that time cotton had progressed to the point where some picking had commenced. There was concurrently, however, a great political campaign going on, and as in 1867, employers complained to the Freedman's Bureau about time lost from work by their hands who met to hear discussion on the proposed new constitution for the state. Freed-

75. *Ibid.*
76. Gen. Alvan C. Gillem to George W. Brooks, January 24, 1868, Vol. 20, RG 105 (Miss.), NA.
77. Gen. Alvan C. Gillem to Oliver O. Howard, March 31, 1868, Vol. 20, RG 105 (Miss.), NA.
78. *Ibid.*, July 14, 1868.

174   Enclave: Vicksburg & Her Plantations

men likewise complained to the Bureau about being fired for deciding to vote for the constitution, which would have disfranchised and barred from elective office some of the white residents of the state. According to General Gillem, freedmen who were working on shares had their jobs returned to them, but those who were employed for wages by the day, week, or month had no recourse.[79]

All told, 1868 was, in spite of its difficulties, the best year for agriculture since the War's end. Many planters had taken Gillem's advice earlier in the year and had planted corn, and as the Freedmen's Bureau head had stated, "where corn is abundant, meat will not be scarce."[80] There had been "a marked improvement in the material prosperity of this State," wrote Gillem to the U.S. Adjutant General in November of the year. The cotton crop had survived the worm half intact, and corn was abundant.[81] The proposed new state constitution had been defeated by the voters, and whites, pleased by the fact that many blacks had voted, albeit unwillingly, against the proscriptive constitution, were inclined to accord freedmen better treatment in the year ahead, though it is doubtful whether the economic situation of the ex-slave improved much.[82]

The following year, freedmen seemed to have little reluctance about signing contracts, and issues of the *Daily Times* from the end of 1868 through the first months of 1869 carried very few

79. Gen. Alvan C. Gillem to Oliver O. Howard, October 14, 1868, Vol. 21, RG 105 (Miss.), NA; William C. Harris, "The Reconstruction of the Commonwealth 1865–1870," in *A History of Mississippi*, ed. Richard A. McLemore (Hattiesburg; University & College Press of Mississippi, 1973), I, 562–63.
80. Circular #1, General Gillem, January 25, 1868, published in *Vicksburg Daily Times*, January 29, 1868.
81. General Gillem to adjutant general, November 1, 1868, *Book A, 1868*, RG 98 (Miss.), NA.
82. Wharton, *The Negro in Mississippi*, 66–73.

notices of plantations for sale or lease — proof perhaps that the ease or difficulty of obtaining farm laborers was a primary reason for wanting to give up agriculture. "B," undoubtedly Benjamin Montgomery, who was experimenting with the crop at the time, suggested in the *Daily Times* that broom straw would make a good crop for the cotton planter, for it matured "about the time the cotton crop is laid by" and "would be worth . . . about one hundred dollars clear gain in the work of each hand."[83]

Floods along the Big Black River caused problems in that portion of Warren and Hinds counties in May of 1869,[84] but by August, the *Daily Times* was able to report that "everything here wears a cheerful aspect, and the farmers are already making mamoth [sic] preparations for cropping next year; they are renewing their contracts with the freedmen," it was stated, "who seem to be well pleased to retain their present situation, and are making efforts to induce others of their race to come into this portion of the country. They have redeemed their reputations as laborers among the farmers this past year, by fulfilling their contracts and remaining closely at work during the summer and most particular season on the farm, and thus show the World that they know their duty and are willing to work for their real friends, the white farmers."[85]

This panegyric to the freedmen was all the more remarkable because it followed by only forty-five days the same newspaper editor's ecstatic announcement that 500 Chinese laborers were coming down the river to work in Louisiana. "This is but a beginning," the editor had stated. "The tide will swell in volume until these immigrants are counted by the tens of thousands, for the basis of supply can never be exhausted. . . . We do not take Chinamen by choice," continued the writer, "but from necessity.

83. *Vicksburg Daily Times*, March 12, 1869.
84. *Ibid.*, May 2, 1869.
85. *Ibid.*, August 12, 1869.

176   *Enclave: Vicksburg & Her Plantations*

. . . Emancipation has spoiled the negro, and carried him away from fields of agriculture."[86]

Though the Chinese laborers never arrived in Vicksburg, the city's chamber of commerce sent Gen. W. R. Miles to California to investigate the situation. Even before he returned, however, planters began to have second thoughts about the cost and efficacy of importing a horde of non-Christian, non-English-speaking workers who knew little about the South's way of cultivating the cotton plant. Then word leaked out that the U.S. Government was prepared to oppose the importation of Chinese labor, and the entire scheme was quickly abandoned.[87]

The 180 degree turn of the *Daily Times* is remarkable, all the same; and even the appearance of the army worm two days after its unprecedented praise of the freedmen failed to dampen the spirits of those who had been involved with cotton cultivation this year.[88] By late August cotton was everywhere in the city. The "Snow of Southern Summers" was still "King," reported the *Daily Times*, and cotton from the plantation of J. G. Ferguson and Col. L. Price was being readied for shipment to the St. Louis Fair, where the editor was sure that this sample of the area's staple, of a "Creamy rich appearance, with an exceedingly fine fiber," would do well in the competition.[89]

By fall the cotton crop had proven so unmanageably large that labor was again at a substantial premium, and pickers could receive for their efforts a rate of a penny a pound.[90] With this development the story had come full circle, for seven years earlier, in the fall of 1862, those first few ex-slaves who picked cotton

---

86. *Ibid.*, June 30, 1869.
87. *Ibid.*, August 27, 1869; Wharton, *The Negro in Mississippi*, 97–98.
88. *Vicksburg Daily Times*, August 14, 1869; Warren County farmers raised 28,601 bales of cotton in 1869, together with 213,153 bushels of corn and 66,862 bushels of sweet potatoes. 1870 Census of Agriculture (manuscript).
89. *Vicksburg Daily Times*, August 26, 1869.
90. *Ibid.*, September 26, 1869.

Post-War Agriculture 177

for white businessmen with whom General Grant had contracted also received a penny per pound for their work.[91]

Agriculture had made the necessary adjustments under the new order, and a somewhat uneasy relationship was developing between black tenant and white landowner which would endure to the present.[92] Neither black man nor white would get rich from either wage labor, share rent, or the sharecrop system, and the crop lien may have had a mysterious effect on all, but Warren County's farmers were getting by. Agriculture had adapted to the changes of the War, and those within the city of Vicksburg had to do likewise: to confront the situation and work to make necessary adjustments.

---

91. Livermore, *My Story of the War*, 351.
92. William Lincoln Giles, "Agricultural Revolution, 1890–1970," in *A History of Mississippi*, ed. Richard A. McLemore (Hattiesburg: University & College Press of Mississippi, 1973), II, 180–181.

Politics in Black and White

POLITICS AND FREEDMEN were inseparably linked in Reconstruction-era Vicksburg, for one of these subjects could hardly be discussed without involving the other. Indeed, the courses of both Presidential and Congressional Reconstruction in Mississippi can largely be read in terms of conflict over black-white status, for the most obvious change wrought by the Civil War and the most enduring source of friction between native white citizens and U.S. authorities was the new position of the Negro.

The political and social changes to which Vicksburg's citizens had been forced to adapt in the last two years of the War were a prelude to the coming years of Reconstruction in Mississippi, which began in June 1865 when President Andrew Johnson appointed former Mississippi Supreme Court Justice William Sharkey as provisional governor of the state.[1] Shortly afterward, voters in Vicksburg elected a full slate of new municipal officials, including a mayor and seven councilmen.[2] There was still, however, a great deal of uncertainty over the relative status of civil versus military authorities, and many informed citizens saw great po-

---

1. Garner, *Reconstruction in Mississippi*, 77; Marmaduke Shannon to Gov. William Sharkey, July 1, 1865, RG 27, MDAH.
2. Marmaduke Shannon to Gov. William Sharkey, July 1, 1865, RG 27, MDAH.

tential for conflict between the two powers, particularly in areas involving the rights and responsibilities of freedmen.

Judge D. O. Merwin of the Warren County court expressed the opinion that there was "little occasion to fear any collision between the Military and Civil authority," but he was, ironically enough, at the center of the first important controversy over the extent to which the military commander at Vicksburg still controlled the lives of the citizens thereof.[3]

The case arose out of a killing which took place in Washington County, in the Mississippi Delta, on the Fourth of July 1865. Joseph L. Jackson shot and killed "in defence of his own life," stated his attorney, one of the freedmen on the plantation, a man who had formerly been his slave. Jackson was subsequently arrested by the military authorities and taken to Vicksburg for trial, because the court which had jurisdiction in Washington County would not admit the testimony of freedmen.[4]

Jackson's attorney applied to Judge Merwin for a writ of habeas corpus to release the accused from jail, since he was not a U.S. soldier. Merwin issued the writ, based upon his belief that "they [the military authorities] may make any military order they please, but its violation by a citizen, is not a violation of military law."[5] The writ ordered Gen. Henry W. Slocum to appear with Jackson in Merwin's court on July 19, an invitation which Slocum declined, stating that martial law was still in effect and that as long as freedmen were denied equality in the courts he would continue to use military tribunals.[6]

3. D. O. Merwin to Governor Sharkey, June 30, 1865, RG 27, MDAH.
4. T. A. Marshall and W. Brooks to Governor Sharkey, July 15, 1865, RG 27, MDAH.
5. Joseph L. Jackson to D. O. Merwin, July 18, 1865, in Senate Executive Document #26, p. 57, 39th Congress, 1st Session; D. O. Merwin to Governor Sharkey, June 30, 1865, RG 27, MDAH.
6. D. O. Merwin to Clerk of Criminal Court, Warren County, July 18, 1865, and Gen. Henry Slocum to Merwin, July 19, 1865, both in Senate Executive Document #26, pp. 57–58, 39th Congress, 1st Session.

Slocum then arrested Merwin for issuing the writ, an act which the judge described as "a blow by the mailed hand of military power against the civil authority in the exercise of its most valued and hitherto respected function."[7] Governor Sharkey immediately wrote to both General Slocum and U.S. Secretary of State William Seward. To Slocum he stated that "I have the honor to inform you that Judge Merwin issued the writ under express instructions from me,"[8] while to Seward the governor protested vigorously the course of events to that time. He stated, "It will be seen that General Slocum regards 'martial law' as still in force in Mississippi. This law makes the civil subordinate to the military power, but if it ever did exist here, of which I am not aware, outside of the army, the President's proclamation appointing me to office certainly abolished it. In that he expressly declares that the military shall not interfere with, but aid and assist, the civil authority."[9]

The answer from Seward was not long in coming, and in it he informed the governor that President Johnson was upholding Slocum in this case. "The government of the state will be provisional," stated Seward, "only until the Civil authorities shall be restored, with the consent of Congress. Meanwhile military authority cannot be withdrawn."[10] Judge Merwin was soon released from custody, but disposition of the charges against Jackson is not available.

There was no attempt in the first months after the War to provide the complete spectrum of political equality for freedmen, such as was done later with passage of the civil rights legislation in Congress, but the military authorities and Freedmen's Bureau in Mississippi were committed to insuring that freedmen enjoyed

7. D. O. Merwin to Governor Sharkey, July 20, 1865, *ibid.*, pp. 56–57.
8. Governor Sharkey to General Slocum, July 22, 1865, RG 27, MDAH.
9. Governor Sharkey to U.S. Secretary of State William Seward, July 21, 1865, Senate Executive Document #26, p. 56, 39th Congress, 1st Session.
10. William Seward to Governor Sharkey, July 24, 1865, Senate Executive Document #26, p. 60, 39th Congress, 1st Session.

in court the same privileges accorded to whites. Several months after the Merwin case, for example, Col. Samuel Thomas informed Lt. Col. R. S. Donaldson that he was "to give the Civil Authorities of this state all the cooperation and assistance in your power. You will instruct all officers under you to do the same. . . . All courts that will admit negro testimony are to take up cases where Freedmen are interested."[11]

There were continuing problems along these lines, and Maj. T. S. Free, who was in charge of the provost marshal's court in Vicksburg, soon received a petition for trial from one Giles Henry, a freedman in the city who was involved in a court case. Henry had been sentenced by the Mayor of Vicksburg, without a hearing, "to pay a fine of $200.00 dollars, or in default thereof to be confined in Jail until the first Monday in December next, to await trial before Circuit Court, supposed to be in session at that time." Major Free granted Henry's petition, released him from the city jail, and conducted the trial himself, the outcome of which is unknown.[12] Governor Sharkey in September 1865 ordered freedmen's testimony admitted in cases where their interests were involved, and, on the supposition that all courts in the state would comply with Sharkey's order, Colonel Thomas abolished the special provost marshal courts effective October 31. This action, however, was quite premature on Thomas' part, for it soon became evident that many judges would not accept even the limited extent of black testimony required by Sharkey's proclamation.[13]

Mayor Thomas Randolph of Vicksburg, for example, refused to allow a freedman's testimony in a case, and he was questioned by Major Free on his refusal. "He did not know whether he would

11. Col. Samuel Thomas to Lt. Col. R. S. Donaldson, September 21, 1865, RG 27, MDAH.
12. Endorsement, September 1865, *Civil Docket, Provost Court, E & M, MAJOR T. S. Free, AIG,* Vol. 280, RG 105 (Miss.), NA.
13. *Meridian Clarion,* October 1, 1865, and November 5, 1865, cited in Wharton, *The Negro in Mississippi,* 134.

receive such testimony or not," stated the major, "it would depend on the witness. I then asked him whether he would comply with the requirements of your order relating to negro testimony or whether he had done so in his courts. His answers were evasive and in the negative."[14] Public officials in Mississippi, especially away from the military headquarters at Vicksburg, paid little attention to the requirement of admitting Negro testimony in their courts. They were warned by William Manlove, editor of the *Vicksburg Daily Journal*, that "in less than a year you will be compelled to do that which you have refused voluntarily to do.... The negro is in the Courts now, and he will stay there, whether you acquiesce or not."[15] There were, however, judges who would accept the testimony of witnesses without regard to color, and John Trowbridge, a visitor to the South, was pleased to discover one of these exceptional individuals in Vicksburg. This man was William Yerger, an eminent jurist who had been one of only a few delegates who voted against secession at the convention in 1861.[16] Yerger's action was not the rule in 1865, but as months passed and the military authorities applied pressure, more courts across the state decided they had little choice but to go along with the idea. There was considerable foot-dragging, however.

Justice of the Peace A. M. Dowling in Macon wrote Gov. Benjamin Humphreys, an ex-Confederate brigadier who had been elected to replace Sharkey in November 1865, that "I have uniformly admitted Negro testimony in all cases when a Freedman or his interests are the Subject of a Contest, have issued subpoenas for them, and in all respects have endeavoured to do them full justice, and Shall continue to do so."[17] This conditional acceptance

14. Endorsement, October 28, 1865, Major Free, *Civil Docket, Provost Court*, RG 105 (Miss.), NA.
15. *Vicksburg Daily Journal*, November 17, 1865, quoted in Harris, *Presidential Reconstruction in Mississippi*, 133.
16. Trowbridge, *The South*, 373.
17. A. M. Dowling to Gov. Benjamin Humphreys, January 6, 1866, RG 27, MDAH.

Politics in Black and White 183

of Negro witnesses was practiced in other courts as well, and freedmen's testimony was not allowed, even in criminal cases, unless he was "a party to the transaction." This restriction sometimes worked against justice, as in a case in Columbus where a freedman was the only witness to a dispute between two whites. He was not allowed to testify, and this action resulted in the court's failure to resolve the case on its merits.[18]

In Oxford, Mississippi, however, a freedman was convicted of murdering his twin infant children and was sentenced to hang. Circuit Judge Alex M. Clayton assured Humphreys that "the trial was conducted in all respects, as if the accused had been a free white man, the proceedings were impartial, and the verdict founded upon evidence sufficient to justify it."[19]

Shortly after, Circuit Judge Josiah A. P. Campbell admitted in his Warren County court testimony of freedmen in the homicide trial of a white man accused of killing another freedman. The defense attorneys in the case attempted to have the Negro testimony barred, but Judge Campbell would not grant their objection. They then appealed directly to the jury, asking them to disregard the freedmen's testimony. All their pleadings were to no avail, however, and the defendant was convicted of manslaughter and sentenced to a year in the county jail.[20] The importance of the case lay not in the sentence handed down, but in the fact that an all-white jury had convicted a white man solely on the testimony of freedmen.

Finally, the Mississippi legislature which had been elected under President Andrew Johnson's plan of Reconstruction, repealed in 1867 all laws making a distinction in legal rights between blacks and whites except for those pertaining to voting and juror

18. Lt. Col. Henry A. Brinkerhoff to HQ Vicksburg 52 U.S.C.I., March 6, 1866, RG 27, MDAH.
19. Alex M. Clayton to Governor Humphreys, May 5, 1866, RG 27, MDAH.
20. Wharton, *The Negro in Mississippi*, 136.

qualifications. It was even then difficult, wrote Gen. Alvan C. Gillem, Freedmen's Bureau commander in the state, "to impress upon the more ignorant classes of the white population, and in some cases, also upon the petty magistrates throughout the State, the true intent and meaning of this law."[21] Within two years the proscriptions against jury duty and voting were removed by a new legislature organized under Congressional Reconstruction, and freedmen began to appear at both the ballot box and the jury box, a situation that remained until the 1890 constitution disfranchised them again.[22]

A second area of controversy between military and civilian authorities in Vicksburg arose out of the desire of white residents, who did not have confidence in the black troops in Mississippi, to band together into militia units and patrol the country against the freedmen, who allegedly posed a threat to peace and order. Some of these "militia" organizations were formed almost as soon as the War ended. John Allen of Nanechehaw plantation wrote to Governor Sharkey early in July 1865 that he had organized the militia in his part of Warren County. There were 160 men in the group, stated Allen, divided into three companies, and he believed "the community is more quiet and much better satisfied and the negroes in much better order than they were a month ago."[23]

Shortly afterward L. M. Hall, "Colonel, 1st Regiment, Enrolled Militia of the District of Vicksburg," wrote the governor in distress: "The militia force of this City are about to be disbanded. They are the only organized white force at present in the County that can be relied upon for the enforcement of civil authority. There is now in the Armory of the Enrolled Militia of the District of Vicksburg a sufficient quantity of arms to arm at least one thousand men. There is at present an available force of about

21. Gen. Alvan C. Gillem to Gen. Oliver O. Howard, October 10, 1867, Vol. 20, RG 105 (Miss.), NA.
22. Wharton, *The Negro in Mississippi*, 137.
23. James Allen to Governor Sharkey, July 11, 1865, RG 27, MDAH.

Eight Hundred men in the two regiments E Mi D V, which can easily be organized into a state militia. I would most respectfully recommend that this course be pursued."[24]

I. M. Patridge endorsed Hall's idea, informing the governor that "there are no infantry troops here except negroes and a disorganized body of white troops worse than the negroes waiting here to be mustered out."[25] A. H. Arthur likewise urged the governor to act promptly on the matter, stating that "When all the white troops leave here, it is very important that some organization, such as the Enrolled Militia heretofore have been organized, be kept up in this City for its protection."[26]

Sharkey soon responded to such appeals as these, and on August 17 he issued a proclamation calling upon the people of the state "to organize under the militia laws a force for the apprehension of criminals and the suppression of crime."[27] Gen. P. J. Osterhaus reacted quickly to Sharkey's proclamation and reminded the governor that "the State of Mississippi is still under military occupation and that martial law is still in force, and that no military organizations can be tolerated which are not under the control of United States officers." The number of troops stationed about, assured the general, was "amply Sufficient to give the Civil authorities all the Assistance they may possibly need."[28] Sharkey immediately shot back with a claim that "for twelve or fifteen consecutive nights, passengers travelling in the stages between here [Jackson] and Vicksburg have been robbed, and these things have occurred within twelve or fifteen miles of your headquarters."[29]

24. L. M. Hall to Governor Sharkey, July 25, 1865, RG 27, MDAH.
25. I. M. Patridge to Governor Sharkey, July 25, 1865, RG 27, MDAH.
26. A. H. Arthur to Governor Sharkey, July 25, 1865, in letter of L. M. Hall to Governor Sharkey, July 25, 1865, *ibid.*
27. Garner, *Reconstruction in Mississippi*, 99.
28. Gen. P. J. Osterhaus to Governor Sharkey, August 21, 1865, RG 27, MDAH.
29. Governor Sharkey to Gen. P. J. Osterhaus, August 22, 1865, RG 27, MDAH.

The governor also took the matter to higher authority and wrote President Johnson on August 30. "In our last interview," he reminded him, "you distinctly stated to me that I could organize the militia to suppress the crime if necessary. Deeming it necessary I issued a proclamation on the 19th Inst. calling on two companies, one of cavalry" for each county.[30] Whereas the President had upheld the military authorities in the Merwin case, here he sustained Governor Sharkey. Johnson sent the message to Slocum, Osterhaus' superior: "If you have issued any order countermanding the proclamation or interfering with its execution you will at once revoke it."[31]

Militia groups flourished statewide under the President's policy of noninterference,[32] but there was still much potential and actual conflict of authority between military and civil officers. The "Militia Captains of Vicksburg," for example, informed Sharkey with astonishment that "The Provost Marshall [sic], Captain Couch of this City has arrested young Hullum, Simmons and Reed of Warren County, upon the charge of disarming a Negro."[33]

In an attempt to prevent and resolve such problems as these, Governor Sharkey had begun the process by which Mississippi was to be Reconstructed under Presidential auspices. Within a month after taking office he had called a special election to select delegates to a convention set for August 1865. The voter turn-out in Vicksburg and Warren County was quite sparse, only 308 persons casting ballots. Former Whigs were chosen to represent Warren County and Vicksburg at this election, the pre-War Demo-

30. Governor Sharkey to President Andrew Johnson, August 30, 1865, RG 27, MDAH.
31. President Johnson to Gen. Henry Slocum, September 2, 1865, RG 27, MDAH.
32. William E. Bayless to Governor Sharkey, September 13, 1865, RG 27, MDAH.
33. Militia captains of Vicksburg to Sharkey, October 8, 1865, RG 27, MDAH.

crats not even putting forward a slate of nominees.[34] Likewise in the fall, Warren County sent three former Whigs, all of whom had opposed secession, to represent her in the state legislature.[35] In the gubernatorial race which took place at the same time, Benjamin G. Humphreys, an unpardoned ex-Confederate brigadier, received 843 of 868 votes in the county, for an astounding 95.8% of the vote.[36] Humphreys was a Union Whig in 1860 who had gone with the South when war broke out, and of three candidates in the race, he was in the middle on questions involving Reconstruction and the status of freedmen. Humphreys received a large majority of the vote across the state and took office on October 16, 1865.[37] Interestingly enough, the U.S. Government continued for several months to deal with the state through William Sharkey, though Sharkey had notified U.S. Secretary of State Seward of the change in the governorship the day after his successor's inauguration.[38]

Ex-slaves were the primary subject of consideration at the legislative session in October 1865, the main result being a law entitled "An Act to confer Civil Rights on Freedmen, and for other purposes." The "other purposes" were a euphemistic way of describing the act, for it was the basis for the Black Code, passage of which gave Mississippi the dubious distinction of being the first state in the South to restrict the freedom of former slaves and free blacks.[39] The Black Code was a severe blow to the freedmen, prohibiting as it did their leasing or renting of lands except inside

34. Garner, *Reconstruction in Mississippi*, 77; "Certificates of Election of Delegates to Convention (August 1865)," Legislative Records, RG 47, MDAH; Harris, *Presidential Reconstruction in Mississippi*, 49.
35. "Tabular View of the Mississippi Legislature Begun and holden at the City of Jackson, on Monday, the 16th Day of October, A.D. 1865," in Broadsides Collection, 1831–1870, MDAH.
36. Harris, *Presidential Reconstruction in Mississippi*, 112.
37. Harris, "Reconstruction of the Commonwealth," 547–48.
38. Garner, *Reconstruction in Mississippi*, 95–96.
39. Harris, "Reconstruction of the Commonwealth," 548–49.

a city, allowing judges to bind out minor children as apprentices, strengthening laws against vagrancy, and requiring black men who were not otherwise employed to enter into yearly labor contracts.[40]

Freedmen reacted immediately to these measures, a convention in Vicksburg petitioning President Johnson that "it will be virtually returning us to slavery again."[41] White citizens of Vicksburg, too, were stirred by the legislation. The Rev. J. P. Bardwell of the American Missionary Association was amazed at the way "the Negro is the topic of conversation everywhere — in Hotels Rail Roads and Steam Boats, wherever you see a group of men together, the Nigger is the everlasting theme."[42] Men of prominence in both Vicksburg and Jackson sought repeal of the Black Code laws not only because of their inherent unfairness, but also because they were afraid of the political impact they were having in other parts of the country. William Manlove, editor of the *Vicksburg Daily Journal*, denounced the codes on several occasions, while the *Daily Herald* saw the laws as "a useless piece of legislation" and felt they put the state "in antagonism to the policy of the Government, just at the time when we need friends in Washington." Mayors of smaller towns throughout the state, however, insisted on the letter of these laws, and the legislature soon responded to their wishes with additional restrictive measures.[43]

Despite the Vicksburg newspapers, however, the attitudes of many citizens were inimical to the desires and wishes of the freedmen for the right to live and work as they pleased. "The great trouble," wrote Freedmen's Bureau Sub-commissioner Samuel G. Swain to his brother, "is, these people are not whiped [sic] enough yet, or rather the Gov't has been to magnamamous [sic]

---

40. *Ibid.*; Wharton, *The Negro in Mississippi*, 84–86.
41. G. W. Blackwell to President Andrew Johnson, November 24, 1865, quoted in Harris, *Presidential Reconstruction in Mississippi*, 144–145.
42. J. P. Bardwell to M. E. Strieby, November 20, 1865, AMA Papers (Miss.).
43. Harris, *Presidential Reconstruction in Mississippi*, 104, 144; *Vicksburg Daily Herald*, December 5, 1865, quoted in *Natchez Democrat*, December 7, 1865; Wharton, *The Negro in Mississippi*, 84–90.

toward them since they were whiped which has spoiled the good effect of the whipping."⁴⁴ Lieutenant Swain then described the recent visit to the city of Gen. Oliver O. Howard, head of the Bureau of Refugees, Freedmen, and Abandoned Lands, revealing as he did so his own estimation of the freedmen and the white citizens among whom he worked:

He addressed the Colored Citizens of this place, but I do not think his address was of much benefit to them, because it was not adapted to thier [sic] minds, altho' it would have been very good indeed delivered to an intelligent white audience. The Colored people as a general thing cannot comprehend only the most common language, if spoken by a person that is not accostomed [sic] to them or raised among them. Every church in the city was refused Gen. Howard as a place to address the Colored citizens. We of the Freedmen's Bureau are glad of it because it shows to the Gen. what the feelings and actions of these Mississippians are when they are at home. They go to Washington seeking pardons or the restoration of their property with a very sweet face, and pretend that they represent the feelings of the mass of the people, but when they get home again they are bitter against every thing that is done to advance the condition of the Freedmen.⁴⁵

Gen. Thomas J. Wood, who assumed command of the military forces in the state shortly before the Black Code was passed in November 1865,⁴⁶ declared null and void in January 1866 those portions of the recently passed legislation which applied specifically to freedmen. Still in effect, however, were the stringent vagrancy statutes, which ostensibly regulated the idleness of both races; and in towns where there was no U.S. garrison, Wood's order was generally ignored altogether.⁴⁷

In Vicksburg itself, as Swain indicated, there was opposition to things "done to advance the condition of the Freedmen," one

44. Samuel G. Swain to George Swain, November 12, 1865, Swain Papers, WSHS.
45. *Ibid.*
46. Garner, *Reconstruction in Mississippi*, 97.
47. Wharton, *The Negro in Mississippi*, 90–91.

of which was schools conducted by Northern-based societies. Samuel G. Wright of the AMA mission there often heard the idea expressed that "'just as soon as civil power is fully restored there shall be an end to Nigger schools and the presence of Nigger teachers.'"[48] This feeling had been evident all during the period from mid-1863 when the first freedmen's schools were established in the area, and the ending of the War did little to change it. What did change, however, was actual violence against the missionary teachers, for as Joseph Warren, State Superintendent of Education for the Freedmen's Bureau, put it, "The Mississippi people will take care not to allow violence, because they are anxious to get rid of us all, which they can only do by behaving in such a way as to get civil government fully restored."[49]

Money for the schools came largely from Northern mission societies, but in Vicksburg the freedmen initiated soon after the War a direct tax upon themselves in support of the educational effort.[50] With the encouragement of the military authorities and the enthusiastic support of the black population of the city, the school system begun in Vicksburg during the War soon expanded in size, and by November 1865 over 2,200 black residents were enrolled in courses ranging from elementary reading and arithmetic to high school subjects.[51]

The white population did not, at least in the months immediately after the War, attempt by violence to discourage schools for the blacks, but other tactics were successfully employed, such as a refusal to lease buildings or rooms for school purposes.[52] This development worked a substantial hardship on those who were

48. Samuel G. Wright to George Whipple, November 11, 1865, AMA Papers (Miss.).
49. Joseph Warren to Samuel G. Wright, August 23, 1865, AMA Papers (Miss.).
50. Palmer Litts to M. E. Whiting, September 8, 1865, AMA Papers (Miss.).
51. Report of Colored Schools in Vicksburg, Mississippi, for Nov. 1865," AMA Papers (Miss.).
52. Trowbridge, *The South*, 377.

Noon at the Primary School for Freedmen — It was difficult to find buildings in which to conduct classes, but the teachers somehow succeeded. Courtesy: Library of Congress

conducting the schools, for many of the previous locations had to be vacated when rebel owners returned to the city, pardon in hand. Even the U.S. Government was forced to evict a freedmen's school from its quarters in the hospital when the space was "required for the reception of the sick." The Episcopal Church, too, was ordered by Gen. Marion Smith to be turned back to its congregation, a move which prompted J. A. Hawley, Superintendent of Colored Schools for the District of Vicksburg, to enter a vigorous protest. "If the Episcopal Church is taken from us," stated Hawley, "I see little reason to hope that the other churches can be retained and consequently most of the children now taught by the benevolence of the North will be turned loose to be governed and restrained from mischief, instead of being educated. Is not

192 *Enclave: Vicksburg & Her Plantations*

the School the cheapest method of government?" he asked. The order was carried out despite Hawley's plea, but other accommodations were soon located, and the number of students in the school system did not diminish.[53]

Freedmen's education made remarkable progress in the Vicksburg area during the last months of 1865 and into the early spring of 1866, but by April of that year a concerted and often violent opposition to black schools began to manifest itself within the white population.[54] It was perhaps not coincidental that an outspoken conservative movement was developing throughout the state at this same time, as illustrated in the March gathering at Vicksburg of 200 prominent persons who applauded President Johnson's veto of the bill to extend the life of the Freedmen's Bureau. The speakers at this meeting "represented the South as being cruelly injured, insulted, and oppressed, and the North as her wanton oppressor."[55] April brought an increase in opposition to schools for the freedmen and marked the beginning of a series of minor incidents such as rock throwing and window smashing. By May the violence had begun to be directed against the teachers themselves, and even Clara Kimball, whose school for freedmen had grown from 230 pupils in January of 1866 to 280 by the end of April of that year, was forced to concede that "I don't know as any will be able long to teach in this state."[56]

Opposition to black schools was certainly not limited to Vicksburg, for a similar situation prompted the AMA to consider closing its schools in Meridian, 140 miles east near the Alabama line. Addie O. Warren, the teacher there, who was described by a

53. Endorsements, Provost Marshal, April 18, and April 20, 1865, *Endorsements, Provost Marshal, Vicksburg, Mississippi (1865)*, Vol. 73, RG 105 (Miss.), NA.
54. Swint, *The Northern Teacher*, 122–23.
55. Dennett, *The South*, 354–55.
56. Swint, *The Northern Teacher*, 122–23; reports of Clara B. Kimball, January, February, March, and April 1866, all in AMA Papers (Miss.); Clara B. Kimball to Anonymous, May 4, 1866, AMA Papers (Miss.).

Missionary Association correspondent as "never . . . quite satisfied she was not made a *Man*,"[57] was outspokenly against the proposal to accede to threats and abandon Meridian. "I wish that you would try," she wrote the Rev. J. P. Bardwell, "to persuade the Association to keep up its schools a little longer. I am not in favor of bringing joy to the hearts of the Rebs by letting them think they have 'cleaned us out.' My private opinion," she continued with vehemence, "is that the powers of darkness are let loose upon this God forsaken, distracted, demoralized, half-civilized country."[58]

In Canton, too, a town twenty miles north of Jackson and fifty miles from Vicksburg, the white residents were violently opposed to freedmen's schools. The black population of Canton was in a very large majority, wrote J. J. Fultz, who had gone there to teach the freedmen. Freedmen there had "formed a society for Educational purposes, and were raising money for the purpose of building a school house, when they were warned that it would be burnt." Fultz himself was approached by a group of fifteen or twenty men, "headed by a Mr. Luckett, a lawyer," and was informed that he would be hanged on the spot unless he agreed to leave town immediately. The group told him they were "determined not to have any freedmen's schools, or any damned Yankees in the place."[59] Lt. M. R. Williams investigated Fultz's story of the threat and found it to be true. "The principal cause," he stated in a report to the military headquarters in Vicksburg, "appears to be that he had offended the sensibilities of some of the people, by appearing on the street too much with Colored men." The school there remained only a dream for the freedmen, stated Lieutenant Williams, because "they could not find a Southern teacher and were told that no Yankee would be tolerated." One of those from

57. AMA Report, March 10, 1866, AMA Papers (Miss.).
58. Addie O. Warren to J. P. Bardwell, May 6, 1866, *ibid.*
59. J. J. Fultz to Gov. Benjamin Humphreys, May 12, 1866, RG 27, MDAH.

194 *Enclave: Vicksburg & Her Plantations*

whom Williams obtained his information was Amos Drane, "a colored storekeeper of the town, a man very well spoken of by the Citizens." Drane was quite disappointed by the attitude of the white townspeople, and it is ironic that less than two years later he represented Madison County at the 1868 Mississippi Constitutional Convention, where his experiences in Canton undoubtedly molded into him the radicalism he displayed at the state capital.[60]

The progress of black schools in the state is almost an index of the course of Reconstruction, for once Congress took control in 1867 white opposition seemed to melt magically away and reveal "a very thorough earnestness on the part of the white people . . . to see the freedmen properly educated."[61] By October of 1867, in marked contrast to conditions of the previous year, Gen. Alvan C. Gillem, military commander of the state, was able to report to Gen. Oliver O. Howard that "among the intelligent white citizens the subject of education of the freedmen meets with no opposition, but on the contrary is encouraged by them."[62] Some opposition to freedmen's schools developed again in 1871 and 1872, after the state had been readmitted to the Union,[63] but by this time the establishment of free public schools for both races had been made a part of the state constitution.[64] This provision was one of many which came out of the Constitutional Convention of 1868, a group which had met as one of the first steps in the process by which

60. Lt. M. R. Williams to Lt. Stuart Eldridge, May 16, 1866, RG 27, MDAH; James T. Currie, "Conflict and Consensus: Creating the 1868 Mississippi Constitution" (unpublished M.A. Thesis, Univ. of Virginia, 1969), 92.

61. An inspector from the Freedmen's Bureau, quoted in Swint, *The Northern Teacher*, 127.

62. Gen. Alvan C. Gillem to Gen. Oliver O. Howard, October 10, 1867, Vol. 20, RG 105 (Miss.), NA.

63. Swint, *The Northern Teacher*, 132.

64. State of Mississippi, *Journal of the Proceedings in the Constitutional Convention of the State of Mississippi. 1868* (Jackson: E. Stafford, Printer, 1871), 638.

Mississippi was Congressionally Reconstructed under the leadership of Maj. Gen. E. O. C. Ord.

The appointment of General Ord to head the Fourth Military District had come from congressional passage of the Reconstruction Acts of March 23 and July 19, 1867, and had originally been received with favor by conservatives in Mississippi.[65] Ord was basically more of a conservative than not, but he attempted as best he could to carry out the aims of Congressional Reconstruction in the state. In a circular dated July 29, 1867, for example, he warned public officials that "any attempts to render nugatory, the action of Congress designed to promote the better government of the States lately engaged in the rebellion, by speeches or demonstrations at public meetings in opposition thereto, will be deemed good and sufficient cause for their removal from office."[66]

Ord did not remove many officeholders in the state, but of the twenty-five or so he evicted from office, eleven were in Vicksburg. In early September 1867 the military commander, "for the purpose of securing an equal, just administration and execution of the laws upon all alike in the city of Vicksburg, Mississippi, and to secure the best interests of the citizens thereof" removed the city marshal, three justices of the peace, five of the seven city councilmen, and a member of the board of police. The mayor, E. W. Wallin, then resigned, and Ord appointed former Union general A. J. Maltby in his place.[67] Less than two weeks later Ord ousted Warren County sheriff M. H. Dixon for "inefficiency in the discharge of the duties of his office, and for neglect of duty in failing to securely keep prisoners entrusted to his custody."[68] Ord managed to fill most of the Vicksburg offices he vacated, but he was forced

---

65. Garner, *Reconstruction in Mississippi*, 59–60, 93–95, 120–21, 161; Jackson *Daily Clarion*, April 4, 1867.

66. Circular from Gen. E. O. C. Ord, July 28, 1867, RG 27, MDAH.

67. Garner, *Reconstruction in Mississippi*, 164; Special Orders #122, Gen. Ord, September 3, 1867, Records of the War Department, U.S. Army Commands, Fourth Military District, 1867–1870, microfilm, MDAH.

68. Special Orders #132, Gen. Ord, September 14, 1867, *ibid.*

to inform General Grant on September 27 that it was "difficult to find competent men who can qualify to fill the vacancies in the civil offices."[69]

Ord's actions could certainly not be classed as extremist, but William T. McCardle of the *Vicksburg Times*, whose newspaper proclaimed itself "a journal devoted to the interests and supremacy of the white man,"[70] was outraged and denounced Ord as "a usurper and a despot."[71] For these and other statements the general hauled McCardle before a six-member military tribunal, which found him guilty of attempting to hinder Reconstruction. McCardle's attorney attempted to gain his client's release from military custody on a writ of habeas corpus, an action which quickly evolved into a challenge of the constitutionality of Congressional Reconstruction. After various appeals in the civil courts, McCardle's case reached the U.S. Supreme Court. Congress, however, quickly passed a law removing the high court's jurisdiction in cases involving writs of habeas corpus, thereby avoiding the larger constitutional question. McCardle was soon released anyway.[72]

A short time later, however, McCardle and James Dugan, editor of the rival *Vicksburg Republican* were arrested by Ord for "disturbing the public peace by publishing and uttering libelous assaults each upon the other." Each man was freed upon the posting of a $1,000 peace bond, but General Gillem, Ord's successor, soon revoked the order and returned the money.[73]

McCardle had, to put it mildly, both political and personal

69. Ord to Maj. George K. Leet, September 27, 1867, Fourth Military District, *Book A, 1867*, p. 220, RG 98 (Miss.), NA.
70. *Vicksburg Daily Times*, January 21, 1868.
71. Garner, *Reconstruction in Mississippi*, 168.
72. *Ibid.*; for a fuller discussion of this case see Stanley Kutler, "*Ex Parte McCardle*: Judicial Impotency? The Supreme Court and Reconstruction Reconsidered," *American Historical Review*, 72 (1967), 835–57.
73. Special Orders #198, Gen. Ord, December 5, 1867, and Special Orders #17, General Gillem, January 27, 1868, both in Records of the War Department, U.S. Army Commands, Fourth Military District, 1867–1870, microfilm, MDAH; *Vicksburg Daily Times*, January 31, 1868.

animosity toward the convention and its efforts, but many other Caucasian residents of the city were also angered by its actions, their anger increased by the frustration they had experienced in November 1867 when the election for delegates to the convention had taken place. The theory espoused by the *Daily Times* and other newspapers throughout the state was that if less than a majority of the state's voters participated in the election, Congress would have to declare the vote null and void and Congressional Reconstruction would be delayed. The attempt failed statewide, and the convention took place according to plan. Nowhere, however, had conservative whites been as successful in their boycott as in Warren County and Vicksburg, and nowhere were whites more disappointed with the result.

The county had a total of 6,227 registered voters by election time — 1,433 white and 4,794 black. Only 8 white voters, according to the *Daily Times*, cast ballots in Vicksburg, and the county approved the convention by a margin of 4,515−0, the most one-sided vote in the state. As a result of the white boycott, most counties, Warren among them, sent to the convention delegations which did not represent a cross-section of the population.[74]

The Vicksburg and Warren County delegation to this important convention consisted of five persons, three white and two black. The three white delegates were Benjamin Leas, about whose background nothing can be found; George C. McKee, a former Union general, practicing attorney at Centralia, Illinois, and a graduate of Knox College; and Alston Mygatt, who was foreign-born but a long-time resident of the city. The two black delegates, among seventeen of their race at the convention, were Albert Johnson, a preacher who later served in the state legislature; and T. W. Stringer, described by Vernon Wharton as "the most influential Negro in the convention." Stringer was a minister in the African Methodist Episcopal Church, for which he came to Mis-

74. James T. Currie, "The Beginnings of Congressional Reconstruction in Mississippi," *Journal of Mississippi History*, 35 (August 1973), 273−74.

sissippi as general superintendent of missions and presiding elder. "The man had a genius for organization," stated Wharton. "After a distinguished career in religious and fraternal organizations in Ohio, he led in the development of the African Methodist Episcopal Church in Canada before his move to Mississippi. Wherever he went in the state, churches, lodges, benevolent societies and political machines sprang up and flourished. His influence upon the constitution of 1868 was as great as that of any other man in the convention."[75]

Four of the delegates from Warren County — Johnson, Leas, Mygatt and Stringer — were among those whose voting record at the convention identifies them with the more radical group, while McKee was much more moderate.[76] They chaired 6 of the 40 special committees within the convention and 2 of the 13 standing committees[77] and contributed to the ideas considered by the convention. Thomas Stringer, for example, failed in his attempt to have a compulsory education provision inserted in the Constitution, but Alston Mygatt was successful in inserting into the Bill of Rights a pioneering section which protected the property rights of married women.[78] These men were on the whole as capable as any in the convention, but this fact did not endear them any more to the white citizens of Vicksburg. The men were for the most part outsiders; they had been elected by the black population; and the conservatives were infuriated that their own scheme had gone awry. They were in no mood to support with their taxes a group to which they had given no support with their ballots.

The convention completed its work in mid-May 1868, and the

75. Currie, "Conflict and Consensus," 83–84; Wharton, *The Negro in Mississippi*, 147–49.
76. For an analysis of the voting patterns among the delegates to the convention, see Currie, "Conflict and Consensus," 85–94.
77. *Ibid.*, 92–93.
78. Wharton, *The Negro in Mississippi*, 150; Mississippi, *Journal of the Proceedings in the Constitutional Convention, 1868*, 345.

document which came out of it was then submitted to the voters of the state for ratification. Almost before the convention had begun, however, conservative white citizens had organized an opposition group, with Warren County supplying much of the leadership. The ratification campaign itself was largely a case of Democrats versus Republicans.

As early as February 3, seventy persons met in Vicksburg in a "White Men's Meeting" to discuss possibilities for the constitution, and at the Democratic state convention later that month Warren County was represented by twenty delegates — more than any other county except Hinds, site of the meeting.[79] The Democratic press in Vicksburg, too, was militantly outspoken on the convention's efforts, promising that the "outraged and plundered people will wither, with their imagination, all who attempt, with puny arms, to resist the great uprising of the white men of Mississippi."[80] One specific cause of Democratic opposition was the officeholding and franchise provisions in the proposed new state constitution. The first of these sections, adoption of which prompted a walk-out among the conservative delegates at the convention, provided that no one should be allowed to hold office who had given "voluntary aid, countenance, counsel or encouragement to persons engaged in armed hostility to the United States," or who had held any office under the Confederacy or in the state after it had seceded. Exceptions to this proscription were to be given those who had voted in favor of calling the convention or who "openly and publicly advocated, and who does now, and shall continue to advocate the reconstruction measures of the 39th and 40th Congress of the United States." In addition the "private soldier of the late so-called Confederate States army" was not to be barred unless he had voted for or signed the Ordinance of Secession.[81]

79. *Vicksburg Daily Times*, February 4 and 21, 1868.
80. *Ibid.*, February 15, 1868.
81. Mississippi, *Journal of the Proceedings in the Constitutional Convention. 1868*, 519–21, 523, 543–44, 556.

The net result of this portion of the constitution was that most of the white voters in Warren County and other areas of the state would lose their right to seek elective office, and even the *Vicksburg Weekly Republican* argued that the provisions affected too many people.[82] Estimates of the number of men barred statewide by the new document ranged from the 16,000 suggested by the *Weekly Republican* to the 20,000–30,000 counted by the conservative Jackson *Daily Clarion*.[83] The suffrage provision, too, was a great source of contention between Democrats and Republicans, requiring as it did an oath on the part of the voter admitting "the political and civil equality of all men." Some 2,500 persons, it was estimated, would be disfranchised by this section.[84]

The campaign for and against ratification was fiercely waged throughout the state, and Vicksburg and Warren County were no exception. The issue was not white against black, editorialized the *Weekly Republican* but rather wealthy against poor. "Only with the black man's help," stated the editor in a refrain which foretold the ideology of the Populists, "can the poor white man ever gain his just political influence in Mississippi."[85] In an appeal "To the laboring Men of the South" the same newspaper called on all citizens to remember both that the slaveowners were the ones who had brought on the War and that these men despised the laboring white men. "Remember that the Republican Party is pledged," it continued, "to elevate labor, to educate the masses, and to enact such laws as will secure . . . your just and legal rights under the government."[86]

Opponents of the constitution, however, were determined that

---

82. *Vicksburg Weekly Republican*, May 21, 1868.
83. *Ibid.*, June 2, 1868; Jackson *Daily Clarion*, June 25, 1868.
84. Mississippi, *Journal of the Proceedings in the Constitutional Convention. 1868*, 732; Harris, "Reconstruction of the Commonwealth," 563.
85. *Vicksburg Weekly Republican*, April 28, 1868.
86. *Ibid.*, April 7, 1868.

this election would not be a repeat of the previous year and engaged in a most thorough campaign against the document. Violence and threats of violence, economic intimidation, ostracism, and the recently organized Ku Klux Klan all took their toll among pro-constitution voters, and the *Vicksburg Daily Times* even promised to publish a list of businesses which employed black voters or Loyal League members, with the suggestion that white citizens boycott them.[87]

Businessmen throughout the state threatened to fire blacks who voted in the election, while the *Weekly Republican* attempted to minimize the effect of these threats by assuring the freedmen that whites needed their labor and could not afford to discharge them. After the election, however, the editor was forced to admit that the threats had been "pretty effectually carried into execution" in much of Warren County.[88] As a result of the opposition's efforts the constitution was defeated by a vote of 63,860 to 56,231, though in Warren County the document was endorsed by a 4,851 to 1,316 margin,[89] a proportion of votes closely in line with black/white voter registration.

The state remained under the military government of Gen. Alvan C. Gillem, whose benevolent and somewhat conservative hand was preferred over that of local government under the defeated constitution. Gillem continued his command in Mississippi until after U. S. Grant's inauguration in March 1869. Before he left, however, conservative citizens in Vicksburg honored him at a public meeting presided over by Wirt Adams, a former Confederate brigadier. The chairman, in a "brief but earnest and eloquent speech" praised the U.S. commander and gave him a resolution of thanks. "The citizens of Vicksburg and the county

---

87. Currie, "Conflict and Consensus," 58; *Vicksburg Daily Times* quoted in *Vicksburg Weekly Republican*, June 23, 1868.
88. *Vicksburg Weekly Republican*, June 23, and November 1, 1868.
89. *New York Times*, July 22, 1868, p. 1.

of Warren," stated the resolution, "desire to place upon record, an enduring memorial of their appreciation of his ability, impartiality and well directed efforts for the public good."[90]

The new commander in Mississippi was Adelbert Ames, soon to be Ben Butler's son-in-law, and the Democrats quickly decided that they needed to get the state readmitted to the Union. Ames was a West Point graduate and served with great distinction during the War, winning a medal of honor for his bravery at First Bull Run. He served in South Carolina immediately after the conflict, and though he did not like the unfriendliness of the native whites, Ames was no Radical. Colonel Ames was sent to Mississippi late in 1867 and promoted to brevet major general. His early experiences in the state began to turn him more toward the Radical position, and General Grant, who had known Ames during the War, secured his appointment as provisional governor when Gillem removed Humphreys. When Gillem left, Ames assumed the powers both of governor and of military commander.[91]

Ames was dedicated to a literal interpretation of the Reconstruction Acts and did not hesitate to remove from office all those who could not take the "iron clad" oath of July 2, 1862. He antagonized conservatives by removing nearly all the state officers, plus hundreds on the county and local level, including most of those holding office in Vicksburg.[92] In their places he appointed loyal men, many of whom were carpetbaggers or freedmen.[93] Con-

90. General Orders #10, March 5, 1869, Records of the War Department, U.S. Army Commands, Fourth Military District, 1867–1870, microfilm, MDAH; *Vicksburg Daily Times*, March 11, 1869.
91. Richard N. Current, *Three Carpetbag Governors* (Baton Rouge: Louisiana St. Univ. Press, 1967), 67–69; Blanche Ames Ames, *Adelbert Ames, 1833–1935* (New York: Argosy-Antiquarian, Ltd., 1964), 235, 240, 259, 269.
92. *Vicksburg Daily Times*, April 6, 23; May 4; August 13, 14, 26; November 7, 1869.
93. McNeily, "War and Reconstruction," 359; Garner, *Reconstruction in Mississippi*, 230–32.

gress had meanwhile passed a bill authorizing the President, at such time as he might desire, to resubmit the constitution to a vote, allowing a separate vote on any sections he might choose.[94]

In mid-July 1869, President Grant issued orders designating November 30 for the revote on the constitution and state offices and directing that separate votes be taken on three proscriptive clauses and on the provision forbidding the pledging of state credit to private endeavors.[95] The campaign was a spirited one, but the election itself was quiet. The constitution was adopted 113,735 to 955, the proscriptive clauses were overwhelmingly rejected, and a prohibition against pledging state credit won by a vote of 70,427 to 10,834. James L. Alcorn, a prominent member of the pre-War Whig Party, was elected governor.[96] Reconstructed to Congressional satisfaction, Mississippi reassumed her place in the Union, and Vicksburg ended its role as Headquarters of the Fourth Military District on February 20, 1870, when that organization ceased to exist.[97]

---

94. Garner, *Reconstruction in Mississippi*, 227–28.
95. *New York Times*, July 15, 1869, p. 1; Garner, *Reconstruction in Mississippi*, 238–39.
96. *New York Times*, December 2, 1869; Lillian A. Pereyra, *James Lusk Alcorn, Persistent Whig* (Baton Rouge: Louisiana St. Univ. Press, 1966), p. 376; J. L. Power, "The Black and Tan Convention," *Publications of the Mississippi Historical Society*, 3 (1900), 81–82.
97. General Orders #25, February 26, 1870, Records of the War Department, U.S. Army Commands, Fourth Military District, 1867–1870, microfilm, MDAH.

City of Promise

VICKSBURG, which had experienced fantastic growth after the siege was lifted in 1863, showed promise of becoming a substantial city in the post-War South. Orderly development, however, had been out of the question, for the population of the city had risen from 4,500 in 1860 to 50,000 late in the War, then had fallen to approximately 12,000 by the end of 1866.[1]

The civilian government of the city had been in suspension during the two years of occupation following July 1863. It was revived in July 1865, however, with the election of Thomas J. Randolph as mayor and Gerard Stites, A. A. Royall, E. R. Johnson, W. G. Binder, S. Spengler, Charles A. Manlove, and John Porterfield as members of the council.[2] All of these men were long-time residents of the area, and they had possessed considerable wealth in the pre-War period. The average of their real property in 1860 was $51,326; of their personal property it was $45,907.[3] Mayor Randolph was full-time, receiving $2,500 per year for his services while the seven councilmen were unpaid.[4]

---

1. U.S. Census Bureau, *Eighth Census of the United States, 1860: Population*, I, 271; *Census Returns, 1866, Sunflower, Tallahatchie, Tippah, Warren, Washington, and Wayne Counties*, RG 28, MDAH.
2. City of Vicksburg Minute Book, July 3, 1865, City Hall, Vicksburg, Mississippi.
3. 1860 Census of the Population (manuscript), Warren County.
4. City of Vicksburg Minute Book, July 5, 1865.

Washington Street — Vicksburg's main thoroughfare boasted many businesses, such as that of the Bavarian-born Max Kuner. Courtesy: *Harper's Weekly*

Though military rule had not been inefficient in Vicksburg, many problems confronted the new city administration. The streets were dilapidated; the city landing needed "immediate and extraordinary repairs"; and when the city hospital, which had been occupied by the military for two years, was given back to the city, it was found to consist only of "the bare and empty buildings . . . and the deserted ground on which they stood."[5]

Before any problems could be addressed, however, a source of revenue had to be found. Antebellum Vicksburg had depended largely on a real property tax, but the new administration discovered this to be a limited source both because of the dilapidated condition of many of the buildings and because many structures

5. *Ibid.*, March 15, and 16, 1866.

were still in the hands of U.S. Government lessees. "We were therefore compelled," noted the city council, "to look to the 'licenses' for the requisite funds to meet the demands."[6]

Fees were set at $500 per year for banks, brokers, and exchange offices; $500 for bars; $200 on Keno games; $50 on cotton brokers; $40 each on hotels and family groceries; $25 on hacks; and $10 on street peddlers. Wharf boats had to pay a $1 landing fee every time they touched the dock, plus a $10 per year license fee.[7]

New categories of fees were periodically added, rates for licenses were often amended, and the fee system yielded almost $100,000 per year to the city.[8] Residents of the city seemed to accept with no more than the usual grumbling the revenue measures imposed by their local government, but this was definitely not the case when in 1868 the Mississippi Constitutional Convention then meeting in Jackson levied a sweeping, statewide tax in support of its efforts. Section 8 of the Reconstruction Act of March 23, 1867, allowed this action as a means of paying for the convention, and the Mississippi group took full advantage of the provision.[9]

Taxes were levied on an enormous variety of goods and businesses including cotton gins, gristmills, railroads and distilleries, and the convention continued the practice of collecting a state sales tax by imposing a levy of $2.50 per $100 on the gross receipts of dry goods, grocery, drug, and provision stores. A bit later the group imposed a special tax of one-half percent on the value of the stock on hand in each of these stores.[10]

    6. *Ibid.*, March 16, 1866.
    7. *Ibid.*
    8. City Council Minute Book, April 9, 1866.
    9. U.S. Congress, House, Committee on Reconstruction, "Condition of Affairs in Mississippi," *Miscellaneous Documents of the House of Representatives for the Third Session of the Fortieth Congress,* 1868–69, p. 17.
    10. Mississippi, *Journal of the Proceedings in the Constitutional Convention of the State of Mississippi. 1868,* 71–73, 215–17.

City of Promise 207

Opposition to this taxation arose almost immediately in Vicksburg, the *Daily Times* urging citizens not to pay the taxes because it felt the convention had no constitutional right to levy such. Two weeks later, on February 1, 1868, a "Taxpayer's Meeting" took place in the city, at which speakers counseled resistance to the taxation attempt. The *Times* again advised the populace not to pay, stating with great confidence that if the appointed tax collector attempted to sell anyone's property to satisfy the tax, no one would bid upon it. Finally, three weeks after the controversy had begun, the collector attempted to seize the press of the *Daily Times* to fulfill the amount owed for taxes. The newspaper quickly secured an injunction against the action, and Vicksburg enjoyed a respite until May 24, when Gen. Alvan C. Gillem, commander of the Fourth Military District of Arkansas and Mississippi, ordered the county sheriffs to carry out the will of the convention. Some additional taxes were then paid.[11]

The vehemence with which the business community of Vicksburg resisted the convention's taxation effort can be attributed to several factors. Most obvious, of course, is that it was another form of taxation which came when the city was already heavily burdened with such. William T. McCardle, editor of the *Daily Times*, was outspoken against the tax, but even after the problem was temporarily resolved he asserted that "excessive taxation by the city is driving away business."

Taxes, however, continued to be a fact of existence in the city, and though one might be hard-pressed to discover the uses to which the Constitutional Convention put its levy, other than paying the salaries and per diem of its members, there is no such problem with the city of Vicksburg. The budget of the city was between $80,000 and $100,000 per year in the immediate post-War period, with most of the city's revenues, as previously indicated,

11. *Vicksburg Daily Times*, January 15, 1868; February 2, 4, 7, 9, 1868; Gillem to sheriffs, May 24, 1868, Fourth Military District, *Letters Sent, Volume 26, Civil Affairs*, p. 216, RG 98 (Miss.), NA.

coming from license fees or privilege taxes and most of its expenditures going into four areas: street repair, police protection, fire protection, and health and welfare.

The largest city expenditure in the years after the War was for street repair, a recurring nightmare for any city administration, then and now. The city made a valiant effort to maintain the public thoroughfares, but the steep hillsides of Vicksburg encouraged swift run-off from the frequent and heavy rains of the area, washing off the gravel and eroding the filled-in soil beneath. Private owners were responsible for their own sidewalks and gutters, but the city placed stepping stones at intersections, hauled in dirt and gravel for the streets, and generally devoted almost 50% of its revenues to the problem.[12] None of these efforts met with complete success, however, and citizen dissatisfaction surfaced periodically in the pages of the local press. "Awful ravines have been washed into the middle of . . . [Crawford] street," wrote one anonymous complainant in 1869, "rendering it entirely unfit for use, and every succeeding rain washes them still deeper. A perfect 'Niagara' of water rushes down the street, and [it is even worse] when we consider that this street is the principal thoroughfare to and from the river—nearly all the heavy hauling being done upon it."[13]

The second largest item in the city's budget was law enforcement, with about 30% of Vicksburg's revenues going to support a fifteen-man police force (at $75 each per month) and the city jail.[14] No one suggested, either, that too much was devoted to the police force, for Vicksburg had a serious crime problem in the years after the War, as during the antebellum period. The city's ability to cope with it, however, was inhibited by the refusal of General Slocum to return the Warren County jail to civil control.

12. *Vicksburg Daily Times*, May 7, September 17, December 3, March 16, 1866, and June 3, 1867. From March 19, 1866, to March 19, 1867, Vicksburg spent $39,885.79 on street repair from a total budget of $82,404.49.
13. *Vicksburg Daily Times*, April 30, 1869.
14. City of Vicksburg Minute Book, March 18, and June 3, 1867.

China Street Hill—Stepping stones were emplaced by the city, for few of Vicksburg's streets were hard-surface. This is the block between Mulberry and Washington streets. Over the hill was #15 China Street, a most elegant and infamous bordello. Courtesy: J. Mack Moore Collection, Old Court House Museum, Vicksburg

Slocum had issued in August 1865 his General Orders #11 which placed "the entire charge of municipal affairs . . . with the people." The general, nevertheless, would not relinquish the jail, and Mayor T. J. Randolph wrote heatedly to Gov. William Sharkey about the problem. "Our city is full of thieves," he stated, "both white and Black large numbers of them are brought before the Mayors Court for trial; many have been bound over for their appearance at the Circuit Court; I have repeatedly called on the Sherriff of the county to take charge of the State prisoners he *positively refused* to do so; while I am perfectly satisfied that the *slightest effort* on his part would get for the County the immediate possession of her jail now my dear sir I have at this time a very large number of these unfortunate persons crowded together in a small room in the City Work House; and if they are not *immediate* taken charge of by the proper authorities; common humanity will compel, me to run them out of a confinement which they can no longer endure; there by turning lose on our community a large band of notorious thieves."[15]

Sheriff Marmaduke Shannon, too, wrote Governor Sharkey about the problem, stating that General Slocum had rejected the idea of turning the jail over to him and had said that he "did not intend to give up the jail until all the troops left here."[16] A month later the sheriff still did not have a suitable facility in which to lodge his prisoners, and was threatening to turn them loose unless something were done.[17] Both Shannon and Randolph were especially concerned because the city was experiencing an increase in both petty crimes and felonies, and it did little good to apprehend the malefactors if there were no place to keep them.

15. T. J. Randolph to Governor Sharkey, September 17, 1865, RG 27, MDAH.
16. Marmaduke Shannon to Governor Sharkey, September 22, 1865, RG 27, MDAH.
17. Marmaduke Shannon to Gov. Benjamin Humphreys, October 18, 1865, RG 27, MDAH.

City of Promise 211

John Trowbridge commented on the criminality of the city when he passed through in December 1865. Of its 15,000 inhabitants, he stated, 8,000 were black, compared with 1860 totals of 1,433 blacks and 3,158 whites. Yet the Negro population did not commit nearly as many crimes as did the white. On Christmas day, for example, blacks made up only 5 of the 19 prisoners who were brought in; while the next day saw only 1 black among 10 who were incarcerated. "The usual proportion of white criminals," he stated, "was more than two third."[18] Testing this idea in the columns of the *Vicksburg Daily Times*, which reported happenings of the mayor's court, revealed that in fact Trowbridge was correct so far as minor crimes were concerned.

Proceedings of the municipal court appeared 15 times in issues of the *Vicksburg Daily Times* for 1866, 1868, and 1869.[19] A total of 87 cases was brought before the mayor on these occasions, of which 78 were for minor offenses punished by a fine of $5 or $10 or a few days in jail. Whites committed 58 of these crimes, while blacks were charged only 20 times.

Other interesting observations can be made from these proceedings, such as the disproportionate representation of the Irish-surnamed population in the mayor's court. Of the 58 whites who were convicted of misdemeanors, such as drunkenness, disorderly conduct, or fighting, 25 bore such names as Flannagan, Finnegan, Connelly, Donovan, Riley, and O'Shea. Women of Irish ancestry, too, were represented in the group, with Mary McDonald and Ann McGrancy appearing in the list for fighting.

There seems to have been little difference in the type of minor crimes for which blacks and whites were hauled into court, and punishments appear to have been fairly equal. A black man who used "abusive language" toward a white, however, was fined $5 plus court costs, while using "abusive language" toward another

18. Trowbridge, *The South*, 376.
19. Issues of the *Daily Times* for 1867 are not available.

black merited a fine of only $2.50.[20] It cost William Mitchell, who was black, $5 plus costs for striking another freedman; but William White, who was Caucasian, was fined $50 for "striking a colored man named Black," and George W. Carras, also Caucasian, was charged a similar amount for "getting on a spree and striking a colored man on the nose." Interestingly, Bolden McClane, a freedman, was fined $10 for "striking a colored woman."[21] In the Vicksburg of this era those who fought only with their own race and sex seemed to come out better in court.

A rather amusing crime which took place in December 1866 illustrates in part the continuing attitude of some white citizens that freedmen existed only to serve them. An arrogant planter from the Yazoo area rode up to the wharf on a big brown and white horse and handed the reins to a "boy" about 5'6" tall with "an old army coat on." Telling him something like "Hold this," the planter strode off. When he returned neither the "boy" nor his horse was anywhere around. He offered a $125 reward for return of his animal and conviction of the thief, but there is no record of those ever occurring.[22]

Examination of the criminal court docket for Warren County from 1865 through 1869 confirms the general trends established in the city court. Caucasians dominated the list, and though many of the citizens hauled before the circuit court were charged with such offenses as "Unlawful retailing" and "Unlawful gaming," the most common charge was larceny. Blacks were usually designated in the record by the initials "F.M.C." or "F.W.C.," meaning free man or woman of color, though some individuals, and these were presumably black, are listed only by their first names.

In addition to the usual crimes of larceny, assault, attempted murder, and even duelling, a particularly puritanical streak was evident in the charges listed. Mississippi law, for example, made

20. *Vicksburg Daily Times*, December 4, 5, 1865.
21. *Ibid.*, December 5, 6, 1866.
22. *Ibid.*, December 13, 1866.

City of Promise 213

it a crime to hunt or fish on Sunday, and 73 men found to their distress that Warren County's law enforcement officials were determined to enforce this prohibition.[23] Belle Forrest, Molly McDonald, Ellen Golden and other women likewise discovered that "keeping a disorderly house" would sometimes — but not always — result in arrest and a subsequent fine of $25-$50.[24] And the Bedenfield brothers, Faraby and Arthur, found that "cohabitation" was a punishable offense. The former was charged with "cohabiting with negro," while the latter was "cohabiting with white woman." The men were Caucasian.[25]

The Warren County jail was undoubtedly not the best or most luxurious place in which to lodge, but while he was sheriff, Marmaduke Shannon spent an average of $20 per month feeding each of his prisoners.[26] During 1867, however, and the early part of 1868 the council decided to crack down on crimes in the city and make the jail a less popular place in which to spend a cold winter's night. To this end the city marshal was authorized to purchase "six balls and chains to be used at workhouse," and the food ration for those in the workhouse was cut in half — to 30¢ per day, to consist of 22 ounces of bread and either 12 ounces of salt meat or 16 ounces of fresh.[27]

The city council then adopted a strong antivagrancy ordinance, based upon the idea that "idleness, if not itself a crime, has a wonderful tendency to demoralize and lead to habits of vice and immorality." The ordinance stated that "if any person shall be seen to stand about any of the streets of Vicksburg on three

---

23. Criminal Court Docket, Warren County; 1857 Miss. Code, Ch. 64, art. 229. Mississippi law still forbids such. 1972 Miss. Code (Ann.), §49-7-61.
24. Criminal Court Docket.
25. "Receipt of Dixon Sheriff for Prisoners in Jail, January 7, 1867," Crutcher-Shannon Papers, MDAH.
26. "Prisoners," March 1866, Crutcher-Shannon Papers, MDAH.
27. *Vicksburg Daily Times*, February 9, 20, 1868.

successive days, unemployed, not having any visible means of support, he shall be considered a vagrant." Further sections of the ordinance called upon "all good citizens" to report such idle individuals so that they could be "arrested and compelled to earn an honest living by their labor."[28] All these measures failed, however, to stem the growing crime rate in the river city, for a year later the *Daily Times* was still complaining that "thieves and burglars abound." Twelve such had been arrested the day before, stated the paper, and twenty-one the day before that.[29] The advice given by an innkeeper at Vicksburg to journalist John Dennett in March of 1866 remained valid throughout the years following the Civil War. "Gentlemen, I warn you," he had urged. "Take care of your money. . . . Let me beg you look out for your money."[30]

Arsonists, too, were a constant threat in the wooden cities of the nineteenth century, and Vicksburg was certainly no exception. Fires made a good distraction for the police and local officials, and the aftermath of incendiarism provided opportunities for looting. It was no wonder, then, that fire protection was the third largest item in the city budget, generally falling between 8% and 10% of the total.[31] The city administration decided in August 1865 to buy 1,500 feet of rubber fire hose and distribute it among the volunteer fire companies of Vicksburg, and a few months later it directed the removal of the wooden shacks which created a fire hazard on Levee Street.[32] The city also constructed public cisterns to provide a source of water to fight fires,[33] but preventing and extinguishing conflagrations, like the maintenance of good streets, was a goal which was never attained.

Winter, as might be expected, saw the greatest number of

28. *Ibid.*, February 22, 1868.
29. *Ibid.*, May 21, 1869.
30. Dennett, *The South*, 349.
31. City Council Minute Book, March 16, 1866, and June 3, 1867.
32. *Ibid.*, August 21 and November 20, 1865.
33. *Ibid.*, June 3, 1867.

fires because of the stoves which blazed away in every shop and dwelling. An arsonist apparently set fire to Shawver and Pollock's store in November 1866, but the blaze was extinguished before doing much damage. An accidental fire at R. Adam's house late in the same month was also controlled, but December saw a rash of fires, culminating in one just two days before Christmas.[34]

The blaze began about 8:00 P.M. in Hank Myers' house on Levee Street when a kerosene lantern exploded. This in itself could probably have been controlled; but the wind suddenly freshened, and Myers' house was wholly ablaze. An eye-witness described "the heavens . . . lit up with the glare and the air . . . filled with the crash of falling buildings" as the flames spread from one building to the next. Before the flames had spent themselves, houses and buildings on Levee, Mulberry, Washington, Clay, and Crawford streets — some seventy in all — had been destroyed by the blaze.[35]

Members of the 24th Regiment, stationed in the city, had turned out with fixed bayonets to help patrol the streets, and one of the soldiers shot and killed a white man who was attempting to loot a building. Peter Casey, a tavern keeper, killed two would-be robbers, though in the fray one of them managed to wound Casey; and two freedmen also lost their lives in shooting sprees.[36]

The fire itself caused an estimated $1,500,000 in property damage, while thieves and looters made off with an untold sum above that in portable goods. So much had been stolen during and after the fire that a committee of merchants requested that Mayor E. W. Wallin appoint a "committee of citizens" to search "every house in town" for pilfered articles. The mayor agreed to the request, and some searches were conducted, though without much success. Brig. Gen. N. A. M. Dudley cooperated with the

34. *Vicksburg Daily Times*, November 13 and 29, 1866.
35. *Hinds County Gazette*, December 28, 1866; *Vicksburg Daily Times*, December 27, 1866.
36. *Vicksburg Daily Times*, December 27, 1866.

citizens in this project by posting "guards at all the roads leading to the country, also at the landing, to prevent stolen goods being taken out of town."[37]

The U.S. troops stationed at Vicksburg came in for rare praise at a "Public Meeting" on December 24, when a resolution of thanks was unanimously adopted by the assembled citizens. In addition to lauding Generals Wood and Dudley for their "zealous and skillfully directed labors," the assemblage "Resolved, That the rank and file of the U.S. troops, who cordially cooperated with our citizens in trying to arrest the fire, by their good conduct, merit our appreciation and grateful acknowledgements."[38] Five Vicksburg merchants went a step further and presented General Dudley with the sum of $100, to be given to his command "as a slight appreciation of their services." The "enlisted men of the regiment," however, stated Dudley, wanted it given to the mayor "for the benefit of the 'Poor,' who suffered by the conflagration."[39]

The city council quickly voted $1,000 to help those who had suffered from the fire; twenty-six families in the city gave $560; Vicksburg's sister city of Natchez sent $500; and the City Hotel in New Orleans donated another $500.[40] The mayor was also directed by the council to solicit contributions for a new fire engine, which was presented to the Phoenix Fire Company in May.[41] An additional sum of $193.50 was soon voted by the council in payment of a bill for "whisky drank by firemen and soldiers on the night of 23rd December last,"[42] an expense which may explain why the blaze was not better contained.

The *Vicksburg Daily Times*, while lamenting the damage wrought by the fire, yet saw in its aftermath a hopeful sign. "The

37. *Ibid.*
38. *Ibid.*
39. *Ibid.*, December 30, 1866.
40. City Council Minute Book, December 24, 1866, and January 7, 1867.
41. *Ibid.*, January 7 and May 6, 1867.
42. *Ibid.*, February 4, 1867.

spirit of our citizens is progressive," stated editor McCardle, "and despite the depression in business — the uncertainty of National affairs — and the appalling calamity of the fire — the progress of the Hill City will be onward and upward. — Baptized and consecrated in the storm of war; standing out in bright relief upon the scroll of historic fame, Vicksburg will yet be true to her manifest destiny, and sit enthroned above the Father of Waters, a Queen City of the South."[43]

Within two months, even the *Daily Times* was feeling the effects of the fire, for all the newspapers in the city were forced to reduce their size because of the loss of advertising revenues from businesses damaged or destroyed in the blaze.[44] Soon, however, Louis Scharff, who sold ladies' wear in Vicksburg, took advantage of the situation and announced a sale of goods which were "more or less DAMAGED BY REMOVAL AT THE FIRE."[45] Incendiarism continued to plague the city over the next few years, so that by the spring of 1869 the city council voted to issue $7,000 in scrip to pay for an additional "steam fire engine,"[46] thus lessening somewhat the danger of conflagration.

The fourth major budget item for the city of Vicksburg, ranking behind street repairs, police protection, and fire protection, could broadly be termed "health and welfare." There is no "education" in the phrase, for public schools had not yet made their appearance in the city. The city hospital had been under military control for two years, and when it was returned to civilian hands in September 1865 the buildings had to be completely refurnished, a task which cost the city some $5,000.[47] This hospital was not available to indigent blacks, and in February 1866 the council agreed to share

43. *Ibid.*, December 28, 1866.
44. *Hinds County Gazette*, February 15, 1867.
45. *Ibid.*, March 8, 1867.
46. *Vicksburg Daily Times*, January 1, 3, 30, 1868; February 22, 1868; December 15, 1868; April 6, 1869.
47. City Council Minute Book, September 6, 1865, and March 15, 1866.

218   *Enclave: Vicksburg & Her Plantations*

equally with the Freedmen's Bureau in erecting a hospital for the "pauper black population." The city then agreed to assume the continuing cost of running it.[48] Indigents, both black and white, were a sizable expense to the city, for the regularly employed city sexton buried an average of twenty-three paupers per month from 1865 through 1869, the cost running almost $2,000 a year.[49]

In what seems to have been a burst of progressive spirit, the council authorized the mayor to pay for medicines prescribed for indigent citizens by physicians of the city; created a board of health consisting of two persons per ward; and employed more "city scavengers" to help clean the streets.[50] There was no municipal sewerage system, the wooden gutters which ran along the sides of the streets being the city's answer to drainage. Neither was there any system of piped-in water, and each family either had its own well or was dependent upon the public cisterns for drinking water.[51]

Vicksburg was not a refined city in 1865, nor was it one by 1870. Some visitors from other parts of the country, like John Dennett who visited the city in March 1866, were repelled by its rawness. Arriving in the city after dark, said Dennett, "It was not till the next morning that we could really perceive the repulsiveness of the place."[52] Packs of dogs did run wild through the town, and swine rooting in the gutters became so numerous that the city council was forced to outlaw their running loose;[53] but Vicksburg after the War was much as it had been before and during it: a river town barely bridled by the touch of civilization; a splendid place to make a fortune, or to lose one.

"The town is lively," stated a Methodist minister who visited

---

48. *Ibid.*, February 19, 1866.
49. *Ibid.*, March 16, 1866, January 21, 1867, April 13, 1869.
50. *Ibid.*, August 5 and May 7, 1866, and June 3, 1867.
51. *Ibid.*, March 16 and May 7, 1866.
52. Dennett, *The South*, 349.
53. City Council Minute Book, September 16 and November 27, 1867.

there shortly after the War. "A large number of Northern men have come here to open business houses, and Washington Street looks as if much trade was being carried on."[54] The Rev. J. P. Bardwell, however, was not so enthused by the business activity of the city, for he arrived in Vicksburg at 10:30 P.M. and was forced to sleep with eleven other men on the floor of a room in the Washington Hotel.[55]

There were difficulties in finding proper accommodations, for business in Vicksburg had simply outgrown the facilities available to travelers. Advertisements for the city's merchants appeared in newspapers across the state, with everything from monuments and tombstones ("satisfaction guaranteed") to "Old Monongahela" whiskey for sale, always at "the very best prices."[56] As historian William Harris put it, "No town in the state felt the impact of postwar commercial optimism as much as Vicksburg, the gateway to the southern alluvial region, and to several non-Delta counties in Mississippi and Louisiana."[57] The headquarters of the military district and the Freedmen's Bureau was there, and several regiments were mustered out at Vicksburg, adding their population as well as their savings to the city's growth.

The Bank of Vicksburg, boasting "a *steel* burglar and fireproof box," opened its doors in November 1866,[58] while the Vicksburg branch of the ill-fated Savings and Trust Company which was set up for freedmen's savings, received more deposits than did any other of the fifteen branches across the nation.[59] Col. Oliver Matthews built in the fall of 1866 a new saw mill, capable of

54. Quoted in McNeily, "War and Reconstruction," 246.
55. J. P. Bardwell to M. E. Strieby, November 4, 1865, AMA Papers (Miss.).
56. *Hinds County Gazette*, January 13, 1866; *Meridian Daily Clarion*, October 12, 1865.
57. Harris, *Presidential Reconstruction in Mississippi*, 220.
58. *Vicksburg Daily Times*, November 5, 1866.
59. U.S. Congress, Senate, Executive Document #27, pp. 122–23, 39th Congress, 1st Session.

processing 10,000-15,000 feet of lumber per day,[60] but for the years after 1865, cotton was the undisputed mainstay of the Vicksburg economy.

During July 1865, for example, a total of 15,733 bales of cotton was shipped off the Vicksburg wharves, a quantity which was matched in other good months.[61] One problem which plagued and hindered the cotton merchants during this time, however, was the poor freight train service from the east. The bridge across the Big Black River, twelve miles east of Vicksburg, had been destroyed during the campaign of 1863, and not until October 1865 did the Army succeed in erecting even a pontoon bridge across the stream.[62] Railroad service, however, was not a fast and dependable means of shipping freight or people between Vicksburg and Meridian even after service was officially restored.

An editorial in the *Hinds County Gazette* pointed out that "The detention which freight meets with between Vicksburg and this point [Raymond] with the rough useage and high rates, have conspired to turn the attention of our merchants and traders to the other route. It is now thought preferable to go to Byram and thence to New Orleans by the New Orleans Railroad, and the reverse, to trying the uncertainties and vexations of the Vicksburg route."[63] The published schedule for the Southern Railroad offered little refutation of the *Gazette*'s complaint, for it showed that the train left Vicksburg at 5:30 A.M. and was scheduled to arrive at Jackson at 10:15 A.M. — almost five hours to cover the 40 miles. Meridian, ninety miles east of Jackson, could be reached from that city in just over eight hours, assuming the train was on time. A standard joke, however, concerned the "accident" which took place on the Southern Railroad. It seems the train once made the run from Vicksburg to Jackson according to schedule.[64]

60. *Vicksburg Daily Times*, November 19, 1866.
61. *Meridian Daily Clarion*, August 8, 1865.
62. Harris, *Presidential Reconstruction in Mississippi*, 198.
63. *Hinds County Gazette*, January 13, 1866.
64. *Ibid.*, February 16, 1866.

The railroad's poor performance was not altogether the fault of the railroad officials, for the line had suffered greatly during the War. Not only was there no replacement of equipment until after the cessation of hostilities, but many Union generals, and especially Sherman, made the rail lines a special target. Dr. M. Emanuel, President of the Southern Railroad, explained that over 180,000 new crossties had been put into place in an attempt to restore service after the War, not counting the new rails and bridges necessary.[65]

The railroad, such as it was, however, was not the key to Vicksburg's commercial success in the years immediately following the War, though it did play a specific role in the city's economy. Perched on the greatest river on the continent, half-way between Memphis and New Orleans, situated astride the mouth of the Yazoo River, down which came cotton from the Mississippi Delta, Vicksburg's fortune lay with the steamboat, of which there was no dearth at the city's wharf. On the Mississippi, the *Magenta*, *Fashion*, *Quitman*, *Grey Eagle*, and *Robert E. Lee* plied the New Orleans trade; the *Dan Able* and *St. Patrick* went to Memphis; the *Welcome*, *Platte Valley* and *Rubicon* went all the way to St. Louis.[66] Among the smaller steamers, the *Calumet* went semi-weekly into the heart of the Delta, visiting Greenwood, Tchula, and Yazoo City; the *Hope* went to Yazoo City every other day; the *Emma No. 2* visited the same town on a tri-weekly basis; and the *Marmora* called at Skipwith's Landing semi-weekly. "Vicksburg," stated the *Daily Times*, "can boast of the finest packet lines in the country."[67]

The levee at Vicksburg fairly ran over with cotton, and boats like the *Robert E. Lee* could load 1,000 bales in one day and not even make a dent in the supply.[68] The smaller vessels which plied

65. Reprint of letter written to the *Vicksburg Herald* by M. Emanuel, found in RG 27, MDAH.
66. *Vicksburg Daily Times*, October 31, 1866; November 1, 1866.
67. *Ibid.*, November 1, 1866; October 31, 1866.
68. *Ibid.*, October 27, 1866.

Steamboat *Robert E. Lee* — This was perhaps the most famous boat on the Mississippi River, and it carried cargo as well as passengers when it called at Vicksburg. Courtesy: J. Mack Moore Collection, Old Court House Museum, Vicksburg

the interior waterways of the state brought out cotton to feed the larger ones, but there were many cotton-producing areas not traversed by navigable streams, and to bring cotton from these places to Vicksburg the railroad had to be called upon. Figures[69] supplied by George D. Lawrence, the general freight agent for the Southern Railroad, illustrate the decline of this business:

69. *Ibid.*, November 3, 1866.

Cotton Receipts for October at Vicksburg by Rail

1857	25,984 bales
1858	16,796 bales
1859	21,323 bales
1860	12,945 bales
1866	1,574 bales

Shippers in other parts of the state simply could not depend on the Southern Railroad, and as the *Hinds County Gazette* pointed out, they shipped their cotton to New Orleans on another line.[70]

Even shippers close to Vicksburg were at a disadvantage, for the public roads and highways were also in disrepair following the War. The antebellum system had depended on each property owner's furnishing a certain amount of labor for their upkeep, but this had been completely disrupted by the War. The board of police, analogous to present-day Mississippi's board of supervisors, was responsible for the county's administration, but it had great difficulty in securing the necessary support. Though each property owner was in theory still required to maintain the roads which passed through or by his land, in practice he did not.

Freedmen were sometimes compelled to work on the roads, but this system, too, proved less than satisfactory and met with great resistance on the part of the ex-slaves. The situation became bad enough by 1869 that a group of some seventy-five citizens from the neighboring counties of Hinds and Claiborne submitted to the Warren County board of police a petition for better roads. They were, said the petitioners, "desirous of hauling their cotton and produce to Vicksburg for sale and shipment but have found great difficulty in getting to and from said City owing to the almost impassable condition of the roads &c."[71]

The condition of the roads and lack of a dependable rail service boded ultimate ill for the city. But when the *Robert E. Lee* was floating at the wharf, gorging itself on cotton bales, few people could see an unfavorable future for Vicksburg.

70. *Hinds County Gazette*, January 13, 1866.
71. Minutes, Board of Police, Warren Co., microfilm, MDAH.

224   Enclave: Vicksburg & Her Plantations

The last two years of the decade were vital in shaping the future of the city. Vicksburg was in a strong position during this time, but her merchants did not push their advantage. According to one student, the city had a "virtual monopoly" of the cotton and provisions trade in the southern part of the Mississippi Delta. Northern manufacturers came there in hopes of eliminating the New Orleans middlemen and selling directly to the planter; and wholesalers and cotton buyers thronged the city. Foreign cotton buyers, too, descended upon the area, and one firm from Liverpool was soon handling much of the area's cotton.[72]

As the decade drew near its close the city once again felt the effects of poor rail service, and in 1869 the bridge across the Big Black River was out for several weeks, adding to the aggravation of those who tried to ship cotton and other goods into the city from other parts of the state.[73] The New Orleans, Jackson, and Great Northern Railroad, was the principal competitor to the Southern Railroad, which served Vicksburg from the east, and once again it was making it cheaper for planters to ship their cotton directly to New Orleans by rail rather than sending it to Vicksburg then down the river.[74]

Local newspapers saw and felt the decline in the city's economy as well as did anyone, and the editor of the *Daily Times* berated local merchants for their lack of aggressiveness. So lackadaisical and complacent had they become that merchants from the Memphis area were stealing trade all the way down to Yazoo City, and retailers from New Orleans, St. Louis, and even Cincinnati were moving into what formerly had been Vicksburg's exclusive business area.[75] It soon became obvious that the "Gibraltar of the Confederacy" would never fulfill the promise which earlier years had held out so teasingly.

72. Harris, *Presidential Reconstruction in Mississippi*, 222–24.
73. *Vicksburg Daily Times*, September 12, 1869.
74. Harris, "The Reconstruction of the Commonwealth," 555.
75. *Vicksburg Daily Times*, September 12, 1869.

Epilogue and Conclusion

THE READMISSION OF Mississippi into the Union had little visible effect upon Vicksburg and Warren County other than that of removing the last garrison of Federal troops. The city during the 1870s was still the lusty, brawling river town it had always been, and, if anything, it was wilder than before. A letter to the editor of the *Daily Times* in March 1870 complained of the city's "gambling houses and brothels," and urged that "if the evil cannot be stopped, let it be mitigated; if it cannot be eradicated, let it be licensed."[1] The mayor still held court each day and ruled on the guilt or innocence of the usual series of drunk and disorderly individuals, but an average day brought in even more persons than ever.[2] Edward King, who visited the city in 1873 on his tour through the Southern states, was appalled by Vicksburg. It had, he stated, "a not altogether enviable notoriety as a town where shooting on sight is a popular method of vengeance. . . . There is still rather too much of this barbarism remaining in Mississippi. . . . The Vicksburg method seems not to be the duel, but cold-blooded murder."[3]

In politics, the "Vicksburg ring," though not in the same

1. *Vicksburg Daily Times*, March 29, 1870.
2. *Vicksburg Daily Times and Republican*, July 9, 11, 14, 1871.
3. Edward King, *The Southern States of North America: A Record of Journeys* (London: Blackie & Son, 1875), 288–89.

financial league with the group at Tammany Hall, gave the city, in the measured words of historian James Garner, "as corrupt and incompetent a government as ever afflicted an Anglo-Saxon community."[4] According to Vernon Wharton, though, the city "seldom knew an honest government before the war, and has almost never had one since."[5] Nevertheless, county and city officials there indulged in such an orgy of extravagance and corruption that the more conscientious citizens of the community, white and black — but mostly white — organized a "taxpayer's league" to oppose the incumbents in the 1874 city elections. Passions ran high in the city, and semi-military groups paraded constantly back and forth through town in a show of strength. After much feinting and demonstrating the election took place on August 5 with few incidents, and the reform group was largely successful in its efforts.[6]

The Warren County Grand Jury had already indicted several county officials on charges of corruption. A county group quite similar in composition to the one which had been successful in the city then met in a taxpayer's convention and decided to remove from office some unindicted officials they believed to be corrupt, including the sheriff, the chancery clerk, and the coroner. Peter Crosby, the black sheriff of Warren County, at first refused to resign, so a group of some 500 persons descended upon the courthouse and forced him to accede to their wishes. Crosby went immediately to the state capital at Jackson to see Gov. Adelbert Ames, who advised him to return to Vicksburg and summon a posse to his aid. The sheriff thereupon sent notices to all of the black churches, asking their congregations for assistance, a call to which many persons responded. Sunday, December 6, 1874, was filled with false alarms, but the next day brought armed

4. Garner, *Reconstruction in Mississippi*, 328.
5. Wharton, *The Negro in Mississippi*, 171.
6. Garner, *Reconstruction in Mississippi*, 329–30; Wharton, *The Negro in Mississippi*, 171–72.

conflict between large groups of blacks and whites, as a result of which two whites and twenty-nine blacks were killed.[7]

The Vicksburg troubles continued for several weeks longer, during which time the county board of police ordered and held a special election to fill Crosby's office. The man selected in the contest, which was ignored by the black voters, was a Mr. Flannagan. He served less than three weeks in the post, however, for on January 18, 1875, Maj. George E. Head, acting on orders issued by Gen. Philip Sheridan, Commander of the Department of the Gulf, entered Vicksburg with a group of U.S. soldiers, ousted Flannagan, and reinstated Crosby as sheriff. Charges that Crosby was short in his accounts proved totally false, and he finished his term without further difficulty.[8] The entire episode, however, had damaged the Republican party in Mississippi by seeming to pit black against white and further diminished the waning popularity of Governor Ames. Though no lasting changes had resulted from the bloodshed at Vicksburg, the city once again had been the state's pioneer, for the conflict which occurred there in 1874 was a forerunner of similar events elsewhere in the state in 1875. Vicksburg was itself "redeemed" from Republican rule in 1875, again with the help of street violence and bloodshed. The difference this time was that the United States did not step in to reverse the outcome as it had done earlier in the year.[9]

Despite the rejoicing of many of her citizens over the change in the city's political alignment, Vicksburg had, as previously mentioned, already lost much of its preeminence in business and trade, so that soon enough she exerted less influence on affairs in the state. Part of this economic decline was certainly attributable

---

7. David G. Sansing, "Congressional Reconstruction," in *A History of Mississippi*, ed. Richard A. McLemore (Hattiesburg: University and College Press of Mississippi, 1973), 585; Garner, *Reconstruction in Mississippi*, 331–36.

8. Wharton, *The Negro in Mississippi*, 171–72.

9. *Ibid.*, 181–98.

Vicksburg, 1876 — View from the steeple of St. Paul's Catholic Church, looking toward the Court House. Courtesy: Mississippi Department of Archives and History

Epilogue and Conclusion 229

to the success of the New Orleans railroad, but merchants in the hill city believed too optimistically that once the Vicksburg, Shreveport, and Texas line was complete the city would become "one of the greatest railroad centers of the Southwest." The tracks, however, came too late to arrest Vicksburg's decline.[10] Then, too, even nature seemed to be working against the city. The Mississippi River, which for millenia had flowed south, then curled north and down past the city, suddenly changed. Just as it had done at Davis Bend a few years earlier, the river rose in the spring of 1876 and flowed across DeSoto Point, where U. S. Grant had spent so much time digging a canal in 1863. Just as at Davis Bend, the Mississippi chose not to return to its old channel when the water receded, but, following its natural tendency to shorten the distance to the sea, began flowing permanently across the point. As a result the waterfront at Vicksburg became silted-in, and steamboats were no longer able to dock at the foot of Crawford Street but had to unload their cargoes three-fourths of a mile from the business district.[11]

The railroad was many years in coming to Vicksburg from the west and the steamboat trade soon declined on the Mississippi. Vicksburg had promised greatness in the years following her near destruction by U. S. Grant. Her planters had been forced to learn early about the use of free black agricultural labor, and indeed many of her planters had been freedmen. Vicksburg had lost its opportunity, however, to become a great city in the South, though it had possessed more advantages than Memphis. Perhaps the merchants never were really in control of the area. Perhaps those obtuse, independent planters in Warren County who held out so long against the sharecrop system and who did not embrace the crop lien preferred to do their business with suppliers from New Orleans and Memphis. Perhaps their lack of dependence upon

10. Harris, *Presidential Reconstruction in Mississippi*, 209, 222.
11. Map File, Corps of Engineers, Vicksburg, Mississippi.

Vicksburg was what ultimately caused the city to fall short of its promise.

For the long-range political future, Vicksburg's status as an enclave does not seem to have made a great difference, for after the overthrow of the Reconstruction government in 1875, Republican votes were quite scarce in Warren County. Rutherford B. Hayes, for example, received only 623 votes in Warren County in 1876, while Grant had gotten 4,709 four years earlier. Republican voting, which was almost synonymous with black voting, showed an even more precipitous decline in 1880, falling to only 74 votes.[12] Long-term Union occupation, then, does not seem to have been of any benefit once the troops were removed, and there is no indication of any lasting black-white cooperation as a result of the force of Reconstruction.

Of infinitely more benefit to the area would have been land programs modeled after the experiment at Davis Bend, which with a bit of Government aid on the levees might ultimately have succeeded. Not all men were as capable as was Ben Montgomery, but there were undoubtedly many others whose effort could have met with success, had they been given the chance.

The "ifs" and "maybes" are plentiful in any study of the Reconstruction period, for it is, more than any other, the one short span of years which has the most influence on the present in Mississippi, and perhaps in the South. Vicksburg never reached its potential, and if we can ever fully understand the reasons for this, perhaps we will know why the whole area of which it is a part is still on the bottom in so many categories. To understand the cause is to reach toward the cure; and perhaps this study will be a part of that understanding.

---

12. Old Election Returns, RG 28, MDAH.

Selected Bibliography

MANUSCRIPT MATERIAL
Library of Congress
Samuel D. Barnes Papers
John Covode Papers
Benjamin Montgomery Family Papers
Slave Narrative Collection, Vol. IX (Rare Book Collection)
Booker T. Washington Papers

Louisiana State University; Baton Rouge, Louisiana
Henry D. Mandeville Family Papers

Mississippi Department of Archives and History; Jackson, Mississippi
James Allen Plantation Book, 1860–1865 (typescript), Nanechehaw Plantation, Warren County
Frank W. Battaile Papers
Charles-Crutcher-McRaven Papers
Crutcher-Shannon Papers (Marmaduke Shannon and Family)
Joseph E. Davis and Family Papers
Charles Delano Papers
Mrs. H. B. DeLonne Manuscript

Ellett-Jefferies Family Papers
Fonsylvania Plantation Diary, January 26– June 13, 1863 (Diary of Alfred Quine, Overseer)
Samuel G. French Papers
U. S. Grant Papers
William Burr Howell Collection
George Wilson Humphreys and Family Papers
James M. Kennard Papers
Lusk Family Papers
William H. McCardle Papers
J. Warren Miller Papers
George W. Modil Diaries, 1863–1864
C. A. Montross, "Plot of Vicksburg District for Leasing Abandoned Plantations, 1864," Map File
A. J. Paxton, Sr. Manuscript
Mahala P. H. Roach Memorandum, August 22, 1897
Swanson-Yates Family Papers
Alanda Timberlake Papers, "Experiences of Mrs. Eliza Ann Lanier during the Siege of Vicksburg. Written by herself. She 84 years old at the time"
Ida Barlow Trotter Papers
William T. Walthall Papers
Record Group 27, Governors Correspondence
Record Group 28, Records of the Secretary of State. Census Returns, 1866, *Sunflower, Tallahatchie, Tippah, Warren, Washington, and Wayne Counties*
Record Group 28, Old Election Returns (microfilm)
Record Group 47, Legislative Records, "Certificates of Election of Delegates to Convention (August 1865)"
Records of the War Department, U.S. Army Commands, Fourth Military District (Miss. and Ark.), 1867–1870 (microfilm)
Warren County Chancery Court Records (microfilm)

Southern Illinois University; Carbondale, Illinois
   Joseph Skipworth Papers

State Historical Society of Wisconsin; Madison, Wisconsin
   Samuel Glyde Swain Papers (microfilm copy also in Mississippi Archives)

Swarthmore College (Friends Historical Library); Swarthmore, Pennsylvania
   Edward F. Stratton Papers

University of North Carolina (Southern Historical Collection); Chapel Hill, North Carolina
   Roach-Eggleston Papers

University of Virginia; Charlottesville, Virginia
   Abraham Lincoln Papers (microfilm); originals in Library of Congress
   American Missionary Association Manuscripts (microfilm); originals at Dillard University, New Orleans, Louisiana

National Archives: Washington, D. C.
Eighth Census (1860), Slave Inhabitants, Mississippi, Vol. 5 (manuscript)
——(1860), Agriculture (manuscript) (Recorded production for 1859)
Ninth Census (1870), Agriculture (manuscript) (Recorded production for 1869)
Record Group 94 — Commission on Corrupt Practices in the South (Smith-Brady Commission)
Record Group 98 — War Department
   Department of the Tennessee, Letters Sent, Vol. 2
   Records of the U.S. Army Commands, Fourth Military District

Selected Bibliography

>*Book A, 1867*
>*Book A, 1868*
>*Letters Sent, Vol. 25, Civil Affairs*
>*Letters Sent, Vol. 26, Civil Affairs*
>*Record of the Election for the State of Mississippi, 1867*
>*Voter Registration and Report, Miscellaneous Civil Officers, Mississippi, 1867–1868*

Record Group 105 — Bureau of Refugees, Freedmen, and Abandoned Lands

>*Freedmen's Department, 1863–1865, Box 36, "Report of D. O. McCord, Med. Dir. & Insp. of Freedmen, Dept. of Miss."*
>*Freedmen's Department, Boxes 35 and 36A*
>*Davis Bend, 1865–1866, Box 39*
>*Boxes 54 and 54A*
>>*Endorsements, Provost Marshal, Vicksburg, Mississippi, 1865, Vol. 73*
>>*Criminal Docket, MAJOR T. S. Free, A.I.G., Vicksburg, Miss. 1865, Vol. 279*
>>*Civil Docket, Provost Court, E & M, MAJOR T. S. Free, A.I.G., Vol. 280*
>>*Pupils, Vol. 289* (consists of lists of pupils from January-May 1865)
>>*Morning Report, Freedmen's Hospital, Vicksburg, Mississippi March 20, 1864–March 1865*
>>*Register of Freedmen's Hospital, Vicksburg, Miss., 1863*
>>*Special Orders: Freedmen's Department (old organization) and Provost Marshal Genl. Freedmen May 3, 1864 to June 16, 1865*
>>*Henry Rowntree Letter Book and Record of Capt. Norton's Business, Davis Bend, Miss.*
>>*Davis Bend, Letters Received*
>>*Record Court of Freedmen, Davis Bend, Miss.*
>>*Record People, Home Colony Davis Bend, Miss., 1864*

Records of the Assistant Commissioner, State of Mississippi
Record Group 366 — Treasury Department,
  Second Special Agency
    Second Special Agency
      Natchez — Boxes 157, 213A
      Vicksburg — Boxes 123, 124, 222A

Vicksburg, Mississippi
U.S. Army Corps of Engineers, Map File
Old Court House Museum
  Crop Lien Records, Warren Co., 1867–73
  Provost Marshal Record Book, 1864–65
  Criminal Court Docket, 1865–69
City Hall
  City Council Minute Book, 1860–69

NEWSPAPERS

Copiah County News (Hazlehurst)
Daily Clarion (Meridian)
Daily Mississippian (Jackson & Meridian, Miss. & Selma, Ala.)
Daily Southern Crisis (Jackson)
Hinds County Gazette (Raymond)
Meridian Chronicle
Natchez Daily Courier
Natchez Democrat
Vicksburg Daily Herald
Vicksburg Daily Times
Vicksburg Daily Whig
Vicksburg Weekly Republican

GOVERNMENT RECORDS (PRINTED)

Mississippi. *Laws of the State of Mississippi Passed at a Called Session of the Mississippi Legislature held in the City of Jackson, October 1866 and January and February 1867*. Jackson: J. J. Shannon & Co., State Printers, 1867.

———. *Journal of the Proceedings and Debates in the Constitutional Convention of the State of Mississippi*, August 1865. Jackson: E. M. Yerger, State Printer, 1865.

———. *Journal of the Proceedings in the Constitutional Convention of the State of Mississippi, 1868*. Jackson: E. Stafford, Printer, 1871.

———. *Reports of Cases Argued and Determined in the Supreme Court, High Court of Errors and Appeals, and the Superior Court of Chancery of Mississippi*. St. Paul, Minn.: West Publishing Co., 1907.

———. "Tabular View of the Mississippi Legislature Begun and holden at the City of Jackson, on Monday, the 16th Day of October A.D. 1865." Broadsides Collection, Mississippi Department of Archives and History.

United States Congress. House of Representatives. 39th Congress. 1st Session. Executive Document #11, "Report of the Committee on the Bureau of Refugees, Freedmen, and Abandoned Lands."

———. House Report #30, "Joint Committee on Reconstruction."

———. House Executive Document #70, "Report of the Committee on the Bureau of Refugees, Freedmen, and Abandoned Lands."

———. 39th Congress. 2nd Session. House Executive Document #1, "Annual Report of the Secretary of War."

———. 40th Congress. 1st Session. House Document #20. "Report of the Adjutant General."

———. 40th Congress. 3rd Session. House Document #1. "Report of the Secretary of War."

———. 40th Congress. 3rd Session. House Committee on Reconstruction. "Condition of Affairs in Mississippi." *Miscellaneous Documents of the House of Representatives for the Third Session of the Fortieth Congress.*
United States Congress. Senate. 39th Congress. 1st Session. Senate Executive Document #2.
———. 39th Congress. 1st Session. Senate Executive Document #26.
———. 39th Congress. 1st Session. Senate Executive Document #27, "Reports of Asst. Commissioners of the Bureau of Refugees, Freedmen, and Abandoned Lands since December 1, 1865."
———. 39th Congress. 1st Session. Senate Report #126. "Levees Along the Mississippi."
———. 39th Congress. 2nd Session. Senate Executive Document #6. "Reports of Asst. Commissioners of Freedmen."
United States Department of the Interior. Bureau of the Census. *Population of the United States in 1860: Compiled from the Original Returns of the Eighth Census, Under the Direction of the Secretary of the Interior.* Washington: Government Printing Office, 1864.
United States Department of Commerce. Bureau of the Census. *1970 Census of the Population: Mississippi.* Washington: Government Printing Office, 1970.
The War of the Rebellion: A Compilation of the Official Records of the Union and Confederate Armies. 73 vols, 128 parts. Washington: Government Printing Office, 1880–1901.

PRINTED MEMOIRS, DIARIES, CONTEMPORARY ACCOUNTS

Abernethy, Byron R., ed. *Private Elisha Stockwell, Jr. Sees the Civil War.* Norman: University of Oklahoma Press, 1958.

Selected Bibliography

Abrams, Alexander S. *A Full and Detailed History of the Siege of Vicksburg.* Atlanta: Intelligencer Steam Power Presses, 1863.

Anderson, John Q., ed. *Brokenburn: The Journal of Kate Stone, 1861–1868.* Baton Rouge: Louisiana State University Press, 1955.

[Benham, George Chittenden]. *A Year of Wreck: A True Story; by a Victim.* New York: Harper & Brothers, 1880.

Bettersworth, John K., ed. *As They Saw It.* Vol. I of *Mississippi in the Confederacy.* 2 vols. Baton Rouge: Louisiana State University Press, 1961.

Boney, F. N., ed. and annotator. *A Union Soldier in the Land of the Vanquished: The Diary of Sergeant Mathew Woodruff, June-December, 1865.* University, Alabama: University of Alabama Press, 1969.

Cable, George Washington, ed. "A Woman's Diary of the Siege of Vicksburg," *Century Magazine*, 30 (September 1885), 767–75.

Cate, Wirt Armistead, ed. *Two Soldiers: The Campaign Diaries of Thomas J. Key, C.S.A. and Robert J. Campbell, U.S.A.* Chapel Hill: University of North Carolina Press, 1938.

Davis, Varina Howell. *Jefferson Davis, Ex-President of the Confederate States of America: A Memoir by His Wife.* 2 vols. New York: Belford Company Publishers, 1890.

Dennett, John Richard. *The South As It Is: 1865–1866.* Henry M. Christman, ed. New York: The Viking Press, 1965.

Eaton, John. *Grant, Lincoln, and the Freedmen.* New York: Longmans, Green and Company, 1907.

Edmonds, S. Emma E. *The Female Spy of the Union Army.* Boston: De Wolfe, Fiske & Co., Publishers, 1864.

Elder, Bishop William Henry. *Civil War Diary (1862–1865) of Bishop William Henry Elder Bishop of Natchez.* R. O. Gerow, ed. N.p., n.d.: Most Reverend R. O. Gerow.

French, Gen. Samuel Gibbs. *Two Wars: An Autobiography of*

Gen. Samuel G. French. Nashville: Confederate Veteran, 1901.
Grant, U. S. *Personal Memoirs of U. S. Grant.* 2 vols. New York: Charles L. Webster & Company, 1885.
Grigsby, Melvin. *The Smoked Yank.* Sioux Falls: Dakota Bell Publishing Co., 1888.
Hepworth, George H. *The Whip, Hoe and Sword; or the Gulf Department in '63.* Boston: Walker, Wise and Company, 1864.
Howard, Oliver Otis. *Autobiography of Oliver Otis Howard, Major General United States Army.* 2 vols. New York: The Baker & Taylor Co., 1907.
King, Edward. *The Southern States of North America: A Record of Journeys.* London: Blackie & Son, Paternoster Buildings, E. C., 1875.
Knox, Thomas W. *Camp-Fire and Cotton-Field.* Philadelphia: Jones Bros. and Co., 1865.
Kuner, Max. "Vicksburg and After: Being the Experience of a Southern Merchant and Non-Combatant during the Sixties," arr. by Edwin L. Sabin, *The Sewanee Review*, 15 (October 1907), 485–96.
Livermore, Mary A. *My Story of the War: Woman's Narrative of Four Years Personal Experience as Nurse in the Union Army, and in Relief Work at Home, in Hospitals, Camps and at the Front, during the War of the Rebellion.* Hartford: A. D. Worthington and Company, 1889.
Lynch, John Roy. *Reminiscences of an Active Life: The Autobiography of John Roy Lynch.* Ed. John Hope Franklin in the Negro American Biographies and Autobiographies series. Chicago: University of Chicago Press, 1970.
Morgan, Albert T. *Yazoo; Or, On the Picket Line of Freedom in the South.* N.p.: by the author, 1884.
Osborn, George C., ed. "The Civil War Letters of Robert W. Banks," *Journal of Mississippi History*, 5 (July 1943), 141–54.

Power, John L. "The Black and Tan Convention," *Publications of the Mississippi Historical Society,* 3 (1900), 73–84.
Reid, Whitelaw. *After the War: A Tour of the Southern States, 1865–1866.* Ed. C. Vann Woodward. New York: Harper & Row, Publishers, Harper Torchbooks, 1965.
Rowland, Dunbar., ed. *Jefferson Davis: Constitutionalist. His Letters, Papers and Speeches.* 10 vols. Jackson: Mississippi Department of Archives and History, 1923.
Sherman, William T. *Memoirs of General William T. Sherman.* 2nd ed., rev. New York: D. Appleton and Company, 1887.
Smedes, Susan Dabney. *Memorials of a Southern Planter.* Ed. Fletcher M. Green. New York: Alfred A. Knopf, 1965.
Strode, Hudson., ed. *Jefferson Davis: Private Letters, 1834–1889.* New York: Harcourt, Brace & World, Inc., 1966.
Taylor, Richard. *Destruction and Reconstruction: Personal Experiences Of the Late War.* Ed. Richard B. Harwell. New York: Longmans, Green and Co., 1955.
Trowbridge, John T. *The South, A Tour of its Battlefields and Ruined Cities, A Journey Through the Desolated States, and Talks with the People, etc.* Hartford: L. Stebbins, 1866.
United States Sanitary Commission, Western Department. *The U.S. Sanitary Commission in the Valley of the Mississippi, during the War of The Rebellion, 1861–1866. Final Report of Dr. J. S. Newberry, Secretary.* Cleveland: Fairbanks, Benedict & Co., 1871.
Vilas, William Freeman. *A View of the Vicksburg Campaign.* Madison, Wisc.: Wisconsin History Commission: Original Papers, No. 1 (August 1908).
Wells, Seth J. *The Siege of Vicksburg from the Diary of Seth J. Wells, including Weeks of Preparation and of Occupation After the Surrender.* Detroit: Wm. H. Rowe, Publisher, 1915.
Winther, Oscar Osburn, ed. *With Sherman to the Sea: The Civil War Letters, Diaries, & Reminiscences of Theodore F. Upson.* Bloomington: Indiana University Press, 1958.

Yeatman, James E. *A Report on the Condition of the Freedmen of the Mississippi presented to the Western Sanitary Commission, Dec. 17, 1863.* St. Louis: N.p., 1864.

SECONDARY MATERIALS (PRINTED)

Ames, Blanche Ames. *Adelbert Ames, 1833–1935.* New York: Argosy-Antiquarian, Ltd., 1964.
Badeau, Adam. *Military History of Ulysses S. Grant, from April 1861 to April 1865.* 2 vols. New York: D. Appleton and Company, 1885.
Beasley, Jonathan. "Blacks — Slave and Free — Vicksburg, 1850– 1860," *Journal of Mississippi History*, 38 (1976), 1–32.
Bettersworth, John K. *Confederate Mississippi: The People and Policies of a Cotton State in Wartime.* Baton Rouge: Louisiana State University Press, 1943.
Bigelow, Martha M. "Vicksburg: Experiment in Freedom," *Journal of Mississippi History*, 26 (1964), 28–44.
Bragg, Jefferson D. *Louisiana in the Confederacy.* Baton Rouge: Louisiana State University Press, 1941.
Brandfon, Robert L. *Cotton Kingdom of the New South. A History of the Mississippi Delta from Reconstruction to the Twentieth Century.* Cambridge, Mass.: Harvard University Press, 1967.
Carpenter, John A. *Sword and Olive Branch: Oliver Otis Howard.* Pittsburgh: University of Pittsburgh Press, 1964.
Catton, Bruce. *Grant Moves South.* Boston: Little, Brown & Company, 1960.
Cornish, Dudley Taylor. *The Sable Arm: Negro Troops in the Union Army, 1861–1865.* New York: Longmans, Green and Co., 1956.
Coulter, E. Merton. "Commercial Intercourse with the Confederacy in the Mississippi Valley, 1861–1865," *Mississippi Valley Historical Review*, 5 (1919), 377–95.
Cox, La Wanda. "The Promise of Land for the Freedmen," *Mis-

sissippi Valley Historical Review, 55 (December 1958), 413–440.

Current, Richard N. *Three Carpetbag Governors*. Baton Rouge: Louisiana State University Press, 1967.

Currie, James T. "The Beginnings of Congressional Reconstruction in Mississippi," *Journal of Mississippi History*, 35 (August 1973), 267–286.

Davis, Ronald L. F. "The U.S. Army and the Origins of Sharecropping in the Natchez District — A Case Study," *Journal of Negro History*, 62 (January 1977), 60–80.

Everett, Frank E., Jr. *Brierfield: Plantation Home of Jefferson Davis*. Hattiesburg, Miss.: University and College Press of Mississippi, 1971.

Fairman, Charles. *History of the Supreme Court*, Vol. 6. *Reconstruction and Reunion, 1864–1888*, Part 1. New York: Macmillan, 1971.

Fleming, Walter L. "Jefferson Davis, the Negroes and the Negro Problem," *Sewanee Review*, 16 (October 1908), 407–27.

Franklin, John Hope. *From Slavery to Freedom: A History of Negro Americans*, 3rd. ed. New York: Random House, Vintage Books, 1969.

Futrell, Robert F. "Efforts of Mississippians to Encourage Immigration, 1865–1880," *Journal of Mississippi History*, 20 (April 1958), 59–76.

Garner, James W. *Reconstruction in Mississippi*. New York: Macmillan, 1901.

Gerteis, Louis S. *From Contraband to Freedman: Federal Policy Toward Southern Blacks, 1861–1865*. Westport, Conn.: Greenwood Press, Inc., 1973.

Giles, William Lincoln. "Agricultural Revolution, 1890–1970," *A History of Mississippi*. 2 vols. Richard A. McLemore, ed. Hattiesburg, Miss.: University and College Press of Mississippi, 1973, II, 177–211.

Halsell, Willie D. "A Vicksburg Speculator and Planter in the

Yazoo Delta," *Journal of Mississippi History*, 11 (October 1949), 231–42.
Harris, William C. *Presidential Reconstruction in Mississippi*. Baton Rouge: Louisiana State University Press, 1967.
———. "The Reconstruction of the Commonwealth," *A History of Mississippi*. 2 vols. Richard A. McLemore, ed. Hattiesburg, Miss.: University and College Press of Mississippi, 1973, I, 542–70.
Hesseltine, William B. *Lincoln's Plan of Reconstruction*. Tuscaloosa, Ala.: University of Alabama Press, 1960.
Hoehling, A. A., and the Editors, Army Times Publishing Company. *Vicksburg: 47 Days of Siege*. Englewood Cliffs, N. J.: Prentice-Hall, Inc., 1969.
In and About Vicksburg. An Illustrated Guidebook to the City of Vicksburg, Mississippi. Its History: Its Appearance: Its Business Houses. Vicksburg: Gibraltar Publishing Co., 1890.
Klingberg, Frank W. *The Southern Claims Commission*. Berkeley: University of California Press, 1955.
Kolchin, Peter. *First Freedom: The Responses of Alabama's Blacks to Emancipation & Reconstruction*. Westport, Conn.: Greenwood Press, Inc., 1972.
Korn, Bertram Wallace. *American Jewry and the Civil War*. Philadelphia: The Jewish Publication Society of America, 1951.
Kutler, Stanley, "*Ex Parte McCardle*: Judicial Impotency? The Supreme Court and Reconstruction Reconsidered," *American Historical Review*, 72 (1967), 835–57.
The Leading Afro-Americans of Vicksburg, Miss. Their Enterprises, Churches, Schools, Lodges and Societies. Vicksburg: Biographia Publishing Co., 1908.
McFeely, William S. *Yankee Stepfather: General O. O. Howard and the Freedmen*. New Haven: Yale University Press, 1968.
McLemore, Richard A., ed. *A History of Mississippi*. 2 vols. Hattiesburg, Miss.: University and College Press of Mississippi, 1973.

McNeily, J. S. "War and Reconstruction in Mississippi, 1863–1890," *Publications of the Mississippi Historical Society, Centenary Series*, II (1918), 165–535.

Miers, Earl Schenck. *The Web of Victory: Grant at Vicksburg*. New York: Alfred A. Knopf, 1955.

Moore, John Hebron. *Agriculture in Ante-Bellum Mississippi*. New York: Bookman Associates, 1958.

Morse, W. E., Sr. "The Fight of Jefferson Davis over the Will of His Brother, Joseph E. Davis, for his Home, 'Brierfield,'" *Journal of Mississippi History*, 33 (May 1971), 141–48.

Murphree, Dennis. "Hurricane and Brierfield, the Davis Plantations," *Journal of Mississippi History*, 9 (April 1947), 98–107.

Pereyra, Lillian A. *James Lusk Alcorn, Persistent Whig*. Baton Rouge: Louisiana State University Press, 1966.

Philippsborn, Gertrude, *The History of the Jewish Community of Vicksburg (from 1820 to 1968)*. Vicksburg: N.p., 1969.

Powdermaker, Hortense, *After Freedom: A Cultural Study in the Deep South*. New York: The Viking Press, 1939.

Quarles, Benjamin. *The Negro in the Civil War*. Boston: Little, Brown and Co., 1953.

Randall, James G. and David Donald. *The Civil War and Reconstruction*. Rev. ed. Boston: D. C. Heath and Co., 1961.

Ransom, Roger L. and Richard Sutch. *One Kind of Freedom: The Economic Consequences of Emancipation*. Cambridge: Cambridge University Press, 1977.

Roberts, A. Sellew. "The Federal Government and Confederate Cotton," *American Historical Review*, 32 (January 1927), 262–75.

Roland, Charles P. *Louisiana Sugar Plantations during the American Civil War*. Leiden, Netherlands: E. J. Brill, 1957.

Rose, Willie Lee. *Rehearsal for Reconstruction: The Port Royal Experiment*. New York: Vintage Books, 1964.

Sansing, David G. "Congressional Reconstruction," *A History of Mississippi*. 2 vols. Richard A. McLemore, ed. Hattiesburg, Miss.: College and University Press of Mississippi, 1973, I, 571–89.
Sefton, James E. *The United States Army and Reconstruction, 1865–1877*. Baton Rouge: Louisiana State University Press, 1967.
Silver, James W. *As Seen In Retrospect*. Vol. II of *Mississippi in the Confederacy*. Baton Rouge: Louisiana State University Press, 1961.
Singletary, Otis A. *Negro Militia and Reconstruction*. Austin: University of Texas Press, 1957.
Smith, Frank E. *The Yazoo River*. New York: Rinehart & Co., Inc., 1954.
Swint, Henry Lee. *The Northern Teacher in the South, 1862–1870*. Nashville: Vanderbilt University Press, 1941.
Sydnor, Charles S. *Slavery in Mississippi*. Baton Rouge: Louisiana State University Press, 1966.
Walker, Peter F. *Vicksburg: A People at War, 1860–1865*. Chapel Hill: University of North Carolina Press, 1960.
Warren, Charles. *The Supreme Court in United States History*. New and revised ed., 2 vols. Boston: Little, Brown & Co., 1926.
Watkins, James L. *King Cotton: A Historical and Statistical Review, 1790–1908*. New York: James L. Watkins & Sons, 1909.
Wesley, Charles H. *Negro Labor in the United States, 1850–1925: A Study in American Economic History*. New York: Russell & Russell, 1927.
Wharton, Vernon L. *The Negro in Mississippi, 1865–1890*. New York: Harper & Row, Publishers, Harper Torchbooks, 1965.
Wiley, Bell I. *Southern Negroes, 1861–1865*. New Haven: Yale University Press, 1938.
———. "Vicissitudes of Early Reconstruction Farming in the

Lower Mississippi Valley," *Journal of Southern History*, 5 (1937), 441–52.
Woodman, Harold D. *King Cotton and His Retainers: Financing & Marketing the Cotton Crop of the South, 1800–1925.* Lexington: University of Kentucky Press, 1968.
Woodward, C. Vann. *Origins of the New South, 1877–1913.* 2nd ed. Baton Rouge: Louisiana State University Press, 1971.
Works Progress Administration. *Mississippi: A Guide to the Magnolia State.* New York: Viking Press, 1938.

UNPUBLISHED DISSERTATIONS & THESES

Currie, James T. "Conflict and Consensus: Creating the 1868 Mississippi Constitution." Unpublished M.A. Thesis, University of Virginia, 1969.
Eubank, Sever Landon. "The McCardle Case: A Challenge to Radical Reconstruction." Unpublished Ph.D. Dissertation, George Peabody College for Teachers, 1954.
Jackson, Maurice Elizabeth. "Mound Bayou: A Study in Social Development." Unpublished M.A. Thesis, University of Alabama, 1937.
Moore, Ross H. "Social and Economic Conditions in Mississippi during Reconstruction." Unpublished Ph.D. Dissertation, Duke University, 1937.
Qualls, Youra Thelma. "Friend and Freedman: The Work of the Association of Friends of Philadelphia and Its Vicinity for the Relief and Education of Freedmen during the Civil War and Reconstruction, 1862–1872." Unpublished Ph.D. Dissertation, Harvard University, 1955.
Sansing, David Gaffney. "The Role of the Scalawag in Mississippi Reconstruction." Unpublished Ph.D. Dissertation, University of Southern Mississippi, 1969.

Index

Abrams, Alexander, 4
Adams County, Miss., 95
Adams, R., 215
Adams Street, xiv
Adams, Wirt, 201
Alabama, xx, 95
Alcorn, James L., 203
Allen, James.
  See Plantations, Nanechehaw
Allen, John, 184
American Missionary Association: missionaries from, 35; and schools, 37, 153, 192–93; and Congregationalists, 38; and lessees, 38; and Davis Bend, 95; mentioned, 63, 188, 190
Ames, Adelbert, 202, 226, 227
Anderson, William, 6
Anderson, William B., 24
Army worm: why so named, 66–67; attempts to control, 67; destruction of crops by, 67, 100, 156, 173; at Davis Bend, 120, 128–29, 132–33, 137
Arthur, A. H., 185
Association (at Davis Bend), 122–23, 126
Atkins, W. P., 147n

Baker, Mary O., 35–36
Balkston, H.J., 29
Banks, Gen. N.P., 61

Bardwell, Rev. J.P.: describes white refugees, 34; comments on black lessees, 76; and freedmen, 188; and conditions in Vicksburg, 219; mentioned, 193
Barnes, Samuel D., 95–96, 105
Beaulings, Lucy, 4
Beckwith, Miss (missionary), 35
Bedenfield, Arthur, 213
Bedenfield, Faraby, 213
Bedford, M.E.S., 105, 111, 112
Bell, John, xvii
Benham, George C., 59, 157
Big Black Island, 94
Big Black River: plantation near, 158, 159; flooding along, 175; bridge over, 220, 224; mentioned, 92
Binder, W.G., 204
Birchett, Judge (at Vicksburg), 148
Black Code: provisions of, 149, 153, 187–88; enactment of, 187; whites opposed to, 188
Blumensteil (Vicksburg citizen), 17
Bobb, John H., 26
Bodford, Elisha, 146
Bolivar County, Miss., 141, 155
Bond, H.L. (family), 7
Bonnie, Mrs. C.R., 7
Bowie, A.T., 160

247

248 *Index*

Boyle, Joseph H., 29
Brady, James T. *See* Commission on Corrupt Practices in the South
Breckinridge, John C., xvii
Brierfield. *See* Plantations
Broom straw, 137
Brown, M.T., 6n
Brown, Thomas, 28
Buck, R.S., 148
Bull Run, First Battle of, 202
Bureau of Refugees, Freedmen, and Abandoned Lands. *See* Freedmen's Bureau
Burns, Thomas, 28
Burwell, Armistead, 4
Butler, Gen. Benjamin, 32
Byram, Miss., 220

Cable, Simon, 102
Callicott, Thomas C., 16, 17, 18
Calvin (Shannon's slave), 46
Campbell, Judge Josiah A.P., 183
Canby, Maj. Gen. E.R.S., 66
Canton, Miss., 193
Carpetbaggers, 156, 157
Carras, George W., 212
Carroll Parish, La., 66
Carruthers, Chaplain, 51–52, 53
Casey, Peter, 215
Caves, 14, 15
"Cedar Grove," xv
Census of Agriculture, 165, 166
Chase, Salmon P., 15
Cherry Street, xiv
Chickasaw Bayou, xix
China Street, xiv, 209
Chinese, 175–76
Churches:
—African Methodist Episcopal, 50, 197–98
—Episcopal, 5, 191
—Presbyterian, 22
—St. Paul's Catholic, 228
—United Brethren, 40
—United Presbyterian, 38
Cincinnati, 11, 224
Cincinnati Contraband Relief Commission, 36
Civil Rights Act, 155, 160
City Council (of Vicksburg), 25, 204
Claiborne County, Miss., 223
Claiter, Mrs. G., 6n
Clay Street, xiv, 215
Clayton, Judge Alex M., 183
Clinton, Miss., 24
Coahoma County, Miss., 155
Cohen, Moses, 17, 18
Coleman, Jenny, 28
Collier, J.D., 147, 148
Colored Planters of the Hurricane Plantation," 109–10
Columbus, Miss., 169, 183
Commission on Corrupt Practices in the South, 68
Confederacy, xix, 83, 199
Congressional Reconstruction, 157, 197
Constitutional Convention: of 1865, 146, 186; of 1868, 71, 195, 206, 207; of 1890, 184
Contracts; consequences of breaking, 155; and planters, 156; and freedmen, 157, 174–75; agricultural, 161. *See also* Crop lien
Cook, T.K., 28
Cook, Mrs. T.K., 28
Corliss, Lt. G.W., 154–55
Corn, 90, 135, 174
Cornwell, Maj. S., 53
Cotton: Mississippi production of, 55, shipping of, 68; difficulties of raising, 72–73; at Davis Bend, 111, 114, 129, 137, 138; price of, 112, 162, 166; crop of 1867, 130; crop of 1866, 156; as payment for lease, 159; crop of 1868, 174; sent to exhibition, 176
Couch, Capt. (provost marshal), 186
Courts: replacement of civilian judges in, 25; citizens of Vicksburg petition

Index 249

about, 30; and freedmen, 179–83, *passim*
Covode, John, 74
Crawford Street, xiv, 208, 215, 229
Crimes: drunkenness, 24–25; statistics on, 26; by civilians, 28, 29; cruelty to animals, 29; wife beating, 29; by soldiers, 46; fraud, 79, 113, 116; on Davis plantations, 87; at Davis Bend, 134; in Vicksburg, 210, 213; vagrancy, 213–14; arson, 214; prostitution, 225. *See also* under specific types of crime. *See also*, Soldiers.
Crop lien: suggested, 160; enacted, 161; in Warren County, 161–67; mentioned, 177
Crosby, Peter, 226, 227

Dabney, Thomas, 140
Daily Clarion (Jackson), 200
Dana, George, 7
Dana, Gen. N.J.T.: and citizens of Vicksburg, 6, 7; and price controls, 11, 12; and smuggling, 18, 70; criminal court system of, 30; and schools, 40; and guerrillas, 66; and Davis Bend, 100–101; mentioned, 25
Dana, Mrs. N.J.T., 8
Daughters of Zion, 50
Davenport, Daniel, 102
Davis Bend: marriage performed at, 49; and U.S. Grant, 83; condition of slaves at, 91; freedmen at, 91, 106–07; legal system at, 91, 101–03; defensive advantages of, 92; Home Farm at, 92, 94–95; rules governing, 92–94, 101; cotton crop at, 100, 111, 120, 132–33, 137–38; profits of Freedmen at, 100; number of freedmen at, 104; insects at, 109; report to Congress of experiment at, 114–15; closing of military post at, 114; closing of hospital at, 119; registration of voters at, 130; Wood plantation at, 131; present condition of, 142; isolation of, 145; mentioned, 82, 145, 156, 229, 230
Davis Island, 127
Davis, Jefferson: plantation of, 83; becomes Confederate President, 88; poem about, 97; imprisonment of, 121; and Benjamin Montgomery, 134; and lawsuit against Joseph Davis' will, 140–41; mentioned, 4
Davis, Joseph: plantation of, 83; slaves of, 83; picture of, 89; leaves Davis Bend, 90; pardoning of, 115, 121; sells plantation, 121–22; and ex-slaves, 125; will of, 136–37; death of, 140; mentioned, 91, 92, 145, 160
Davis, Varina Howell, 85
Deer Creek, 74
Deer Creek Planters Association, 72
Delta: planters in, 79, 155; plantation in, 146; floods in, 158; gateway of, 219; steamboats in, 221; trade in, 224; mentioned, 68, 173
Democrats, 186–87, 199
De Moss, Ada, 7
Dennett, John, 214, 219
Dennis, Gen. (Union Army), 63
Department of the Gulf, 61, 227
DeSoto Point, 229
Disease, 13, 38, 54
Dixie, 24
Dixon, M.H., 195
Dobson (planter), 59
Donaldson, Lieut. Col. R.S., 109, 181
Douglas, Stephen, xvii
Dowling, Justice A.M., 182
Drane, Amos, 194
Dudley, Gen. N.A.M., 215–16
Dugan, James, 196

Eagle Lake, 73
Eaton, Col. John: appointment of, xxiv; and refugee relief, xxiv, xxvi; photograph of, xxv; and freedmen, 34, 47, 50, 51, 62, 77; and relief efforts, 35;

Index

and missionaries, 36; and schools, 42, 43; and lessees, 57; and Davis Bend, 98, 102, 103, 142; mentioned, 60
Eggleston, Elizabeth, 7, 8
Elder, Bishop William Henry, 34, 59–60
Emanuel, Dr. M., 7n, 221
Enrolled Militia of the District of Vicksburg, 184–85
Enterprise, Ala., 145

Farragut, Adm. David G., xx, 88, 90
Farrar, A.K., xxn
Ferguson, J.G., 176
First East Street, xiv
Flannagan (sheriff), 227
Flood: of 1859, 88; of 1867, 125–26; and price of land, 158; of 1869, 175
Forrest, Belle, 213
Forrest, Gen. Nathan Bedford, 6
Fort St. Pierre, xiii
Fourth Military District, 195, 203, 207
Fourth of July, 31, 96
Franklin, John Hope, 117–18
Franklin, La., 160
Franklin, Tenn., 22
Free, Maj. T.S., 181
Freedmen: and schools, 40, 41–42, 190, 193; occupations of, 46; independence of, 48; marriage of, 48, 49; attendance at theater of, 49; and the military, 50–51, 147; number of in Vicksburg, 54n; and plantations, 64, 70, 77, 78, 79, 81, 147n, 155; as lessees, 75; defrauding of, 79, 113; wages of, 78, 98, 150–51, 157; at Davis Bend, 103–04; accused of crime, 108; and contracts, 149, 157, 171, 175; and rumors of insurrection, 169; rights of restricted, 187; hold convention, 188; hospital for, 217–18
Freedmen's Bureau: courts of, 146–47; and labor contracts, 150; and Black Code provisions, 153; agents of, 154, 155, complaints to, 171, 173; and legal equality, 180–81; official of visits Vicksburg, 189; Superintendent of Education of, 190; mentioned, 75, 80, 188–89
Freedmen's Department, 34, 38
Friends Freedmen's Association, xxiv, 63–64
Fultz, J.J., 193

Gaiter, Philip, 113
Garner, James W., 29, 90, 226
Georgia, xx
Germans, 159
Gla, J.A., 102
Glasscock's Island, 76
Gillem, Gen. Alvan C.: and scarcity of labor, 173; and freedmen's political activity, 174; urges planting of corn, 174; and legal equality, 184; and schools, 194; and William McCardle, 196; leaves Mississippi, 201; and taxation, 207; mentioned, 169, 170
Goodrich's Landing, 18
Golden, Ellen, 213
Goodrum & Stout, 162
Grand Caillou, La., 67
Grant, Gen. U.S.: picture of, xviii; and campaign against Vicksburg, xix; and racism, xxiii; and Vicksburg citizens, 5, 15; and Confederate prisoners, 9; and trade, 15, 20; and Reconstruction, 30; and black troops, 43–44; and contracts for picking cotton, 56; and Davis Bend, 92; becomes President, 201; appoints Ames, 202; Warren County votes for, 230; mentioned, 25, 90, 96, 114, 142, 177, 196, 229
Green, Duff, xiv, 3
Green, Mrs. E., 147
Greenwood, Miss., 147, 221
Gregory, G.W., 28
Grove Street, xiv

Index 251

Guerrillas: raids of, 62–63, 64, 66, 92; problems caused by, 62–63, 145; records of, 64; attempts to control, 65

Hall, L.M., 184
Halleck, Gen. Henry W., xxiii, 30
Hamilton, Minnie, 28
Harris, William, 219
Hawley, J.A., 191, 192
Hawley, Mr. (financier), 108–09
Hayes, Rutherford B., 230
Head, Maj. George E., 227
Henry, Giles, 181
Hewitt, "Aunt Florida," 87
Hill, Charles, 168
Hill, Judge Edwin, 141
Hinds County, 175, 199, 223
Hinds County Gazette: and Benjamin Montgomery, 124; and labor, 150; and sharecropping, 170; mentioned, 159, 220
Hinton, John, 169
Hoenish, E.A., 6
Holland (theater manager), 22
Holly Springs, Miss., xvi
Home Farm. *See* Davis Bend
Hospital, 119, 217–18
"House that Jeff Built, The," 96–97
Hove, Henry, 17
Howard, Gen. Oliver O.: and military personnel, 80; visits Vicksburg, 189; mentioned, 154, 155, 173, 194
Huddleson, Miss (missionary), 96
Hudson, Thomas J., 145
Hullum (militia member), 186
Humphreys, Gov. Benjamin G.: as source of insurrection rumors, 169; Warren County vote for, 187; removal from office of, 202; mentioned, 160, 168, 182, 183
Humphreys, George W., 150, 159
Hurlbut, Gen. Stephen A., 5, 30–31
Hurricane. *See* Plantations

Ike (a slave), 146
Indiana, 96
Indianola, Miss., 79
Island 102, xxvi
Israel (a slave), 74

Jackson, Joseph L., 179
Jackson, Miss., 185, 220
Jackson Street, xiv
J.H. Carter & Co., 97, 98, 99–100
Johnson, Albert, 197, 198
Johnson, Pres. Andrew: and pardoning of Joseph Davis, 121; vetoes Civil Rights bill, 155; appoints Provisional Governor, 178; upholds Gen. Slocum, 180; plan of Reconstruction, 183; petition of freedmen to, 188; and veto of Freedmen's Bureau bill, 192; mentioned, 186
Johnson, Jacob, 28

Kansas, 141
Kelley, William, 29
Kentucky, 60
Kimball, Clara, 192
King, Edward, 225
Kline, Miss (smuggler), 6n
Knox College, 197
Knox, Thomas, 58, 68, 79
Ku Klux Klan, 201

Labor, 99, 173
Lake St. Joseph, La., 133, 160
Land: cost of, 152, 158; freedmen forbidden to lease, 153, 187–88
Lanier, Eliza, 24, 168
Lauderdale County, Miss., 146
Law, 29, 87. *See also* Black Code
Lawrence, George D., 222
Lease, Benjamin, 197, 198
Lee, Robert E., 104
Lee, Miss (missionary), 96
Legislature, 183–84, 187

252 Index

Lessees: and guerrillas, 64–65; statistics on, 75; cheat freedmen, 79; at Davis Bend, 116; and conflicts with owners, 147
Levees, 131, 134
Levee Street, xiv, 214, 215
Lewis, William, 113
Liberty, 32
Lien. *See* Crop lien
Lincoln, Pres. Abraham: and freedmen, 60; and planters, 71; election of, 88; toast offered to, 96; reaction to death of, 104–05; and John Eaton, 105n; mentioned, 31
Livermore, Mary, xxi
Liverpool, England, 224
Locust Street, xiv
Logan, Maj. Gen. John A., 10
Louisiana, xxi, 95, 175
Lovell, Joseph, 131
Loyal Leagues, 171, 201
Luckett (Canton resident), 193
Lum, William, 3
Lynch, John Roy, 131

McCall, Lt. Dougal, 64, 81
McCardle, William T., 171, 196, 207, 217
McClane, Bolden, 212
Macon, Miss., 182
McConnell, Mr. (missionary), 96
McCord, Dr. D.O., 38, 79, 104
McDaniel, C.C., 28–29
McDonald, Mary, 211
McDonald, Molly, 213
McGowan, John, 28
McGrancy, Ann, 211
McKee, George, 197
McNutt, Gov. Alexander, xv
McNutt, Austin, 156
McPherson, Gen. Edward N.: banishes women, 5, 6; orders rations for citizens, 9; and Davis Bend, 90–91; mentioned, 25

McQuirk, Ellen, 6
McRae, Dr. (planter), 172
McWillie, Gov. William, 160

Madison County, Miss., 194
Madison Parish, La., 66
Main Street, xiv
Maltby, Gen. A.J., 195
Manlove & Hobart, 163
Manlove, Charles A., 204
Manlove, William, 182, 188
Marriages, 99
Masonic Lodge, 24
Matthews, Col. Oliver, 219–20
Mellen, William, 16–17, 60, 61
Memphis, Tenn., xiii, 221, 229
Meridian Daily Clarion, 111
Meridian, Miss., 192–93, 220
Merwin, Judge D.O., 179–80, 186
Militia, 184, 186
Militia Captains of Vicksburg, 186
Milliken's Bend, 18, 62–63, 81
Miner, Robert, 76
Missionaries: description of, 35; number of, 35; character of, 36, 39; raids on, 63–64; at Davis Bend, 95–96
Mississippi River: flooding of, 107, 125, 141; and Davis Bend, 125; and plantations, 151–52, 158, 168; steamboats on, 221; and Vicksburg, 229; mentioned, xiii, 92, 104, 153
Mississippi Valley, xix, 59, 71
Mitchell, William, 212
Monroe Street, xiv
Montgomery, Benjamin: business ability of, 87, 117, 136n; as plantation manager, 90, 91, 105, 116; returns to Davis Bend, 101; and Freedmen's Bureau, 110, 116; background of, 117; as an inventor, 117; relationship with Joseph Davis, 120, 129, 133, 137–38; seeks to lease Davis plantations, 120–21; finances of, 121–22; purchases Davis plantations, 121–

22; and the Association, 122–23, 159–60; appointed Justice of the Peace, 130–31; as a planter, 138, 140, 175; death of, 141; mentioned, 145, 156, 230
Montgomery, Isaiah: goes to Ohio, 118; joins Union Navy, 118; delegate to 1890 Constitutional Convention, 123; leadership of, 141; paternalism of, 142; photograph of, 143; mentioned, 90
Montgomery, Mary, 118
Montgomery, Thornton, 90, 130
Morgan, Albert T., 156–57
Mound Bayou, Miss., 142
Mulberry Street, xiv, 215
Mules, 107, 108, 152, 165n
Musgrove, Henry, 156
Myers, Hank, 215
Mygatt, Alston, 71, 197, 198

National Freedmen's Relief Association, 49–50
Natchez Daily Courier, 63
Natchez; schools at, 23, 41; judges at, 25; Home Farm at, 35; missionary at, 36; corruption at, 69; freedmen at, 81; refugees from, 95; Benjamin Montgomery bought at, 117; sends aid to Vicksburg, 216; mentioned, xvi, 48, 57, 68
New Orleans, La.: as market for cotton, 68, 223; corruption at, 69; merchants at, 119; railroad to, 220; steamboats to, 221; mentioned, xiii, 32, 61, 216, 224, 229
New Orleans, Jackson, and Great Northern Railroad, 220, 224
New York Tribune, 97
Norton, Capt. Gabriel, 114
Newton, Henderson, 125
Northwestern Freedmen's Aid Society, 10

Oath of Allegiance, 3, 5, 18

Ohio, 95, 153
Oliver, Hamilton, 49
Oliver, Maggie, 6n
Omega Island, xxvi
Ord, Maj. Gen. Edward O.C.: appointees at Davis Bend, 130–31; issues stay of foreclosure, 168–69; compels freedmen to contract, 170; appointed Fourth Military District Commander, 195; removes disloyal men from office, 195; denouncement of by McCardle, 196
Ordinance of Secession, 199
Orme, William, 16
Osterhaus, Gen. Peter J., 185, 187
Ousley, Ben, 138
Overseers: prefer employment by Northern men, 58; have trouble adjusting to emancipation, 58; warned by L. Thomas, 62; sometimes called "superintendent," 77; at Davis Bend, 88
Oxford, Miss., 183

Palmyra. *See* Davis Bend
Patridge, I.M., 185
Paw Paw Island, xxvi
Paxton, A.M., 74
Pemberton, Jim, 85, 88
Pemberton, Gen. John C., 9
Pennsylvania, 96
Pettit, I.C., 162
Pettus, Gov. John J., xxn
Phoenix Fire Company, 216
Pierce, I., 146
"Plain Gables," xv
Plantations: problems of, 72, 73–74; abandonment of by owners, 145; price of, 151–52, 158–59; cost of operating, 152; lists of for sale and rent, 157–59; financing of, 164; number of in Warren County, 164;
—Balmoral, 133
—Bazinsky, 66

—Blakely, 154, 155
—Brierfield: acquisition of, 85; crops at, 85; description of, 85; slaves on, 88; Union troops at, 90; toast to, 96; Fourth of July at, 96–97; photograph of, 97; sale of, 121–22
—Buckner, 64
—Bums and Maher, 81
—Fonsylvania, xxii–xxiii
—Glen Mary, 168
—Hurricane: acquisition of, 83; crops at, 85; description of, 86–87; Hall of Justice at, 87; burning of, 88; slaves at, 88; leasing of, 97; sale of, 121–22; burial of Joseph Davis at, 140
—Liverpool, 159
—Nanechehaw, 74, 184
—Palmetto, 76, 78, 79
—Prince, 171
—Roach, 73
—R.Y. Wood, 88
—Sligo, 159
—Turner and Quitman, 88, 92
—Villa Rosa, 162
Planters: Benjamin L.C. Wailes, xxii; John Winn, 76, 77n, 78; problems of, 81, 107; and schools, 153, 154; Henry Musgrove, 156; George C. Benham, 157; William C. Smedes, 158; George W. Humphreys, 159; I.C. Pettit, 162; William Whitaker, 162; Charles Hill, 168; Dr. McRae, 172; J.G. Ferguson, 176; Col. L. Price, 176; and decline of Vicksburg, 229. *See also*, Davis, Jefferson; Davis, Joseph; Montgomery, Benjamin; Plantations
Port Gibson, Miss., 108
Port Hudson, La., xxvii
Porterfield, John, 204
Powdermaker, Hortense, 79
Presbyterians, United, 95
Price, Col. L., 176

Prostitution, 28, 29, 209, 213
Provost Marshal, 11, 12, 25–26

Quine, Alfred, xxii

Race Course, Evergreen, 22
Randolph, Mayor Thomas, 181–82, 204, 210
Raymond, Miss., 220
Read, J.T., 23
Reconstruction, 30, 184, 195, 206
Reed (militia member), 186
Refugees: suffering of, 33, 34, 35; return with Gen. Sherman, 37; hospital for, 38; related to soldiers, 45; unwilling to go to camps, 45; at Davis Bend, 94–95, 104
Reid, Whitelaw, 81–82
Republican Party, 227, 230
Reynolds, Mrs. W.F., 6n
Richards, Rachel, 28
Robert E. Lee (steamboat), 221, 222, 223
Robinson, Col. Harrai, 69
Roland, Charles, 80
Richardson, John F., 69, 78
Riley, C.H., 6
Rountree, Henry: dislike for Vicksburg, 21; on unmarried women missionaries, 36; work among refugees, 37; favors gradual emancipation, 46; at Davis Bend, 94, 96; and freedmen, 99
Royall, A.A., 204
Rules and Regulations . . . for the Government of the Freedmen at Davis Bend, Miss., 92
Russell, Mrs. M.A., 6n

St. Louis, Mo., 11, 36, 221, 224
St. Louis Fair, 176

Salmon, Willie, 6
Salmon, Rose, 6

Index 255

Sanitation, 14
S.B. Howe's Great European Circus, 22
Scott, Dr. R.B., 147
Schools: white private, 23; subjects taught in, 23, 36, 190; established for freedmen, 40; tuition at, 40; attendance at, 41, 190; needs of, 41; white citizens reaction to, 43, 190, 192, 194; lack of, 217
Seward, William, 180, 187
Shannon, Alice, 4, 23, 24, 42–43
Shannon, Anne, 4, 5, 7
Shannon, Emma, 47
Shannon, Lavinia, 23, 31, 47
Shannon, Marmaduke: and oath of allegiance, 5, 5n; sends daughters to school, 23; and murder of John Bobb, 26; and freedmen in Vicksburg, 53, 53n; as Sheriff, 210, 213; mentioned, 31
Shakers, 37
Sharecroppers, 79. *See also* Sharecropping
Sharecropping, 151, 168, 170
Sharkey, Gov. William L.: and Gen. Slocum, 148; appointed as Governor, 178; and arrest of Judge Merwin, 180; and testimony of freedmen, 181; and militia, 185, 186; and Presidential Reconstruction, 186; and U.S. Government, 187; mentioned, 146, 184, 210
Sharpe (theater manager), 22
Sheehan, Barney, 29
Sheridan, Gen. Philip, 227
Sherman, Gen. William T.: on necessity of loyalty to the U.S., 8; brings back refugees, 37; describes an irregular military force, 44; and guerrillas, 63; withdraws troops from Vicksburg, 63; destroys railroad, 221; mentioned, 25
Shipley, Samuel, xxiv
Shreveport, La., 229

Shuler, Mrs. (Confederate sympathizer), 6n, 7
Simmons (militia member), 186
Skipwith's Landing, 18, 221
Skipworth, Joseph, 9, 10
Slavery, 146
Slaves: escape of, xix; execution of, xxn; freed by Union soldiers, xxii, 56; Northern attitudes toward, xxiii; Southern attitudes toward, xxiii
Slocum, Gen. Henry W.: on black soldiers, 26; and lessee, 148; and Judge Merwin, 179, 180; and militia, 186; and city jail, 208, 210; mentioned, 25, 180
Smedes, William C., 158
Smith, Gen. Marion, 191
Smith, Brig. Gen. Morgan L., 53
Smith, Maj. Gen. William F., 69. *See also* Commission on Corrupt Practices in the South
Smith, William H., 28
Soldiers: crimes of, 9, 20, 26, 28; and trade permits, 16; attendance at theater, 21; and literary association, 22–23; executions of, 27, 28; found dead, 27; arrested in house of prostitution, 28; used to work on fortifications, 43–44; First Mississippi Cavalry of African Descent, 44–45; at Davis Bend, 104; serve arrest warrant, 148; and fire fighting, 215, 216
South Carolina, 202
South Street, xiv
South Union, Ky., 37
Southern Railroad, 220, 221, 223, 224
Spencer, William, 103
Spengler, S., 204
Sports, 22
Stanton, Edwin, 44, 60, 74
Steamboats, xx, xxi, 139, 221–22
Stevens, J.H., 69
Stier, Isaac, 149

Stites, Gerard, 204
Streetlights, 13
Streets, 13, 208
Stringer, T.W., 197, 198
Sullivan, M.P., 23–24
Swain, Samuel G.: and smuggling, 20; and freedmen, 149; and Northern immigration, 151; and Southern feelings, 152–53, 188–89; mentioned, 27
Swanson, Maria, 65
Sweeney, Capt. H., 155
Swords, James, 14, 34–35, 54. *See also Vicksburg Daily Herald*
Sydnor, Charles, 78, 158

Tammany Hall, 226
Tchula, Miss., 221
Teachers, 35, 153, 154. *See also* Missionaries
Tennessee, xxiv
Testimony, 182
Texas, xx
Theater, Vicksburg, 21
Thibodeaux, La., 67
Thomas, Adj. Gen. Lorenzo: and schools, 40; and black troops, 44; and leasing program, 57; and freedmen, 60–61; and Davis Bend, 92
Thomas, Col. Samuel: and freedmen, xxvi, 49, 51, 52–53, 79, 80, 81; and Davis Bend, 90, 105–06, 107, 109, 110, 112, 114–15; complaint about, 113; and lessee, 148; and provost courts, 181; orders cooperation with State, 181; mentioned, 64, 81, 147
Thompson, Pvt. Cornelius, 27
Thrasher, J.B., 108
Trade, 19
Treasury Dept.: and speculation in food, 11; and abandoned buildings, 12; and trade permits, 15, 17; and Home Farm, 35; and leasing of land, 57, 61; and freedmen, 60–61; and records of guerrilla raids, 64; and shipping of cotton, 68, 70; agents of accept bribes, 69; mentioned, 75
Trowbridge, John T., 102–03, 182, 211
Tuttle, Brig. Gen. (at Natchez), 41

Union League, 31
Union Literary Association, 22–13
U.S. Colored Infantry, 27, 35
U.S. Supreme Court, 196
Utica, Miss., 65, 156

Vick, Newitt, xiii
Vicksburg, Miss.: founding of, xiii; population of, xiv, 204; characteristics of, xiv, 9, 20, 205, 225; social structure of, xv–xvi; businesses in, xvi–xvii, 75, 219, 224; slaves in, xvii; politics in, xvii, 178, 186, 192, 197, 199, 200, 226–27; strategic importance of, xix; and cotton production, xxi, 67, 70, 151, 220; military operations near, xxiii, xxvi–xxvii, 88; economy of, 10; plantations near, 157–59; crop lien in, 161–67; and Chinese labor, 176; adjustments of people in, 177; crime in, 179, 185, 208, 214; military affairs at, 179, 203; and freedmen, 181, 188, 189; militia at, 184–85; visit of O.O. Howard to, 189; removal of officials in, 195, 202; finances of, 205, 206, 207, 208; fires in, 214, 217; municipal services in, 218; and steamboats, 221–22, 229; levee at, 221; street violence at 227; photograph of, 228; lessons of, 230; mentioned, 68, 74, 81, 87, 98, 145, 148, 152, 193. *See also* Warren County
Vicksburg Daily Journal, 182, 188
Vicksburg Daily Herald: and shipping problems, 7, and profiteering on food, 10–11; and condition of streets, 13;

and crime, 18, 27, 28; and the theater, 21; and Reconstruction, 31; and the army worm, 67; opposes Black Code, 188. *See also* James Swords
Vicksburg Daily Times: and freedmen, 175; opposes election, 197; and taxes, 207; and crime statistics, 211, 214; and fire in the city, 216–17; and steamboats, 221; mentioned, 157–58, 171, 224. *See also* McCardle, William T.
Vicksburg Weekly Republican, 200, 201
Voting: in 1860, xvii; by freedmen, 174, 183, 184; in Warren County, 187, 230; in 1867, 197; on Constitution of 1869, 201, 203

Wages: of freedmen, 61–62, 77, 98, 135, 150, 151, 152, 168, 172, 176; failure to pay, 157
Wallin, Mayor E.W., 195, 215
Walnut Street, xiv
War Department, 60–61, 74, 75
Warren, Addie O., 192, 193
Warren County, Miss.: elections in, xvii, 186, 197, 201, 230; law in, 147, 183, 212–13; agriculture in, 151, 171, 176n, 177; crop lien in, 161–67; flooding in, 175; militia in, 184, 186; elected officials in, 187, 198, 226; politics in, 199, 200; jail in, 208, 213; roads in, 223; conditions in, 225; grand jury in, 226; mentioned, 229. *See also* Vicksburg, Miss.
Warren, Joseph, 57, 96, 153, 190
Washburne, Maj. Gen. C.C., 51
Washington, Booker T., 123, 137–38

Washington County, Miss., 172, 179
Washington, D.C., 188, 189
Washington Hotel, 219
Washington Street, xiv, 71, 205, 215
Watt, Warren, 125
Wells, Pvt. Seth J., xxn, 9
Wenstin, A., 6n
West, Elias, 88
West, Lizzie, 4
West, Mrs. (Vicksburg citizen), 4
Western Sanitary Commission, 10, 57
Wharton, Vernon, 144, 197, 226
Whigs, 186, 187, 203
Williams, Hannah, 42
Williams, John W., 17
Williams, Lt. M.R., 193
Winn, John, 76, 78
Wisconsin Daily Journal, 69
Whitaker, William, 162
White, William, 212
Whiting, Miss (missionary), 35
Wood, Maj. Gen. Thomas J.: and Davis Bend, 119, 224; and planter attitudes, 154; and problem of contracts, 155; and Black Code, 189; praise of, 216; mentioned, 156, 168
Works Progress administration, 149
Wright, Samuel G., 36, 41, 63, 95, 190

Yadkins, P.T., 6n
Yazoo City, Miss., 7, 73, 159, 221, 224
Yazoo River, xiii, 153, 159
Yeatman, James, 57, 76
Yerger, William, 183
Young, Clarisse, 148–49
Young, Col. Van E., 15
Young's Point, Miss., xxvi

www.ingramcontent.com/pod-product-compliance
Lightning Source LLC
Chambersburg PA
CBHW022003160426
43197CB00007B/245